Deciphering Poe

Perspectives on Edgar Allan Poe
Series Editor: Barbara Cantalupo

Embracing interdisciplinary perspectives, cultural studies, and traditional scholarship, Perspectives on Edgar Allan Poe publishes scholarly interpretations of Edgar Allan Poe's works, influences, and contexts to enhance Poe studies within and beyond the parameters of nineteenth-century American literary history.

Titles in the Series

Deciphering Poe: Subtexts, Contexts, Subversive Meanings edited by Alexandra Urakova
Poe's Pervasive Influence edited by Barbara Cantalupo

Deciphering Poe

Subtexts, Contexts, Subversive Meanings

Alexandra Urakova

LEHIGH UNIVERSITY PRESS
Bethlehem

Published by Lehigh University Press
Co-published with The Rowman & Littlefield Publishing Group, Inc.
4501 Forbes Boulevard, Suite 200, Lanham, Maryland 20706
www.rowman.com

10 Thornbury Road, Plymouth PL6 7PP, United Kingdom

Copyright © 2013 by Rowman & Littlefield Publishers, Inc.

All rights reserved. No part of this book may be reproduced in any form or by any electronic or mechanical means, including information storage and retrieval systems, without written permission from the publisher, except by a reviewer who may quote passages in a review.

British Library Cataloguing in Publication Information Available

Library of Congress Cataloging-in-Publication Data

Deciphering Poe : subtexts, contexts, subversive meanings / edited by Alexandra Urakova.
  pages cm
Includes index.
ISBN 978-1-61146-139-8 (cloth : alk. paper) -- ISBN 978-1-61146-140-4 (electronic)
1. Poe, Edgar Allan, 1809-1849--Criticism and interpretation. I. Urakova, A. P., editor of compilation.
  PS2638.D396 2013
  818'.309--dc23
  2013019612

∞™ The paper used in this publication meets the minimum requirements of American National Standard for Information Sciences Permanence of Paper for Printed Library Materials, ANSI/NISO Z39.48-1992.

Printed in the United States of America

Contents

List of Illustrations — vii

Acknowledgments — ix

Introduction — xi
   Alexandra Urakova

1. Poe's Resonance with Francis Quarles: Emblems, Melancholy, and the Art of Memory — 1
   William E. Engel

2. "A snare in every human path": "Tamerlane" and the Paternal Scapegoat — 13
   John Edward Martin

3. Mother Goddess Manifestations in Poe's "Catholic Hymn" and "Morella" — 27
   Amy Branam

4. Poe's 1845 Boston Lyceum Appearance Reconsidered — 41
   Philip Edward Phillips

5. "Torture[d] into aught of the sublime": Poe's Fall of the House of Burke, Ussher, and Kant — 53
   Sean Moreland

6. Poe and Perversity — 67
   Daniel Fineman

7. From the Romantic to the Textual Sublime: Poesque Sublimities, Romantic Irony, and Deconstruction — 75
   Stephanie Sommerfeld

8	The Armchair *Flâneur* *Tim Towslee*	87
9	No Kidding: "The Gold-Bug" Is True to Its Title *Henri Justin*	97
10	"Trust to the shrewdness and common sense of the public": *The Narrative of Arthur Gordon Pym* as a Hoaxical Satire of Racist Epistemologies *John C. Havard*	107
11	Moving Daguerreotypes and Myths of Reproduction: Poe's Body *Lauren Curtright*	121

Index	139
About the Editor and Contributors	147

List of Illustrations

Fig. 4.1	Boston Theatre, Federal Street, c.1824.	47
Fig. 4.2	Odeon, from *Bowen's Picture of Boston*, 3rd ed. (Boston, 1838).	48
Fig. 7.1	Diagram I	82
Fig. 7.2	Diagram II	82
Fig. 11.1	William Abbott Pratt produced the Traylor daguerreotype in his studio in Richmond, Virginia in 1849.	123
Fig. 11.2	William Abbott Pratt produced the Thompson daguerreotype in his studio in Richmond, Virginia in 1849.	124
Fig. 11.3	William Abbott Pratt produced the *Players Club* daguerreotype, a copy of the *Thompson* daguerreotype, for Thomas Dimmock in Pratt's studio in Richmond, Virginia circa 1855.	125

Acknowledgments

I took the editorship of this collection after Barbara Cantalupo had already done the preliminary work of selecting and reviewing the papers. Since that time, her help has been essential to the volume, and I am indebted to her generosity and willingness to give me a hand in the process of preparing the manuscript.

The director of the Poe Museum in Richmond, Harry Lee Poe, supported me from the very beginning; I am particularly grateful to him for helping us obtain permissions for some of the illustrations included in the volume.

The Poe Studies Association was very generous in supporting this project financially, and I would like to thank personally the PSA Executive Committee and the PSA current president, John Gruesser, for their generous gesture.

Introduction

Alexandra Urakova

After the two-hundredth anniversary of his birth,[1] Edgar Allan Poe remains a complex and controversial figure whose work continues to demand careful reconsideration. Much of this complexity stems from a long and sophisticated tradition of analytical readings that address the many undercurrents of meaning in his work, as well as the conundrum that the work both reflected and often subverted the major intellectual, political, and social discourses of his time. *Deciphering Poe: Subtexts, Contexts, Subversive Meanings* is grounded in a scholarly tradition that shares a fascination with the subversive, secret, coded, and controversial in Poe.[2] The aim of this volume, then, is twofold: to expand the contextual framework of Poe's work and to interpret still unrevealed subtexts of his poetry, prose, and social behavior that provide a more attenuated vision of Poe's place and role in nineteenth-century American literature. Contributors to this volume searched for the hidden clues that allowed them to reconsider Poe's literary and intellectual debts, ones that heretofore have escaped critical attention. The authors demonstrate how obscure texts or side elements of Poe's art/discourse influence his exemplary, well-known literary techniques. They examine the parodic, ironic, and hoaxing character of his work, as well as the ways his sophisticated narrative strategies subvert the ideological clichés and stereotypes of his time. Thus, the question of how we should read Poe today remains as essential as ever.

The eleven chapters in this volume vary in their approaches. Rereadings of works like *The Narrative of Author Gordon Pym*, "The Raven," and "The Fall of the House of Usher" alternate with chapters discussing lesser-studied pieces like "Tamerlane" and "Catholic Hymn." Analyses of Poe's short fiction in light of its philosophical background and antebellum social constructions of race and gender are supplemented by investigations in biography and reception. What unites the chapters is their attention to the subversive nature of Poe's art found in the subtle, minute details of his life and work, whether that might be the pseudonym used in the first printing of "The Raven" or the history of the Odeon stage where Poe infamously delivered "Al Aaraaf" in 1845. Close reading techniques have a direct counterpart in Poe's tales when we think of Dupin's or Legrand's meticulous attention to the apparently insignificant material details and facts. Jorge Luis Borges claimed that Poe invented the reader of detective tales;[3] it would not be an exaggeration to say that Poe also invented his future critics, who largely borrow his own methods to decipher his life and work.

Author of the Dupin tales, "The Gold-Bug," and "A Few Words on Secret Writing," Poe possessed what Shawn Rosenheim called "the cryptographic imagination," referring not only to stories that "explicitly include ciphers or codes" but to "a constellation of literary techniques concerning secrecy in writing."[4] In Poe's own words, "secret writing" is the desire "of transmitting information from one individual to another, in such manner as to elude general comprehension,"[5] and this is often seen as a motivating force behind his work. Much work on deciphering political and social subtexts of Poe's writing has been done in the past twenty years, after Poe was restored to the cultural and historical context of the antebellum United States.[6] Reexamining his heritage in its complex interrelation with contemporary notions of race, sexuality, and gender, scholars bring to light subjects and issues that are central to his work but by no means obvious; rather, like the purloined letter, they are exposed and concealed at the same time.

Most of the chapters here offer a textual analysis of Poe's poetry and fiction. The first four chapters form a "poetical" block. It is not surprising that poetry evokes a discussion of biographical allusions and subtexts, such as Poe's complex relations with John Allan or the irrecoverable loss of his mother, Elizabeth Arnold. Poe's poems, from "Tamerlane" to "The Raven," are placed at the junction of biographical, social, and literary contexts; much attention is paid to genetic relations of the early poetical experiments to mature work. From Poe's poetry we move through an account of the actual poetic performance in Boston to the analysis of his prose in the six chapters that follow. *Deciphering Poe* encompasses Poe's detective stories as well ("The Purloined Letter," "The Mystery of Marie Rogêt"), and texts explicitly using codes and secret writing ("The Gold-Bug," *The Narrative of Arthur Gordon Pym*). This block falls into two parts thematically organized around the intellectual subtexts of Poe's fiction, on the one hand, and its social (mainly racial) implications, on the other. Chapters 5 to 7 predominantly consider the question of sublimity in Poe, showing the author's critical and ambiguous attitude to the existing philosophical tradition. Poe's intellectual thought is seen as subversive to the existing philosophical tradition and at the same time as anticipating the theoretical and critical thinking of the twentieth century. Precursor of both the twentieth century's intellectual and mass culture (the latter thesis is developed in chapter 8), Poe at the same time shared many prejudices of his contemporaries, notoriously including those about race. However, the chapters in *Deciphering Poe* reconstruct Poe's radical artistic gesture that placed his work in opposition not only to explicit racist ideology as such but also to the "average racism"[7] nourishing the popular imagination. The last chapter expands the volume's framework by exploring the role that Poe's daguerreotypes played in his reception at the turn of the nineteenth and twentieth centuries. The history of Poe's reception in the United States is notorious for being largely the history of his misrecognition. While much has already been written about the ambiguities of Poe's "afterlife" at home, this study offers a different approach to the subject, showing how attempts to reevaluate Poe as a national genius were themselves not free from stereotypical thinking about gentility and race.

Poe's most often quoted work is "The Raven," the poem that made him famous during his lifetime; however, its first printing in *The American Review* (February 1845) was anonymous, signed "By——Quarles." William E. Engel's chapter, "Poe's Resonance with Francis Quarles: Emblems, Melancholy, and the Art of Memory," not only demonstrates Poe's familiarity with Francis Quarles's poems but claims the centrality of the affinities the former shared—or claimed to share—with the English poet, for his aesthetics. Francis Quarles (1592-1644), a preeminent seventeenth-century English poet, was best known to Poe's audience, according to Engel, for his "jarring comparisons and his seemingly inexhaustible variations on the themes of human mortality and vanity—but most especially for his books of emblems." Discussing potential influences of Quarles and his emblematic poetry on Poe, Engel argues that "Poe adopted the familiar tropes and themes associated with baroque artifice as part of his effort to wean himself away from the sentimental poetics of his own day." Furthermore, "Quarles takes on added significance in the light of Poe's explicit aesthetic concern with 'emblems of mournful and never-ending remembrance' as discussed in the 'Philosophy of Composition.'"

While Engel's chapter focuses on Poe's allusions to a literary predecessor, John Edward Martin, in "'A snare in every human path': 'Tamerlane' and the Paternal Scapegoat," links "Tamerlane"—via Hebrew and Islamic allusions—to Poe's complex and dramatic relations with his stepfather, John Allan. "Tamerlane" (1827), the first test of the pen, is relatively obscure among Poe's poetic works and has certainly not obtained as much critical attention as "The Raven;" yet Martin demonstrates that the poem and its rhetorical strategies are consistent with the author's mature works. He also notes that in "Tamerlane," Poe uses a "confessional" narrative for the first time. Furthermore, at the time he was composing and publishing "Tamerlane," Poe was involved in a long series of painful exchanges with John Allan—exchanges that, as Martin argues, developed the model upon which his poetic theory and gothic aesthetics finally took form in the poem and in his later work. The chapter examines a subversive potential of the poem, which challenges traditional boundaries of paternalistic authority through "a subtle invocation of one of the foundational myths—that of the 'scapegoat'—common to all three patriarchal 'religions of the book.'"

Amy Branam's "Mother Goddess Manifestations in Poe's 'Catholic Hymn' and 'Morella'" shifts our attention from the (anti)paternalistic discourse of "Tamerlane" to feminine allusions in the "Catholic Hymn" and "Morella," respectively. "Catholic Hymn," which first appeared in the early printed version of "Morella," was regarded by critics such as Arthur Quinn and Alvaro Salas Chacón as a manifestation of Poe's personal devotion to the Virgin Mary. Trapping both the poem and the story in the contemporary anti-Catholic discourse, Branam claims the opposite. Once an attendee of the Monumental Church in Richmond, Poe was exposed to the "Mary controversy." The plot of "Morella," embodying patriarchal fears about a powerful female, also proves that he shared a negative attitude to the cult of Mother Goddess. Whereas Martin views Poe's rhetoric as subversive to the paternalistic authority, Branam's feminist reading reconsiders "Morella" in saying that "patriarchal religions had demonized and dethroned the Goddess in an attempt to control her sexuality and, by extension, her autonomy. . . . Poe inherited an array of Mother Goddess imagery that he could use in his tales and poems as literary shorthand to craft a mood of terror tailored precisely for his Protestant audience."

Poe's female figures, powerful yet suffering and dying, are traditionally linked to his childhood memories of Elizabeth Arnold. In "Poe's 1845 Boston Lyceum Appearance Reconsidered," Philip Edward Phillips gives a fresh touch to the theme of Poe's affection for his mother. The Odeon, where Poe read his early poem "Al Aaraaf" on October 16, 1845, before the Boston literati, was once the Boston Theatre, where "his mother had performed to great acclaim." Therefore, by returning to the Odeon, Poe was returning to his origins: he had been on that stage before, *in utero*, when Eliza Poe had delivered so many memorable performances. Rather than reading the Boston "failure" merely as an expression of Poe's contempt for the city of Boston, Phillips considers Poe's performance as an attempt to reclaim his literary and personal birthright as a Bostonian. Remapping Boston as a city of memory and nostalgia, Phillips develops a more nuanced idea of Poe's conflicting feelings—those "of attraction and repulsion"—toward his birthplace.

We encounter another subtle touch on the psychoanalytic return-to-the-womb subject in Sean Moreland's "'Torture[d] into aught of the sublime': Poe's Fall of the House of Burke, Ussher, and Kant." "If Poe's tales trace the return to the womb, as [Marie] Bonaparte insisted, it is finally a textual matrix, a Poetic vor*text*, to which they return, and to which they invite their readers to return." Moreland attempts to historicize this Freudian observation by reading the vortex in Poe's fiction as emblematic of sublimity and showing his engagement in the contemporary discourse on the sublime. The chapter focuses specifically on "The Fall of the House of Usher" for a number of reasons. It is a tale that testifies to Poe's "negative sublimity" (e.g., his rejection and critical revision of theories by Burke, Kant, Coleridge, and Radcliffe). It also encodes the name of James Ussher, English philosopher and author of *Clio*, a treatise on sublimity, written in 1767. Situating the tale in its relation to "a number of contemporaneously prevalent philosophical and aesthetic binaries," Moreland discloses its "elaborate parodic play, meant to trap readers who are, in Poe's phrase, 'theory mad beyond redemption.'"

Daniel Fineman's "Poe and Perversity" continues discussing the philosophical context of Poe's prose and interprets "The Imp of the Perverse" in the light of Burkean irrational sublimity. Tracing perversity on the level of language—as "a constructive deconstruction of the constituents of composition"—he demonstrates how "the initial discourse appears in a form appositional to the last: a path from academic distance to personal threat," from "we" to "I," from rationality to insanity. Fineman describes this shift of the tale's discourse as "the swerve of the perverse," a pattern to be found in Poe's other works and exaggerated in "The Imp of the Perverse." Interestingly, Fineman's chapter, too, swerves from a general discussion of Poe's philosophical ideas and borrowings to a close reading of his story. This repetitive critical gesture should not surprise readers of "The Purloined Letter," with its famous round-robin structure that engaged generations of its critics in a sophisticated metatextual game.

"The Purloined Letter" is the focus of the chapter by Stephanie Sommerfeld, "From the Romantic to the Textual Sublime: Poesque Sublimities, Romantic Irony, and Deconstruction." As is evident from the title, Sommerfeld, like Fineman and Moreland, addresses the question of sublimity in Poe. More specifically, she explores "the interplay of Kantian- and Burkean-infused, diegetic sublimity on the one hand and a textual sublimity that is indebted to Longinian rhetorical sublimity to a certain degree, on the other hand." The signals for sublimity are to be found in the passage that describes the narrator's and the Prefect's astonishment when they see the letter, the motionlessness and speechlessness of the Prefect pointing to the Burkean sublime. Sommerfeld contends that it is the narrator who "passes his capacity of producing sublime effects on to Dupin, who, in turn, loses his sublimity when he becomes just another agent in the diegetic shifting of letters, power, and sublimity." Although Sommerfeld's own reading bears on the high theory interpretations of "The Purloined Letter," she claims that postmodern philosophy is itself rooted in the Romantic irony to which Poe was indebted; the author alienates herself from Derrida's followers, on the one hand, and from G. R. Thompson's tradition of exploring Poesque Romantic Irony, on the other.

While according to Walter Benjamin, "The Purloined Letter" anticipated a famous theoretical dispute, in "The Man of the Crowd" Poe first introduced the figure of the *flâneur*, a would-be symbol of modernity. Following Benjamin, Tim Towslee suggests an alternative term, "armchair *flâneur*," and uses it as a tool to explore "The Mystery of Marie Rogêt," the second tale of the Dupin trilogy. Yet, as Towslee argues in "The Armchair *Flâneur*," "the tale is better aligned with Poe's earlier urban spectator tale and essay 'The Man of the Crowd' and 'The Philosophy of Furniture.'" In Towslee's opinion, "By blending fact and fiction through newspaper voyeurism and armchair *flânerie*, Poe invents a new archetype altogether—detective fiction's antisocial, sedentary cousin the armchair detective, whose stories are based in secondhand particulars of true crime, but written to entertain by allowing the media to do the detective's legwork, and solved (or in Poe's case, not solved) by pure intellect and intuition." Dupin reads newspapers as the narrator of "The Man of the Crowd" reads the crowd or as Poe himself reads the contents of peoples' houses in "The Philosophy of Furniture." The penny press becomes Dupin's window, allowing him "to peer out onto the seedy underbelly of Parisian society without having to leave his library." Towslee defines the genre of "The Mystery of Marie Rogêt" as a "true crime" story. He sees Poe's fiction as a "symptom" of emerging mass culture, in the terms of Jonathan Elmer,[8] his "Marie Rogêt" foreshadowing "the popularity of true crime shows such as *America's Most Wanted*, *Cops*, and the myriad of incriminating video files available on YouTube."

Poe's most popular and commercially successful story during his lifetime, however, was not "The Mystery of Marie Rogêt" but his prize-winning "The Gold-Bug," based on cryptography and secret writing. Like "The Man of the Crowd," "The Gold-Bug" is often compared with the Dupin trilogy, and Henri Justin in "No Kidding: 'The Gold-Bug' Is True to Its Title" follows this tradition when he writes: "Deep down, [Legrand] shares Kidd's criminality. Like Dupin, he has a 'Bi-Part' psyche, half brilliant analytic intellect, half murderous drives." Justin's chapter, with a pun in the title, offers a sophisticated and engaging reading of the story, pointing to its rich "undercurrent of meaning." Justin draws our attention to Jupiter's slip: living bugs are not made of gold, and the one in the tale is only accidentally ancillary to the plot proper. Yet the "goole bug," as Jupiter says in his stereotyped Black English, is a "key to a deeper meaning" and a fit emblem of the tale's unexpected coupling of gold and murder in the closing lines. "Jupiter feels the duality of the bug—he is both fascinated and frightened by the strange insect—but only Poe conflates 'gold' with the 'ghoul,' the legendary being that feeds on corpses." Bringing Roman Jacobson's famous distinction between "contiguity" and "equivalence" to support his argument, Justin not only demonstrates Poe's subversive narrative strategies but expands and challenges Toni Morrison's interpretation.[9] The reader is not expected to side entirely with Legrand (who, according to Morrison, finally restores his "Southern comfort"[10]) but is "kept suspended between two interpretative stances." Claiming that Jupiter finds a function worthy of his name and is responsible for the emblem that could be read "as a tiny, almost private, but insistent emblem of Poe's art," Justin invites us to reconsider the racial issue in the tale.

The next chapter, John C. Havard's "'Trust to the shrewdness and common sense of the public': *The Narrative of Arthur Gordon Pym* as a Hoaxical Satire of Racist Epistemologies," is focused on the problem that has divided Poe's scholars into two camps: those who claim that Poe's texts are proslavery and those who refuse to see them as "average racist." Following the latter view, Havard enters a famous debate on race in *Pym*. Without denying the racist elements encoded in the novel, he argues that *Pym* interrogates proslavery thought through its hoaxing characteristics. "Poe's writing was multilayered and could ostensibly aim to please his readers all the while subversively attacking them." He does so in *Pym* by making his main character, Arthur Gordon Pym, both "a terrible reader" and "a stand-in" for the audience. According to Havard, Poe mocks the common misunderstanding of race by his Southern, and even more so by his Northern, readership.

The last chapter in the collection, "Moving Daguerreotypes and Myths of Reproduction: Poe's Body" by Lauren Curtright, also brings forward the question of Poe and race but in a different context altogether, focusing on Poe's daguerreotypes and their role in his afterlife reception. Reproductions of daguerreotypes of Poe prefigure his image in the twentieth century. This is not surprising, given that photography is by itself "a quintessentially gothic medium." "Poe's alignment with photography seems logical because, like Poe's oeuvre, indexical media are often associated with the supernatural. The discourse on photography envisions this medium as magical, as well as veracious, and endows it with mystery." The chapter concentrates on the journalist Thomas Dimmock's 1895 letter to the *Century Magazine* about the "Thompson" daguerreotype of Poe, taken by Virginian daguerreotypist and Gothic Revivalist architect William Abbott Pratt just weeks before Poe's death. Analyzing Dimmock's "Notes on Poe," Curtright contends that his adaptation of Poe's daguerreotypes into a written narrative attempts to naturalize "white masculinity" as it was consolidated in the turn-of-the-century United States and to make Poe emblematize this identity. "To readers of *Century*, the daguerreotyped image of Poe connotes knowledge of what constitutes an author at the *fin de siècle.*"

Deciphering Poe, thus, invites us to consider Poe as an even more complicated and ambiguous figure than we are used to thinking. Chapters in the collection give a highly nuanced picture of his engagement in major discourses of the time—religious, philosophical, social, and literary—encouraging future readers to render Poe carefully. Poe's *Pym* was not only subversive to proslavery views of the time but could be read as an intended hoax of its readers' racist stereotypes. He did not just embody Burkean ideas of sublimity in his fiction but radically revised them. His attitude toward Boston was as nostalgic as it was hostile, and the hypothesis of Poe's perverse behavior is by no means sufficient to explain the psychological drama he was going through during and after the performance. "The Gold-Bug," a tale about secret writing, discloses its sophisticated narrative strategies with the help of the "codes" developed by Russian structuralism; moreover, instead of being racist as is widely believed, it appears to endow the black slave with supreme poetical function. The nuances of Poe's poems and tales and the controversies of his life, career, and reception become relevant in our attempts to understand Poe the artist and Poe the man when rereading him after a century of critical debates. Offering new insights in the whole range of subjects related to Poe, the chapters eventually demonstrate that there is still much left to be "deciphered" in Poe, even in the twenty-first century.

NOTES

1. The chapters in this collection came from a four-day conference sponsored by the Poe Studies Association, held in Philadelphia in October 2009: "The Third International Edgar Allan Poe Conference: The Bicentennial." The conference was a major Poe-related academic event in the year of Poe's bicentennial; it had an international impact and appeal. This volume certainly benefited from the fruitful panel discussions of each individual paper.

2. At least since Patrick Quinn and G. R. Thompson, scholars have been searching Poe's texts for secret clues. Quinn (*The French Face of Edgar Poe* [Carbondale: Southern Illinois University Press, 1957]) pointed to the undercurrent, symbolic meaning unnoticed by American readers, while G. R. Thompson, a decade and a half later (*Poe's Fiction: Romantic Irony in the Gothic Tales* [Madison: University of Wisconsin Press, 1973]), attempted to reveal the ironic and hoaxing nature of Poe's discourse beneath the layer of conventional Gothic plots. Among more recent studies concerned with "secrecy in writing," we would name John Irvin's *American Hieroglyphics: The Symbol of the Egyptian Hieroglyphics in the American Renaissance* (Baltimore: Johns Hopkins University Press, 1983), Richard Kopley's *Poe's Pym: Critical Explorations* (Durham, NC: Duke University Press, 1992), Shawn J. Rosenheim's *The Cryptographic Imagination: Secret Writing from Edgar Poe to Internet* (Baltimore: Johns Hopkins University Press, 1997), and Louis A. Renza's *Edgar Allan Poe, Wallace Stevens, and the Poetics of American Privacy* (Baton Rouge: Louisiana State University Press, 2002).

3. Jorge Luis Borges, *Borges at Eighty: Conversations*, ed. Willis Barnstone (Indianapolis: Indiana University Press, 1982), 145.

4. Rosenheim, *The Cryptographic Imagination*, 2. Speculating about Poe's "secret writing," Louis Renza also suggests that one of the functions of his numerous puns, doublings, implanted anagrams, obscure citations, and allusions is "to delay any full reading of his text. The tale others read, its immediately apprehensible or aesthetic reading, coterminously encodes the very same reading, and so produces the sense that they have not yet really read it." (See Renza, *Edgar Allan Poe, Wallace Stevens, and the Poetics of American Privacy*, 33).

5. Edgar Allan Poe, *Essays and Reviews*, ed. G. R. Thompson (New York: Literary Classics of the United States, 1984), 1277.

6. Poe is hardly placed any longer "outside the main currents" of the national thought and the literary canon, a thesis effectively debated in critical works from Stephen Rachman and Shawn Rosenheim's *The American Face of Edgar Allan Poe* (Baltimore: Johns Hopkins University Press, 1995) to the most recent *Poe and the Remapping of Antebellum Print Culture*, ed.

J. Gerald Kennedy and Jerome McGann (Baton Rouge: Louisiana State University Press, 2012).

7. The term of Terence Whalen, first introduced in the chapter "Average Racism in Poe, Slavery, and the Wages of Literary Nationalism," in his book *Edgar Allan Poe and the Masses: The Political Economy of Literature in Antebellum America* (Princeton, NJ: Princeton University Press, 1999), 111–47.

8. Jonathan Elmer, *Reading at the Social Limit: Affect, Mass Culture, and Edgar Allan Poe* (Stanford, CA: Stanford University Press, 1995), 1–2.

9. See Toni Morrison's chapter "Romancing the Shadow," in *Playing in the Dark: Whiteness and the Literary Imagination* (Cambridge, MA: Harvard University Press, 1992), 29–60.

10. Morrison, "Romancing the Shadow," 58.

Chapter One

Poe's Resonance with Francis Quarles

Emblems, Melancholy, and the Art of Memory

William E. Engel

> It was upon this principle, it is said, that Simonides founded the first regular system for aiding the memory, of which history makes mention.... We do not now-a-days appeal to mythological fables for the causes and explanations of facts pertaining to the understanding, but only to Logic and to Philosophy.
> —Francis Fauvel-Gouraud, *Phreno-Mnemotechny; or The Art of Memory* (1845)

This essay concerns the pseudonym Poe used in the first printed version of "The Raven."[1] Insofar as this poem "By——Quarles" won celebrity for Poe at home and a reputation as a poet of consequence abroad, the question implicitly posed by his linking the name of "Quarles" to "The Raven" deserves a central place in any serious consideration of his aesthetics. What affinities did Poe share, or want to declare that he shared, with the baroque emblematist Francis Quarles?[2]

Francis Quarles (1592–1644) was best known to Poe's audience for his jarring comparisons and his seemingly inexhaustible variations on the themes of human mortality and vanity—but most especially for his books of emblems.[3] Poe adopted the familiar tropes and themes associated with baroque artifice as part of his effort to wean himself away from the sentimental poetics of his own day.[4] To be sure though, as René Wellek pointed out, "One must acknowledge that all stylistic devices may occur at almost all times.... Much better chances of success attend the attempts at defining baroque in more general terms of a philosophy or a world-view or even merely emotional attitude toward the world."[5] The "general terms of a philosophy" of the baroque informing Poe's craft will be shown to have involved the emblem's place in *The Art of Memory*, a venerable method for coming up with, carefully arranging, and expounding upon "topics of invention."[6]

Poe sought to reclaim something of the latent totemic power associated with one of the most popular poets of the seventeenth century. Even Horace Walpole had to concede, reluctantly, that "Milton was forced to wait until the world had done with admiring Quarles."[7] While Poe clearly was tapping into the revived reputation of Francis Quarles during the mid-nineteenth century,[8] his gambit in substituting Quarles's name for his own should also be seen as a reflection of his inclination toward self-irony and satire. Reminiscent then of the baroque practice of arrogating the name of someone from the past to round out one's composite literary identity (as when Robert Burton chose Democritus Junior for his alter ego in the satirical preface to *The Anatomy of Melancholy* [1621]), Poe took on the loose-fitting mask of Quarles in much the same spirit. Moreover, as Poe well knew, baroque emblems both embodied and bodied forth a combined elusiveness and allusiveness that was recognized as being part of an elaborate game. From their stylized origin in the mid-sixteenth century on, emblems were attended by a kind of festive, intellectual playfulness "pointing to a knowing self-consciousness."[9] While an emblem, strictly speaking, consisted of a picture and a pithy motto along with an explanatory verse clarifying a connection between the two, by the nineteenth century the word "emblem" tended to imply any type of symbol, whether verbal or visual.[10]

Even though Poe used the name of Quarles just this one time, the associations implicitly forged between the work of the celebrated emblematist and Poe's own writing can be seen to have been securely in place throughout his career. And even though anonymous and pseudonymous publication was part of standard magazine practice of the day, the specific name Poe chose as his pseudonym for "The Raven" situates him squarely within an earlier tradition involving the play of paradox and hidden meanings fundamental to baroque rhetorical practices and aesthetic concerns.[11] His gesture of concealing himself initially behind the aegis of Quarles, in part alerting his audience to read "The Raven" with a sympathetic eye toward an emblematic method, provides a compelling instantiation of a larger and consistent strain of literary brinksmanship that has come to be associated with his life and career.

Francis Quarles was an English devotional poet remembered most for his exceedingly popular *Emblemes, Divine and Moral* (1635).[12] Excerpts from it appeared in an anthology Poe reviewed for the *Southern Literary Messenger* in 1836, Samuel Carter Hall's *The Book of Gems: From the Poets and Artists of Great Britain*.[13] In his roll-call of the exemplary poets treated by Hall, Poe mentions Quarles twice, whether because of his enthusiasm for this poet or perhaps owing to some mishap that occurred in the printing house. One of the reasons Poe was drawn to Quarles, especially as regards the cryptic nature of the emblematic method, can be found in the preface to *Emblemes*: "An emblem is but a silent parable."[14] Additionally, Poe declares he was engrossed by this collection of poets "of a former age . . . over which we have been poring for many days with intense delight" ("Review," 585). What Poe delighted in as a literary critic and what, as a poet, he hoped to draw on was "the source of this so shadowy pleasure" ("Review," 585), a notion that resonates sympathetically with his own attitude toward composition. The similar tone and content of the three poems by Quarles found in Hall's anthology indicate something of what Poe valued in poetry. Here we can glimpse what he wanted his readers to value as well, insofar as it mirrors and is in harmony with his own aesthetic sensibilities. Quarles's poems thus can be seen to reify and enrich what Poe deemed most estimable in verse.

The first poem, although unidentified in Hall's anthology, is an elegy on the futility of mortal strivings taken from Quarles's paraphrase of Jeremiah's Lamentations: "People, that travel through thy wasted land, / Gaze on thy ruins, and amazed stand, / They shake their spleenful heads, disdain, deride, / The sudden downfall of so fair a pride."[15] Perhaps, in imitation of Jeremiah's alpha-numeric acrostic style, Quarles composed each elegy within his three threnodies so that the letter "A" is the first letter of the first elegy and so on through the alphabet to "Y," which begins the twenty-second and final elegy.[16] Given Poe's pronounced delight in acrostics, displayed among other places in his puzzle poems concealing a lady's name,[17] it is easy to see how Quarles's emblematic method would appeal to him.

The other two poems excerpted by Hall come from *Emblemes*, thus giving pride of place to this work over the many others by Quarles then available. Again, the theme of restlessness in a fallen world pervades the verse. We can glimpse something of what Poe found worthy of imitation in some typical stanzas from each of the excerpts: "'Tis vain to flee, 'tis neither here nor there / Can 'scape that hand, until that hand forbear; / Ah me! Where is he not, that's everywhere? . . . My glass is half spent! Forbear t'arrest / My thriftless day too soon: my poor request / Is that my glass may run but out the rest."[18] Although Hall leaves the excerpts from *Emblemes* unidentified, they both come from the third book, specifically the emblems numbered 12 and 13. A glance at any of the many editions of Quarles's *Emblemes* (and at least ten were published during Poe's lifetime) reveals that the biblical passages heading each poem come from Job.[19] The first is from Job 14:13 ("O that thou wouldst hide me in the grave, that thou wouldst keep me secret until thy wrath be past!") and the second from Job 10:20 ("Are not my days few? Cease then, and let me alone, that I may bewail my self a little.") Although no biblical tags or illustrations accompany Hall's excerpts, insofar as the poems spin out the implications of the various icons and symbols that collectively render a larger allegorical vignette, readers easily could reconstruct the emblems in their mind's eye.[20]

In his review Poe projects a hypothetical reader who, if called upon to give an account of what was pleasing in such a poem, "would be apt to speak of the quaint in phraseology and of the grotesque in rhythm. And this quaintness and grotesqueness are, as we have elsewhere endeavored to show, very powerful, and if well managed, very admissible adjuncts to Ideality" ("Review," 585). Poe's own aesthetic predispositions, revealed here unmistakably, are consonant with the views expressed in "The Philosophy of Composition" and "The Poetic Principle." The linking of quaintness and grotesqueness as "admissible adjuncts to Ideality" is a prominent feature of Quarles's oddly jarring conceits, typical of the last gasp of what has come to be called metaphysical poetry.

Given the extracts from Quarles that Poe had in Hall's anthology, and taking into account whatever else he could have encountered by Quarles, we can discern an affinity in his work for Quarles's characteristically baroque diction and paradoxes: "Get up my Soul; Redeem thy slavish eyes / From drowsy bondage: O beware; be wise: / Thy Fo's before thee; thou must fight or fly: Life lyes most open in a closed eye."[21] Quarles's conceit here, about the stuff of the imagination being more real than things of the sensuous world, finds a parallel expression in Poe's own work. For example, among other places, in the poem "Alone," a striking lament that "from childhood's hour" the poet has "not been / As others were" nor "seen / As others saw." [22] Like Quarles's recognition of the power within being stronger than the insubstantial allurements of the world, Poe's narrator concludes: "And the cloud that took the form / (When the rest of Heaven was blue) / Of a demon in my view" (ll.20–22). Each must stand alone and confront the inner trial, whether it is figured as an encounter with a great foe or powerful demon; when cast back on one's own resources, one must draw on previous experiences with and recollections of the supremely beautiful, a vision that fortifies one to continue the struggle in the face of, as Poe puts it midway through this poem, "the mystery which binds me still" (l.12). For both Quarles and Poe, their involved poetic conceits bear out that life indeed lies most open in a closed eye and, paradoxically, that it is by means of such highly mannered formulations that we are able to see it for what it really is.

Along similar lines "The Conqueror Worm," in which the worm is figured as the hero of a tragic play called "Man,"[23] bears an uncanny resemblance to the dominant conceit of Quarles's *Feast for Wormes*, a verse paraphrase of Jonah with periodic "meditations" that showcase Quarles's penchant for copiously apostrophizing the luridly desolate:

> Why? What are men, but quickened lumps of earth?
> *A Feast for Wormes*; a bubble full of breath;
> A looking-glasse for grief; a flash; a minute;
> A painted Toombe, with putrifaction in it;
> A mappe of Death; A burthen of a song;

> A winters Dust; A worme of five foot long;
> Begot in sinne; In darknesse nourisht; Borne
> In Sorrow; Naked; Shiftlesse and forlorne:
> His first voice (heard) is crying for reliefe;
> Alas! He comes into a world of griefe:
> His Age is sinfull, and his Youth is vaine,
> His Life's a punishment; His Death's a paine;
> His life's an houre of Ioy, a world of Sorrow;
> His death's a winters night, that findes no morrow:
> Mans life's an Hower-glasse, which being runne,
> Concludes that houre of joy, and so is done.[24]

In this catalogue of *contemptus mundi* commonplaces Quarles refers to the course of our life as culminating in an interminable winter's night that finds no morrow, a conceit incidentally that coincides neatly with Poe's own setting for "The Raven" in bleak December. Moreover, Poe likewise uses a "sorrow/morrow" rhyme to convey a similar sense of the unabating remembrance of loss: "Eagerly I wished the morrow:—vainly I had sought to borrow / From my books surcease of sorrow—sorrow for the lost Lenore."[25]

While this pairing of "sorrow" and "morrow" generally was available to any English-speaking poet, what Quarles and Poe have in common is their use of it principally to express a longing for remission from the burden of consciousness in a world intersected by supernatural stirrings and soulful longings. This can be seen in Quarles's *Feast for Wormes* with some frequency: "Death is a minute; full of sudden sorrow: / Then live to day as thou may'st die to morrow" (D3v); and "Burst forth, my teares, into a world of sorrow, / And let my nights of griefe find ne'r a morrow" (F6v). Another telling "sorrow/morrow" rhyme shows up in Quarles's *Pentelogia*: "So strong is *Man,* that with a Gasping *Breath* / He totters, and bequeaths his Strength to *Death*; / So yong is *Man,* that (broke with *care* and *sorrow*) / He's old enough to day, to *Dye to morrow*" (F7v). And again in *Feast for Wormes* Quarles used the rhyme in an extended conceit that gives further intimations of possible influence on Poe's work, "The Conqueror Worm" in particular. These lines evoke the backdrop of a shifting dream-world so commodious to Poe's own poetic register: "I live on Earth, as on a *Stage* of sorrow; / Lord, if thou pleasest, end the *Play* to morrow. / I live on Earth, as in a Dream of pleasure, / Awake me when thou wilt, I wait thy leisure" (F1v). This passage, as it happens, resonates beguilingly with the conclusion to "Al Aaraaf," where the lovers "whiled away / The night that waned and waned and brought no day," falling into a kind of indeterminate sleep from which one only awakens, if at all, by the grace of supernatural intervention.[26]

These representative examples of "sorrow/morrow" couplets are not cited as evidence that Poe picked up the pattern from Quarles definitively, but to indicate a shared poetic sympathy for using this particular rhyme pair to convey the same sense of unremitting desolation. And even though Poe emphasizes all of the melancholy without giving any of the hope that comes from Quarles's expressions of faith in a gracious God, still both poets point toward a privileged place of contemplation of the highest good, which alone can raise us out of ourselves; or, as Poe put it in "The Poetic Principle: "to attain that pleasurable elevation, or excitement, *of the soul*, which we recognize as the Poetic Sentiment, and which is so easily distinguished from Truth, which is the satisfaction of the Reason, or from Passion, which is the excitement of the heart" [original emphasis].[27]

It was the emblematical method with its quaint conceits elaborated by way of "the grotesque in rhythm" that Poe found so alluring in the "old poets" such as Quarles. In line with this notion of true "Poetic Sentiment," Poe declares in "The Philosophy of Composition" that the raven is to be construed emblematically.[28] He goes on to highlight the bird's overtly iconic aspects and explains its grotesquely echoic features of phraseology. What Poe attributes to the raven finally is the quality of Ideality, such that it is "emblematical of *Mournful and Never-ending Remembrance*" [original emphasis] ("Philosophy," 70). In similar fashion, all of Quarles's emblems admonish his readers to reflect time and again on the lamentable case of our mortality; each one, in effect, is a token to remember some aspect of our alienation from Ideality, some impediment that keeps the Supremely Beautiful just out of reach.

Poe appreciated the quaintness of Quarles's conceits more than did Hall, who prefaced the poems by damning with faint praise: "The faults of Quarles are large and numerous. No writer is either more affected or more obscure. It is only by raking that we can gather the gold; yet it is such as will reward the seeker who has courage to undertake the search" (*Gems*, 194). These are faults one can imagine Poe's detractors using to describe his poetry. Poe himself remarked: "Future generations will be able to sift the gold from the dross, and the 'The Raven' will be beheld, shining above them all as a diamond of purest water."[29] Despite the commonplace nature of this phrase, the similarity between what Poe read in Hall about Quarles and what he said about his own poetic gem, "The Raven," is almost uncanny; as such, it serves to demonstrate another aspect of the affinity between the two poets.

Notwithstanding Hall's critical assessment of Quarles's "large and numerous" faults, *Emblemes* had remarkable staying power. It was first published in 1635 with illustrations, forty-five of which were copied from Herman Hugo's *Pia Desideria* (1624), principally by the famous engraver William Marshall.[30] Although frequently reissued, all later editions follow the original pictures quite closely. The preface to one such mid-nineteenth century edition, a version of which incidentally was reissued the same year as "The Raven," clarifies the value of such emblems for Poe's contemporaries: "Our forefathers in the seventeenth-century, so far as regarded their intellectual capacities, were but children of a larger growth. They needed to be taught, as our little ones now are, by pictures, and they were as easily captivated by them."[31] This condescending assessment at once masks and excuses the delight that contemporary readers would have found in an emblem book; at the same time, it accounts for the time-tested pedagogical practice of using images to stimulate the memory.[32] Quarles maintained that pictures were capable of "catching therein the eye and fancy at one draught."[33] Poe likewise was keen to avail himself of this mnemonic aspect of the image, and in "The Raven" he sought to devise stirring mental images through repetition, augmented further by elaborate echoic aural conceits, which would—and indeed did—captivate his audience.[34]

Closely aligned to his predisposition toward the encoding and deciphering of emblems was Poe's penchant for complex word-play and hidden chiastic designs, for cryptograms and secret writing.[35] He displayed both knowledge of and a debt to baroque writers on these subjects, though his method of exposition is marked by a dizzying blend of self-effacing and self-promotional cunning far too involved to go into here.[36] For our purposes, namely inquiring into Poe's resonance with baroque emblems and the Art of Memory, a single example will suffice. In his run-up to introducing his magazine cryptograms, so much a part of his tongue-in-cheek literary identity,[37] Poe gives clues hinting at Francis Bacon but never names him directly: "He who has been termed the 'wisest of mankind'—we mean Lord Verulam—was as confident of the absolute insolubility of his own mode as our present cryptographist is of his. What was said upon the subject in his *De Augmentis* was, at the day of its publication, considered unanswerable. Yet his cipher has been repeatedly unriddled."[38]

In addition to having an extended section on ciphers, Bacon's *Of the Proficience and Advancement of Learning* also contains a discussion on artificial memory schemes. Such systems, derived from classical rhetoric and oratory, depend on the orderly disposition of lively images (*imagines agentes*) within designated places (*loci*) arranged, for example, in a room, palace, or city.[39] This technique for arranging and embellishing one's compositions clearly was well known to Poe both because of his acquaintance with the works by early modern writers who commented on mnemotechnics such as Francis Bacon and Robert Fludd,[40] and also because he published a review of Francis Fauvel-Gouraud's *Phreno-Mnemotechny; or The Art of Memory*.[41] Indeed Poe was aware, quoting Gouraud, that "by Artificial Memory we understand, simply the power of recollecting facts and events, by means of *conditional associations*, which must first be called for, in order, by their assistance, to get at the facts associated with them" [original emphasis] ("Notices," 327). His review was published three months before "The Raven" and so, as Gouraud's book is seven hundred pages long, it is likely that Poe was thumbing through it at about the same time he was putting the finishing touches on his poem.

Despite its prodigious length, Poe lauds *Phreno-Mnemotechny* as being "beyond doubt, one of the most important and altogether extraordinary works which have been published within the last fifty years" ("Notices," 326). While this topic, like Gouraud's previous compendium on homophones and rhyme words,[42] would have intrigued Poe given his range of interests, his hyperbolic praise may also be due in some measure to the fact that this book was published by the same firm that, on the strength of "The Raven," was in the process of publishing a collection of his prose tales—Poe's first book in nearly five years.[43] All the same, this is high praise coming from the likes of Poe "the Tomahawk Man," so called because of his reputation for writing savagely brutal reviews. Poe is a faithful expositor of Gouraud's method and an ardent apologist for his publicly demonstrated feats of memory as well as for the man himself.

> M. Gouraud is himself a very peculiar man; his idiosyncrasies are marked beyond those of any person we have yet met. And of men such as these, we must be wary how we adopt prejudices—for they radiate prejudices wherever they go. The world always receives with distrust any thing which gives it a startling impulse—any thing which jostles its old conservative equanimity. ("Notices," 327)

It is as if Poe found in Gouraud a kindred spirit no less than a living realization of Maelzel's Chess-Player, for the Frenchman had been accused of tricking—or hoaxing—his audiences: "It is by no means too much to say that the powers of memory, as aided by his system, are *absolutely illimitable*. We earnestly advise our readers to procure M. Gouraud's extraordinary work and decide in the premises *for themselves*" [original emphasis] ("Notices," 327–28). Indeed Gouraud's explanation of the principles of mnemotechny, especially as concerns the rigorous, rational, and systematic application of the most fanciful inventions and grotesque images to achieve a higher end, is wholly consistent with Poe's own ideas about the efficacy of jarring imagery and aural conceits to achieve a totality of effect as discussed in "The Philosophy of Composition." Gouraud wrote about it in precisely these terms: "In order to remember a series of words, they are put in the several squares or places, and the recollection of them is assisted by associating some idea of relation between the objects and their situation; and as we find by experience that whatever is ludicrous is calculated to make a strong impression upon the mind, the more ridiculous the association the better" (*Phreno-Mnemotechny*, 76).

Among the key figures in the history of mnemotechnics to whom Gouraud refers is Poe's own cryptographic touchstone, Francis Bacon. He is praised for having "framed a kind of system of his own, so deeply was he convinced of the utility of artificial processes in aiding and assisting the memory" (*Phreno-Mnemotechny*, 84). Whether from the original source or from Gouraud, Poe would have been familiar with Bacon's view that emblems "reduce conceits intellectual to images sensible, which strike the memory more."[44] And, as is well known, Poe was concerned throughout his career with finding aural patterns and arresting poetic images that would strike the memory with more than the usual intensity—"The Bells" being an extreme case in point.

Poe's knowledge of and allusions to applications of such systems show up, among other places, in "A Decided Loss": "To sharpen my invention, I took down a prize poem on _____, and reading half an hour, found myself fuddled. Jumping up in despair, I hit upon an expedient, and immediately set about carrying it into execution. Being naturally quick, I committed to memory the entire tragedies of Metamora and Miantinimoh."[45] On the surface this might read like one of Poe's extravagant satirical rants in the style of a Blackwood article—and it is. And yet, a little more than a decade after writing "A Decided Loss," as already has been observed, Poe would praise and defend just such a mnemonic method designed for committing to memory and recalling anything whatsoever: "The powers of memory, as aided by his system, are *absolutely illimitable*" [original emphasis] ("Notices," 328).

Poe's confidence where verbal play and emblematic devices are concerned, as with his self-assured if initially self-effacing gesture of assigning "The Raven" to Quarles, reflects, in Wellek's words, "an attitude toward the world" that is quintessentially baroque. He admired the quaint phraseology and grotesqueness in rhythm typical of Quarles; he absorbed it, resonated with it, let it stir his inventions and, in the end, made it wholly his own. Recourse to baroque aesthetics along the lines discussed here offers a compelling way to read and make sense of Poe.

NOTES

This essay is based on a paper presented at the Edgar Allan Poe Society's 2009 Bicentennial Poe Conference held in Philadelphia; I am indebted to George Core and Brown Patterson for reading more than a few versions of this project and making helpful suggestions. For a more fully developed version of this argument, which takes into account the larger critical implications with respect to visual culture and intellectual history, see William E. Engel, *Early Modern Poetics in Melville and Poe: Memory, Melancholy, and the Emblematic Tradition* (Farnham, UK: Ashgate, 2012), 77–156.

1. "Quarles" [Edgar Allan Poe], "The Raven," *American Review*, February 1845, 143–45. See Edgar A. Poe, *The Collected Works of Edgar Allan Poe,* vol. 1., ed. Thomas Olive Mabbott (Cambridge, MA: Belknap Press, 1978). Future quotations from Poe's poems, as well as Mabbott's textual notes and commentaries, refer to this edition.

2. On his life and career, see Karl Josef Höltgen, *Francis Quarles* (Tübingen, Germany: Max Niemeyer Verlag, 1978); on his contribution to the emblematic method, see Ernest B. Gilman, "Word and Image in Quarles' *Emblemes*," *Critical Inquiry* 6, no. 3 (1983): 385–410.

3. Mabbott, *Collected Works*, 360.

4. The word *baroque* is used here principally as a way to continue the dialogue about literary style using the terms in which historically it has been cast. I concur with Jonas Barish, *Ben Jonson and the Language of Prose Comedy* (New York: Norton, 1970), 308: "The energy expended at differentiating such terms has only compounded confusion and darkened counsel."

5. René Wellek, "The Concept of Baroque in Literary Scholarship," *Journal of Aesthetics and Art Criticism* 5, no. 2 (1946): 92–93.

6. The *locus classicus* regarding "topics of invention" is Cicero, *De inventione*, trans. H. M. Hubbell (Cambridge, MA: Harvard University Press, 1949), 7–9, 87–90. On the development of this notion from antiquity up to the early modern period, see Mary Carruthers, *The Book of Memory: A Study of Memory in Medieval Culture* (Cambridge, MA: Cambridge University Press, 1990), 122–55.

7. Peter Cunningham, ed., *Letters of Horace Walpole* (London: Henry G. Bohn, 1861), 3:99.

8. See, for example, Ernest E. Leisy, "Francis Quarles and Henry D. Thoreau," *Modern Language Notes* 60, no. 5 (1945): 335–36, regarding Thoreau's indebtedness to Quarles in *A Week on the Concord and Merrimack Rivers* (1849), a work suffused with the condoling remembrance of his brother, who died in 1842 and with whom Thoreau had made that river journey in 1839.

9. John Manning, *The Emblem* (London: Reaktion Books, 2002), 107.

10. Charles Moseley, *A Century of Emblems* (Aldershot, UK: Scolar Press, 1989), 2.

11. See Rosalie L. Colie, *Paradoxia Epidemica: The Renaissance Tradition of Paradox* (Princeton, NJ: Princeton University Press, 1966), 450–58; and Dalia Judovitz, *Subjectivity and Representation in Descartes: The Origins of Modernity* (Cambridge: Cambridge University Press, 1988), 154–55.

12. Mabbott, *Poems,* 360. See also Bart Westerweel, "William Blake and the Emblem," in *Configuring Romanticism: Essays Offered to C .C. Barfoot*, ed. Theo D'haen et al. (Amsterdam and New York: Rodopi, 2003), 21: "Quarles' *Emblemes* is both the best and by far the most popular English emblem book ever."

13. Edgar Allan Poe, review of S. C. Hall's *Book of Gems*, in the *Southern Literary Messenger* 2 (August 1836): 9; hereafter in the text referred to as "Review" and followed by page number. I am indebted to the Newberry Library for making this work available to me, along with S. C. Hall, *The Book of Gems: From the Poets and Artists of Great Britain*, 3 vols. (London: Bell and Daldey, 1836).

14. Quarles's preface, with this definition of the emblem as a silent parable, appears in all editions of *Emblemes: Divine and Moral* from its first appearance in 1635 well into the nineteenth century (with no fewer than ten editions printed during Poe's lifetime); moreover, it is retained in Johann Abricht's popular abridgement, *Divine Emblems: Embellished with Etchings on Copper after the Fashion of Master Francis Quarles* (London: Thomas Ward & Co., 1838), 2. It should be observed in passing that editions of this particular much-reprinted volume would have been available to Poe from his childhood on, as it was first published in 1800.

15. Francis Quarles, *Sions Elegies Wept by Jeremie the Prophet* (London, 1624), Threnodia II, 15.

16. Lamentations is based on a chiastic plan following the twenty-two letters of the Hebrew alphabet rendered in five sections consisting of sets of 22, 22, 66, 22, 22 verses, thus making it, as it were, an intensified alphabet of woe with a threefold climax of desolation in the central section.

17. See, for example, "A Valentine" and "An Enigma"; Mabbott, *Poems*, 386–91, 424.

18. Hall, *Gems*, 1:197.

19. In addition to the useful information contained in the National Union Catalogue, much about the publication history of Quarles's *Emblemes* during Poe's lifetime can be gleaned from William Thomas Lowndes, *The Bibliographer's Manual of English Literature* (London: William Pickering, 1834), 2:1525–1526. The entries for Quarles's works expand considerably thereafter; for example, see the much enlarged, revised edition of Henry G. Bohn (London: Bell and Daldy, 1865), 4:2020–2023.

20. On this element, concerning internal visualization techniques at the heart of the emblematic method, see William E. Engel, "Mnemonic Emblems and the Humanist Discourse of

Knowledge," in *Aspects of Renaissance and Baroque Symbol Theory, 1500–1700*, ed. Peter Daly and John Manning (New York: AMS Press, 1999), 125–42.

21. Francis Quarles, *Emblemes* (London, 1634), 1:vii, C4.

22. "Alone," in Mabbott, *Collected Works,* 146–47.

23. "The Conqueror Worm," in Mabbott, *Collected Works*, 326.

24. Francis Quarles, *Divine Poems* (London, 1638), B3–B3v.

25. "The Raven," ll.9–10; Mabbott, *Collected Works*, 365.

26. "Al Aaraaf," ll.261–62; Mabbott, *Collected Works*, 115.

27. *Edgar Allan Poe: Critical Theory, The Major Documents*, ed. Stuart Levine and Susan F. Levine (Urbana: University of Illinois Press, 2009), 185.

28. Levine and Levine, *Critical Theory*, 70.

29. George Edward Woodberry, *The Life of Edgar Allan Poe* (Boston and New York: Houghton Mifflin Company, 1909), 2:425; qtd. in Mabbott, *Collected Works*, 351.

30. Marshall's other celebrated works include George Wither's *Collection of Emblemes* (1635) and the allegorical portrait of "King Charles, martyr" for *Eikon Basilike* (1649).

31. Francis Quarles, *Emblemes, Divine and Moral* (London: William Tegg & Co., 1839), xv. The prominent bookseller Thomas Tegg, who specialized in illustrations, published numerous editions of *Emblems* beginning in the 1820s; thereafter his son, William, continued issuing the book steadily in very much the same form.

32. William E. Engel, "Updating Classical Mnemonics," *International Journal of Case Method Research and Application* 20, no. 2 (2008): 174–88.

33. Quarles, *Emblemes*, xvi.

34. Mabbott, *Collected Works*, 350.

35. Regarding the former, see Richard Kopley, *Edgar Allan Poe and the Dupin Mysteries* (New York: Palgrave Macmillan, 2008), 21; and the latter, Peter Ackroyd, *Poe: A Life Cut Short* (New York: Doubleday, 2008), 91.

36. For further elaboration of this important issue, see Jonathan Elmer, *Reading at the Social Limit: Affect, Mass Culture and Edgar Allan Poe* (Stanford, CA: Stanford University Press, 1995), 182–85; and Scott Peeples, "'The *Mere* Man of Letters Must Ever Be a Cipher': Poe and N. P. Willis," *ESQ: Journal of the American Renaissance* 46, no. 3 (2000): 129.

37. John Hodgson, "Decoding Poe," *Journal of English and Germanic Philology* 92, no. 4 (1993): 523–34.

38. Edgar Allan Poe, "Secret Writing [Addendum III]," *Graham's Magazine* (December 1841): 308.

39. Frances A. Yates, *The Art of Memory* (Harmondsworth, UK: Penguin, 1978), 18–28.

40. For a more detailed analysis of Poe's knowledge of writers and works related to this topic, especially as regards the books in Roderick Usher's library, see Engel, *Early Modern Poetics in Melville and Poe*, 109–10.

41. Edgar Allan Poe, "Notices of New Works," *Southern Literary Messenger* May 1845, 326–28, hereafter identified parenthetically in the text followed by page number; Francis Fauvel-Gouraud, *Phreno-Mnemotechny; or, The Art of Memory* (New York and London: Wiley and Putnam, 1845), hereafter identified parenthetically within the text followed by page number.

42. Francis Fauvel-Gouraud, *Phreno-Mnemotechnic Dictionary; being a Philosophical Classification of all the Homophonic words of the English Language* (New York: Houel and Macoy, 1844).

43. Jeffrey Meyers, *Edgar Allan Poe: His Life and Legacy* (New York City: Cooper Square Press, 1992), 176–78.

44. *Works of Francis Bacon*, ed. James Spedding, Robert Leslie Ellis, and Douglas Denton Heath (Cambridge, MA: Riverside Press, 1863), 6:282.

45. Edgar Allan Poe, "A Decided Loss," *Saturday Courier*, November 10, 1832, 2:35; Mabbott, *Collected Works*, 2:55. The 1832 version is quoted here rather than the more canonical "Loss of Breath" because only in this version does Poe deploy the word *invention* which, as my analysis bears out, was integral to the thought processes associated with the Art of Memory. This phrasing, retained only in "A Decided Loss," leaves no doubt that Poe was well aware of the link between "invention" and feats of mnemotechnic gymnastics.

Chapter Two

"A snare in every human path"

"Tamerlane" and the Paternal Scapegoat

John Edward Martin

The most remarkable thing about Poe's "Tamerlane" (1827) is not necessarily its ambition—for what gifted young poet is not ambitious? Nor is it the poem's relative obscurity among Poe's poetic works—because for young, gifted poets, and particularly for Poe, ambition often proves inversely proportional to popular success. Rather, what is most remarkable about the poem is its *consistency* with Poe's more mature writings, particularly in its distinctive rhetorical strategies, which include (apparent) self-revelation, deception, emotional evasion, and subversion of its audience's expectations or conventional assumptions. Specifically, Poe makes use of a nominally "confessional" narrative—one that invokes his favorite themes of ambition, love, visionary idealism, violence, loss, and betrayal—only to reject the traditional premises and benefits of the confessional form, namely, contrition, sympathy, forgiveness, and reintegration of the "lost" self back into the social or spiritual body from which it has been alienated. Instead, Poe uses Tamerlane's unusual confession to challenge the very authority of his confessor— that "holy friar" who, in later versions of the poem, is renamed "holy father"—and to reject the notion of any sort of paternalistic sympathy or identification. He does so, interestingly, through a subtle invocation of one of the foundational myths—that of the "scapegoat"—common to all three patriarchal "religions of the book": Judaism, Christianity, and Islam. In doing so, Poe lays the groundwork for a lifelong poetic project, and a poetic theory, that reimagines the figure of the artist-as-scapegoat, not as an ultimate sacrifice or surrender of artistic integrity, but rather as a viable alternative for preserving that integrity in the face of paternal (and literary) authority.

The critical history of Poe's "Tamerlane" is sparse. The original printed version, as it appears in *Tamerlane and Other Poems* (1827), received no critical notices at all, and its subsequent publications, in revised form, were generally received as merely a sample of Poe's "juvenilia" (a perception that Poe himself encouraged). In the century and a half since Poe's death, only a handful of critics have given the poem any sustained critical treatment outside of an introduction or footnote to Poe's collections of poetry. These rarely go beyond noting its general themes of ambition, loss, and dissolution as typical of Poe's early writing, tracing its literary sources and references as examples of Poe's reading, exploring its relationship to Poe's early romantic disappointments (particularly with Sarah Elmira Royster), or examining its awkward experiments with versification.[1]

Perhaps the reason for this critical neglect is that, as Daniel Hoffman puts it, the poem is an "elephantine failure" and "a poem that nobody would read unless he *had* to."[2] And yet, when we consider those handful of critical readings that have addressed the poem in depth—notably Edward Davidson (1957), David Halliburton (1973), Robert Jacobs (1977), and G. R. Thompson (1984)—a case can be made that anyone who wishes to understand Poe's driving motivations as a poet, his distinctive rhetorical strategies, and the development of his poetic theory and practice will, like the "unfortunate" students in Professor Hoffman's now famous seminars, *have to* read "Tamerlane."[3] Each of these critics makes a compelling argument for the poem's centrality to Poe's thinking about the role and function of the poetic imagination, and each notes the significance of the power dynamics at work within the poem's nominally confessional narrative, although they disagree on precisely what those dynamics are. None of them, however, argue that the poem "works" on any but the most rudimentary conceptual and poetic level. The poem continues to be seen as only a formative stage in Poe's artistic development—a notion that I don't seek to change but rather to complicate and perhaps refocus.

But in order to understand both the "confessional" nature of the poem and its ambivalence toward paternal authority, we must first reflect on some of the biographical and material circumstances of the poem's composition. In the formative years of 1826–1831 (during which time "Tamerlane" was written and revised three times), Poe experienced increasing tensions in his relationship with his foster father, John Allan. Already, the young Poe had a cultivated sense of his own isolation and betrayal by those closest to him, including the birth father who abandoned him; the mother who died early, leaving him a "charity case"; and, of course, the foster father who bullied and belittled him at every opportunity. Even his beloved foster mother, Frances Allan, would die before Poe had the opportunity to pursue his emerging literary ambitions. Thus, it was only with John Allan that Poe was able to carry on, for a time, an increasingly bitter and abject correspondence—one that set a pattern for many of his later relationships, particularly with paternalistic mentors, publishers, editors, and literary friends. These relationships were all intricately tied to Poe's efforts to establish himself in the literary marketplace as a serious man-of-letters and an independent artist—an ambition that, from the beginning, set Poe at odds with the demands of his foster father, as well as those of the marketplace itself.

In his correspondence with Allan, Poe employs a full range of rhetorical strategies and emotional appeals designed to alternately appease, entreat, apologize, accuse, and even threaten John Allan with various forms of embarrassment or guilty complicity. In one early letter, Poe expresses his determination "to leave your house and endeavor to find some place in this wide world, where I will be treated—not as *you* have treated me."[4] How he was actually treated remains a matter of speculation, but for Poe, the salient features were a general lack of "affection," overheard disparagements and insults, and worst of all, the humiliation of economic dependence. Poe dismisses the former abuses as irrelevant to his newfound sense of artistic purpose, but he cannot help but acknowledge the hard reality of his poverty, though he does so with what would become a characteristic hostility and melodrama, not to mention an obscure threat: "Send me, I entreat you, some money immediately—as I am in the greatest necessity—If you fail to comply with my request—I tremble for the consequence."[5]

The consequence, of course, was his enrollment in the army—an ironic embrace of just the kind of authoritarian discipline against which Poe would always rebel (indeed, Poe is later discharged for deliberately disobeying orders). But in this instance, Poe's threat promises something more ominous, not for only for Allan, but for Poe himself—some ultimate degradation or embarrassment, even a tragic death, that might reflect poorly on his image-conscious father. Allan's silence in response to this and later appeals for sympathy, and his repeated refusal to offer anything in the way of financial support, eventually drives Poe to the depths of despairing supplication: "I sometimes am afraid that you are angry & perhaps you have reason to be—but if you will but put a little more confidence in me—I will endeavor to deserve it—"; "I am anxious to abide by your directions, if I knew what they were."[6]

Poe's professed confusion over his father's wishes reveals a deeper desire for his father's "confidence" and "direction"—two things consistently lacking in Poe's personal and literary lives—the denial of which contributes to his growing anxiety that he might not deserve the success for which he longs. So debilitating are his fears and his lack of direction that Poe apparently becomes petrified by his father's continued silence: "You must be aware how important it is that I should hear from you soon—I do not know how to act."[7]

Such paralysis in the face of paternal authority is the presumed situation of most "confessional" models—at least those of Freud, Foucault, and others who have examined such narratives from the standpoint of power relations. Lacking a direct communication with the authoritative other, the typical confessional speaker must ultimately answer his own questions by assimilating his earliest intuitions of paternal authority, confused though they may be, in the form of an overweening "conscience."[8] But interestingly, when confronted with the lack of responsiveness or direction from his foster father, Poe doesn't choose to answer silence with silence; nor does he go about "acting" in any way differently from before. Instead, he repeatedly provokes and cajoles Allan to voice *his* particular complaints, to reveal *his* resentments and suspicions. He demands to hear his own sins spoken aloud by the father.

When Allan at last complies in July of 1829—citing his foster-son's repeated financial failures as well as his harsh words toward Allan himself—Poe takes the opportunity to go on the offensive: "Before I proceed to tell the event of my application, I think it my duty to say something concerning the accusations & suspicions which are contained in your letter. . . . I am conscious of having offended you formerly—greatly—but I thought *that had been forgiven*, at least you told me so" [Poe's emphasis].[9] Here Poe acknowledges a "consciousness" of his own sins against Allan (a fact that belies his earlier "confusion") but at the same time, he takes it as his "duty" to remind Allan that he has already offered "forgiveness"—an act that, Poe implies, cannot be revoked. If Allan's demands are to carry any weight, Poe suggests, they must at least be consistent with his previous words and actions. It is a staggering instance of the sinner *demanding* his rights as a penitent, while simultaneously laying a retaliatory accusation at the feet of the supposed authority: *you forgot your own words.*

This rhetorical strike does little to move the obstinate Allan, but apparently it is one that emboldens Poe to continue his requests and complaints for another six months. In January of 1831, Poe lets fly another angry rant that is part confession, part supplication, and part accusation and rejection:

> Did I, when an infant, solicit your charity and protection, or was it of your own free will, that you volunteered your services in my behalf? . . . I am not about to proclaim myself guilty of all that has been alleged against me, and which I have hitherto endured, simply because I was too proud to reply. . . . You promised me to forgive all—but you soon forgot your promise.[10]

Here Poe takes his "duty" one step further, not only reminding his father of the forgiveness that he has verbally given, but also of the "free will" with which he has given that and all of his previous personal and financial support—a claim that undermines any assumption of obligation on Allan's part (he chose it freely) but also puts him in the tricky position of having to explain his current disavowal of Poe's claims. In asserting his infantile helplessness and his *lack* of free will, Poe denies his own obligation to "reply" to

Allan's accusations, and lays responsibility for any mistakes firmly on Allan's shoulders (*you* are the parent, *I* am the child). Finally, while expressing his own expectation of forgiveness, Poe makes clear in this letter that he has neither forgotten nor forgiven any of Allan's slights against him. Here we see Poe making full use of the rhetorical power at his disposal as a "confessant" and "child" in need of its father's promised protection and blessing.

Nevertheless, Allan never fully accedes to Poe's demands (but for a few grudging dollars sent intermittently throughout their correspondence), which finally leads Poe to disavow not only his father's authority, but even his need for further assistance or support. Understanding that the material battle is lost, Poe nevertheless proclaims his own "moral victory" in one final epistolary lunge that draws upon all the weepy melodrama of the sentimental tradition: "When I think of the long twenty one years that I have called you father, and you have called me son, I could cry like a child to think that it should all end in this. . . . I can write to you with the consciousness of making no application for assistance, that I dare to open my heart, or speak one word of old affection."[11]

The passive-aggressive abjection of this moment recalls Samuel Maio's description of the confessional poet's evocation of pathos as "weeping with one eye on the camera."[12] Poe is fully aware of the manipulative and, he hopes, guilt-inducing effect of his words, and yet he delivers them with a pained sincerity that makes us wonder for a moment if, in fact, he really intends to cause his father pain. But looking over the course of their exchanges, we can see the pattern by which Poe attempts to turn the emotional and moral current in his favor—to take his father's presumed authority and power over him and claim it as his own, at least to the degree that he can, in good conscience, cease to care what his father thinks of him. It is in that eventual "freedom" of his own conscience that Poe claims at least a partial victory.

Poe's rejection of Allan, while it does little to improve his material situation, creates an important template for understanding Poe's later attitude toward authorities of all kinds and his strategies for dealing with their moral and psychological claims over him. If he cannot ultimately free himself from the hard economic and social realities that press upon him, he can at least, through his mastery of the language, perform a kind of rhetorical reversal of their authoritative claims over his conscience and perhaps assert some semblance of "free will." It is a strategy that Poe would apply early and often in his later dealings with the literary marketplace and its symbolic representatives.

More immediately, though, Poe would bring the lessons learned through his correspondence with Allan to bear on his first major poetic undertaking, "Tamerlane"—a poem that evolved over the course of that ongoing struggle with paternal authority, and which reflects, on several levels, the same desires to pacify, evade, and ultimately challenge "the father" on the poet's own terms. As in the letters, Poe would utilize both the dynamics of confessional discourse and the subversive potency of poetic language to shift the terms of Tamerlane's deathbed confession from those of contrition and submission to those of moral defiance and, to a more limited degree, emotional and intellectual liberation.

I am not the first to have noted the poem's biographical associations or its use of a confessional framework. Edward Davidson, in 1957, called the poem "a confused autobiography" that involves "simultaneous concealment and revelation."[13] But he also suggests that the contrived deathbed "confession" is, in fact, "only a device to get the reminiscence under way."[14] As evidence he notes that the speaker, Tamerlane himself, immediately disavows the confession and expresses no desire at all for forgiveness or penance. Instead, the poem as a whole displays what Davidson calls a "self-directional will-to-power"—one that flatly contradicts the confessional impulse, at least as that impulse is traditionally understood. For Davidson, such a contradiction invalidates the meaning or coherence of Poe's clumsy framing of the poem.

I argue, however, that it is precisely through the subverted confessional discourse that Tamerlane, like Poe, seeks to express both his genuine remorse and his lack of "faith" in the power or authority of the father-confessor to offer him any sort of salvation.

> Kind solace in a dying hour!
>   Such, father, is not (now) my theme—
> I will not madly deem that power
>   Of Earth may shrive me of the sin
>   Unearthly pride hath revell'd in—...
> If I *can* hope—Oh God! I can—
>   Its fount is holier—more divine—
> I would not call thee fool, old man,
>   But such is not a gift of thine.[15]

The rejection of the father's "gift" of solace and hope, and indeed his very connection to anything that the speaker considers "divine," is challenged before it is even properly offered. Instead, Tamerlane looks for hope in some "holier fount," some deeper source, that exists outside of his "earthly" father's purview, and perhaps beyond his heavenly father's as well.

David Halliburton, in his classic study *Poe: A Phenomenological View*, sees this rejection of the confessional sacrament as evidence that "Tamerlane" is, on the whole, "the history of a being that negates itself."[16] He argues that far from embracing a will-to-power, Tamerlane's confession represents an ironic realization that "to have power is to be in the power of another, and to know it."[17] In this case, Tamerlane's rejection of the father belies the inheritance that he receives from that father: an "innate nature" that is filled with both a love of beauty and the Ambition that drives him to conquer all that he sees. This "inheritance," however, is perceived by Tamerlane as an external force, perhaps a demonic one, that takes possession of his soul from childhood—"imbibed" through the air and the chilling mists of his native Tagalay. Halliburton's reading suggests that Tamerlane is the victim as much as the perpetrator of his crimes. He emphasizes Tamerlane's lack of a "functional will" and instead suggests that the poem expresses Paul Ricoeur's notion of the "servile will"—the will to self-enslavement or demonic possession that frees the self from moral responsibility for sin, and perhaps, allows for divine intercession or exorcism of that sin."[18] Unfortunately for Tamerlane, as for Poe, there is no intercession by the father, precisely because he has already renounced such a possibility at the opening of the poem. Thus, Tamerlane's confession ultimately serves only to "negate himself."

Robert D. Jacobs, in "The Self and the World: Poe's Early Poems," argues with Halliburton's assertion that Tamerlane displays a "servile will" and instead describes him as "an egotist, like Melville's Ahab, who imposes himself on what he sees."[19] Nevertheless, he agrees on the central fact that Tamerlane's rejection of both Sublime Nature and idealized human Love (both symbolized by the figure of his abandoned lover, Ada), as well as the intercession of the holy father, leads "logically to ontological disaster—a failure in relation to others, and a consequent failure of self."[20] He sees the poem as an early example of that perverse "tendency towards self destruction, and a seemingly uncontrollable impulse towards ego-gratification" that later manifests itself in the tales. In the end, Jacobs says, "Tamerlane has chosen the world, the flesh, and of course, the Devil."[21]

While I agree with all three critics' assessments of Tamerlane's psychological situation and his surrender to those demonic forces that are either the result of his paternal "inheritance" or his overt rejection of the potentially reconciling sacrament of confession, I disagree with the consensus belief that this rejection represents an "ontological disaster" or "negation of self." In fact, I believe that the poem offers an alternative ontological possibility: a self that can exist beyond the influence of paternalistic judgment; a demonic, exiled self that takes on the sacrificial role of the "scapegoat," not as a perverse act of self-destruction, but as a liberating opportunity.

After the poem's initial rejection of the father-confessor's power to console, Tamerlane recounts his early abandonment of his childhood companion, Ada, and the idealized human love that she represents, as well as his embrace of earthly Ambition in its place. Elsewhere, I have argued that this childhood romance is, in fact, representative of a sublimated maternal longing and identification, which creates an early sympathetic bond that allows for the kind of open confession and consolation that Tamerlane cannot receive from the father; it is that "holier fount" that he mentions in the first stanza as an alternative to the father's confessional ritual. [22] But Tamerlane's abandonment of that love, Ada's eventual death, and his later attempt to create a simulacrum in his "queenly city," Samarkand, results in a gothic return of the repressed that threatens to annihilate him. The failure of this maternal/erotic identification opens up that possibility of "a being that negates itself," which David Halliburton suggests. Here, however, I am more concerned with the failure of the paternal identification that, I believe, sets up the closing "demonic" embrace that ultimately offers the dying subject an alternative fate.

Near the end of the poem, after achieving all that earthly Ambition can offer him, Tamerlane finds himself overcome by a "sullenness of heart," haunted by "the sound of coming darkness," and oppressed by a vague sense of "danger nigh." Most disturbing, though, is his vision of a cold, observing presence in the skies above Samarcand:

> What tho' the moon—the white moon
> Shed all the splendor of her noon,
> *Her* smile is chilly—and *her* beam,
> In that time of dreariness, will seem
> (So like you gather in your breath)
> A portrait taken after death.

Here, the moon's deathly gaze brings his vision of triumph and glory to a trembling halt. It recalls the dead (maternal) presence of a former time and casts a pall over his present life. In contrast to his lost love's "quiet eye," this gaze speaks menacingly to Tamerlane's conscience and urges him back to the place that he has abandoned, back to his childhood "home." He guiltily, and with what Peter Brooks would call an "overborne will,"[23] accedes to the demand and seeks out his abandoned birthplace—only to find that it, conversely, has abandoned him:

> I reach'd my home—my home no more—
>   For all had flown who made it so.
> I pass'd from out its mossy door,
>   And, tho' my tread was soft and low,
> A voice came from the threshold stone
> Of one whom I had earlier known—
>   O, I defy thee, Hell, to show
>   On beds of fire that burn below,
> An humbler heart—a deeper wo.

The "undying voice" of remembrance confronts the speaker with his own betrayal and absence. That it speaks from the "threshold stone" of his first home suggests a dark parallel to the "stepping-stone" of Samarcand, upon which his new throne is erected—making them uncanny doubles of one another.[24] As in the later tale "Ligeia" (1838), the voice and gaze of the dead lover take possession here, not only of the new love's form, but of the speaker's mind and will, dispossessing him of all that he has achieved in her absence. Tamerlane seemingly ends the confession with a recognition that "Death, who comes for me" offers the only final truth that he has access to:

the truth of his own guilt and the abandonment of both his spiritualized Love and his earthly Ambition. It is a perfectly tragic ending. Indeed, the original 1827 version of the poem ends after this stanza, with these lines: "What was there left me *now?* Despair— / A kingdom for a broken-heart."[25]

However, the later 1829 and final 1845 versions of the poem do not end here—an additional long stanza takes up the original address to the "Father" (and note, he is no longer a "holy" father or a friar, just an abstracted paternal presence) to whom Tamerlane now teasingly says, "I firmly do believe—/ I *know*," as if he might finally be ready to accept the father's offer of atonement. But instead, what Tamerlane claims to "know" is that,

> —Death, who comes for me
> From regions of the blest afar,
> Where there is nothing to deceive,
> Hath left his iron gate ajar,
> And rays of truth you cannot see—
> Are flashing thro' Eternity—

The claim that his impending death has allowed Tamerlane a view into the "regions of the blest" nullifies the father's implied demand for "faith," or the necessity of relying on a priest's special insight or authority. What's more, the implication that this vision contains "nothing to deceive" suggests that the father's promises (or Tamerlane's own earlier fantasies) might, in fact, have been deceptions. Finally, in response to any claims of authority that the "father" might assert here, Tamerlane instead bears witness to "rays of truth you cannot see." This marks his final rejection of that father-confessor's guidance or redemptive power. The father is never mentioned again in the closing scene of the poem, and Tamerlane's thoughts seem to turn back to his own speculations on the cause of his downfall.

To reject the sacrament of confession upon one's deathbed is, of course, the ultimate renunciation of paternal authority and of the emotional and spiritual salvation that "He" offers. It might, as earlier critics have suggested, be seen as an act of inexplicable self-destruction and an acknowledgment of his own "negation."[26] But as we see in Poe's letters to John Allan, neither he nor his poetic speakers are ever content to *not* have the last word, however desperate and uncertain it may be. For Tamerlane, the choice between a foolish, unfeeling "father" and the annihilating remembrance of the mother/lover, leads him to conclude, ambiguously, that "I firmly do believe . . . that Eblis hath / a snare in every human path."

The word "Eblis" or "Iblis," in Arabic, means "despair" or "deprived" and is often used in the Koran as simply another name for Satan. But in both Judeo-Christian and Muslim demonology, it is also a frequent alias of an earlier demon, Azazel, a subversive spirit and the chief of the Djiin—desert spirits whose name means, among other things, "to conceal or overshadow."[27] Azazel is cast from heaven for refusing to bow down before Adam and for lusting after mortal women, as well as for teaching humans certain forbidden practices, particularly the use of weapons and ornamentation.[28] Notably, these are the same "gifts" (or sins) that Tamerlane demonstrates: the art of war and conquest, the building of a beautiful city, and most importantly, his defiance of all worldly or spiritual authority in favor of his own all-pervading will-to-power.[29] What's different about Tamerlane is that he, like Poe the Romantic poet, still longs for a kind of visionary idealism, a supernal beauty that might transcend the limits of the physical world and its fleeting comforts. He has experienced not only the lust, but the love of a mortal woman, and he longs to return to both the childish innocence and the romantic/maternal sympathetic union that he once knew. He is not "evil," in the ultimate sense of that word, and though he is sinful, he is cognizant and ashamed of that sinful nature. Reconciliation remains a possibility, if he can only locate the appropriate "divinity" with whom to reconcile.

Significantly for my reading here, Azazel is also associated with one of the central ritual myths of Western religion: that of the scapegoat. In the book of Leviticus 16:8, we hear of Aaron casting lots to determine which sacrificial goat goes to God, and which goes to Azazel. The one that goes to God is sacrificed on the altar, but that which falls to Azazel is, first, blessed (or cursed) with a confession of the priest's and the people's sins, and then sent off into the desert. One who is "snared" by Eblis or Azazel, then, is "the scapegoat" who carries the sins of others into the desert, but notably, is *not* sacrificed to "the Father." Instead, the scapegoat represents the eternal exile—his fate is not to die, but to be consumed by "despair," or by those demons whose purpose is to "conceal or overshadow" the truth that the scapegoat represents; that is, the truth imparted to the scapegoat by the confession of the priest and people from whom he has been exiled.

The inescapable "snare" that makes Tamerlane into a "scapegoat," while it dooms him to exile, also allows him the freedom to continue speaking, albeit in a "concealed" fashion—his only audience, perhaps, being fellow exiles or the demonic forces that rule his spiritual desert. But this freedom and lack of concern for the consequences of his words prompts Tamerlane to end his confession, not with a final plea, but with a question:

> How was it that Ambition crept,
> Unseen, amid the revels there,
> Till growing bold, he laughed and leapt
> In the tangles of Love's very hair?

If this closing question is, in fact, aimed at either the father-confessor, or more interestingly, the divine "Father," then what we see, once again, is an inversion of the confessional dynamic—the confessant interrogating his confessor. What's more, he is posing a question that implicates that Father in the speaker's Fall—for how *is it* that, under the watchful gaze of a supposedly loving parent, an impurity creeps into the Edenic scene of his childhood? Who is ultimately responsible for that oversight? Tamerlane, we see, will not take the full blame for his unsought dreams and visions, or for the impulses that drive him to abandon his lover. Though he has, in the rest of the poem, acknowledged his own guilt and condemned himself for it, Tamerlane here evinces a defiant stance and an accusatory gaze that is almost a direct echo of Poe's correspondence with John Allan. Poe, too, asserts that he is not to blame for those failures that took place under the gaze of his father and argues that, if anything, it is Allan who instilled the sense of "ambition" and success that Poe tries to live up to. It might not be absurd to say that Poe partially blames Allan for the fact that he has been alienated from those maternal presences that once offered him comfort. The point here is not that any of these accusations are true or just, but that Tamerlane (or Poe), once freed from the coercive authority of the paternal "conscience," is allowed to *assert the possibility*—to turn the confessional ritual into an act of defiance and questioning.

Though, ultimately, "Tamerlane" offers no viable, or at least attractive, alternative to the Father's ritual of atonement, it does suggest that there are legitimate reasons to question the authority of that ritual. Whether figured as "God," a "holy friar," or a "father," paternalistic authority loses its moral imperative for the exiled scapegoat. Unfortunately for Tamerlane, as for many of Poe's protagonists, any recourse to the maternal, sympathetic other comes too late and in too horrific a guise to do him any good. He is, ultimately, left to "wander the desert" without any authoritative other with whom to reconcile.

"Tamerlane," then, sits at the opening of Poe's poetic career, much like one of his own ghastly marble busts or creaking hinges—a foreboding of things to come. In its defiant rejection of paternal authority, its longing for a primal intimacy and idealized "beauty," its horrific "return of the repressed," and in its subversion of the symbolic order—all via confessional performance—the poem lays out the landscape of Poe's later poetry and poetic theory. It also suggests, for Poe himself, a driving ambition (or compulsion) to overturn those aesthetic assumptions that typically structure the lyric quest for "self-expression"—the demand for "presence" over "absence," the need for sympathetic understanding, and the belief in the efficacy of language itself as a reliable medium. Though his poems would continue to search longingly for an ideal form and a balance between the demands of "innate nature" and external "tyranny," the "undying voices" of the past (or of the repressed) continue to haunt and disrupt such productions.

In order to convey this consciousness of the instability and uncertainty of intimate relationships, including that between poet and audience, Poe would first have to develop a more comprehensive theory of the poetic encounter and the capacity of language to mimic and perform "intimacy." This he does over time through his own frequently reworked theories and "poetic principles"; through a series of later poems that revisit the haunted landscape of love, betrayal, and dissolution that "Tamerlane" first explored; and finally in his experiments with popular narrative forms, particularly the criminal confessional narrative.

NOTES

1. Elizabeth Phillips, "The Poems: 1824–1835," in *A Companion to Poe Studies*, ed. Eric W. Carlson (Westport, CT: Greenwood Press, 1996), 70–71.

2. Daniel Hoffman, *Poe Poe Poe Poe Poe Poe Poe* (New York: Paragon House, 1990), 30.

3. See Edward Davidson, *Poe: A Critical Study* (Cambridge, MA: Belknap, 1957), 5; David Halliburton, *Edgar Allan Poe: A Phenomenological View* (Princeton, NJ: Princeton University Press, 1973); Robert D. Jacobs, "The Self and the World: Poe's Early Poems," *Georgia Review* 31 (Fall 1977); G. R. Thompson, *Circumscribed Eden of Dreams: Vision and Nightmare in Poe's Early Poetry* (Baltimore: Edgar Allan Poe Society, 1984).

4. *The Collected Letters of Edgar Allan Poe*, ed. John Ward Ostrom, rev. by Burton R. Pollin and Jeffrey A. Savoye, vol. 1 (New York: Gordian Press, 2008), 10.

5. Ibid., 11.

6. Ibid., 35.

7. Ibid., 38.

8. See Sigmund Freud, "The Uncanny," in *On Creativity and the Unconscious: Papers on the Psychology of Art, Literature, Love, Religion* (New York: Harper, 1958), and Michel Foucault, *The History of Sexuality, Volume 1: An Introduction* (New York: Vintage Books, 1990). In "The Uncanny," Freud suggests that the uncanny "double" is a result of the ego's emerging capacity for self-observation (in the form of a "conscience" or superego), which is the result of overcoming our primary narcissism through an identification, usually, with the father. But the double also incorporates certain "possible futures that we still cling to in phantasy" and that "nourish in us the illusion of Free Will" (142). "Conscience," then, contains the seeds of both paternal identification and paternal rejection—something we see developing in both Poe and his poetic "double," Tamerlane.

9. Ostrom et al., *The Collected Letters*, 36–38. Though we don't have all of Allan's letters to Poe, it is clear from Poe's correspondence that among the "offenses" Poe has committed, besides his irresponsible behavior, were accusations of drunkenness and adultery against Allan. In fact, Poe was deeply incensed at Allan's apparent ill-treatment of his adopted mother, Frances Allan, who died in February of 1829. Her death prompted a brief reconciliation, but Allan's later remarriage and disinheritance of Poe marked the end of their civil relationship and was no doubt seen as a further sign of "betrayal" by Poe.

10. Ibid., 59.

11. Ibid., 67–68.

12. Samuel Maio, *Creating Another Self: Voice in Modern American Personal Poetry* (Kirksville, MO: Thomas Jefferson University Press, 1995), 26.

13. Davidson, *Poe*, 5.

14. Ibid., 6.

15. This and all other quotations from the poem are from *Edgar Allan Poe: Poetry and Tales*, ed. Patrick F. Quinn, Library of America Edition (New York: Literary Classics of the United States, 1984), 24.

16. David Halliburton, *Edgar Allan Poe: A Phenomenological View* (Princeton, NJ: Princeton University Press, 1973), 51.

17. Ibid., 53.

18. Ibid., 61.

19. Robert D. Jacobs, "The Self and the World: Poe's Early Poems," *Georgia Review* 31 (Fall 1977): 648.

20. Ibid., 652.
21. Ibid., 652.
22. John Edward Martin, *Disquieting Intimacies: Confession and the Gothic Poetic in Edgar Allan Poe and Emily Dickinson*, (PhD diss., Northwestern University, 2006), 84–107.
23. Peter Brooks, *Troubling Confession: Speaking Guilt in Law and Literature* (Chicago: University of Chicago Press, 2001). Brooks defines the "overborne will" as "the nodal moment at which free will, free determination, passed over into compulsion—the narrative, one might say, of the mind twisted to that moment where it breaks" (77). It is also the moment at which the confessant becomes "the unwilling collaborator in establishing his guilt" (68).
24. In the original 1827 version, the voice that Tamerlane hears is that of "a hunter I had known," indicating an old family dependent who informs him of Ada's death. But in later versions, Poe offers this more ambiguous voice emanating from the threshold stone to indicate a more ghostly presence, which I am reading as the "undying voice" of his lost love.
25. Edgar A. Poe, *Collected Works of Edgar Allan Poe*, vol. 1., ed. Thomas Ollive Mabbott (Cambridge, MA: Harvard University Press, 1969), 39.
26. Poe would later offer his own pseudoscientific explanation for such a tendency—"a *mobile* without motive"—when the narrator of "The Imp of the Perverse" posits "a radical, primitive impulse," called "perverseness," in which "the desire to be well is not only not aroused, but a strongly antagonistical sentiment exists" (Quinn, *Poetry and Tales*, 841).This perverse sentiment, while seemingly suicidal, is not wholly self-directed, but rather, exists in an "antagonistical stance," suggesting, perhaps, a position of resistance—a position here evinced by Tamerlane's temporary assimilation of, or by, a lost feminine consciousness that offers annihilation rather than "salvation."
27. Leo Jung, *Fallen Angels in Jewish, Christian, and Mohammedan Literature* (New York: Ktav Publishing House, 1974), 60–62.
28. Jeffrey Burton Russell, *The Devil: Perceptions of Evil from Antiquity to Primitive Christianity* (Ithaca, NY: Cornell University Press, 1977), 191.
29. Although I cannot say definitively how extensive Poe's knowledge was of Hebrew or Arab demonologies, he does demonstrate some familiarity with both the biblical and Koranic myths, not only in "Tamerlane" but also in subsequent poems like "Al Aaraaf" and "Israfel," as well as in his "arabesque" tales, including "Ligeia." Here, it is only necessary to trace the connection between the Arabic Eblis and the Hebrew Azazel—two desert demons with similar origins and characteristics—as possible parallels in this poem.

Chapter Three

Mother Goddess Manifestations in Poe's "Catholic Hymn" and "Morella"

Amy Branam

> All day and long
> Shines, bright and strong,
> Astarte within the sky,
> While ever to her dear Eulalie upturns her matron eye—
> While ever to her young Eulalie upturns her violet eye.[1]
> —Poe, "Eulalie" ll.16–20

In these closing lines to "Eulalie," the subject yearns for her sensual self, which is symbolized by her gaze upon the omnipresent Astarte. However, as a subject within a patriarchal structure, she is expected to disassociate from an important facet of her femininity: her sexuality. The adjective "matron" indicates that she "rightly" chooses chastity. The nineteenth-century virgin/whore dichotomy, discussed at great length alongside the angel/monster bifurcation in Sandra Gilbert and Susan Gubar's *The Madwoman in the Attic*, presents the British and American cultural phenomenon that forced nineteenth-century women to conform to strict gender roles.[2] As part of this changing set of mores, which reached its strictest and most notorious form during the Victorian period, these cultures attempted to limit the older meanings of the signifiers "virgin" and "chastity" by using them synonymously. Although the more antiquated definitions of both words allowed for a woman's sexual desire, the use of these words in literature and other texts, particularly religious, eventually eradicated the component of sexual desire and activity altogether. For example, Miriam Robbins Dexter explains that "virgin" may not have referred to "*virgo intacta*" but to a young woman "who stored untapped energy" and who "guard[ed] her energies before she [chose]."[3] Similarly, "chastity" was used by the sixteenth-century English writer William Baldwin to show that sexuality and chastity were complementary rather than exclusive states. He writes in *A Treatise of Morall Phylosophie, Contayning the Sayinges of the Wyse*: "The first degree of chastity is pure virginity, and the second faithfull matrimony."[4] Poe's poem depicts Eulalie's desire to have her energy stores tapped. However, as Gilbert and Gubar prove in their study, early nineteenth-century standards for a lady separate "wife" from sensuality, thereby repressing the active display of her sexual desires even within the sanctity of marriage. The poem acknowledges Eulalie's virtue, but it also exposes, rather than sanctions, the residual presence of her sexuality.

According to the religious rhetoric of antebellum Protestant America, a woman's ability to be chaste is only possible through a total renunciation of her libido. For instance, this expectation is articulated by Samuel F. B. Morse, a son of a Boston pastor and described by one of his biographers, Carleton Mabee, as "a patriarchal figure."[5] In *Roads to Rome,* Jenny Franchot discusses how Morse reads Eve's fall in connection with her body. She writes, "Morse's use of Edenic imagery to describe Catholicism's serpentine sexual and moral temptations was typical of this time; earlier Americans had also understood the foreign religion as an extension through time of the devil's seduction of Eve."[6] Therefore, in order to be a decorous Protestant nineteenth-century woman, Eulalie must enact a spirit/body split, which illustrates the nineteenth-century expectation that a woman must abnegate this vital part of herself. In fact, rather than read this poem as a warning to other women to renounce Eulalie's residual inheritance through Eve of a predilection to sin, this poem can be read by modern readers as an elegy on Eulalie's sexuality.[7]

This phenomenon of cleaving the female had begun many centuries prior to Poe with the male parsing of the figure of the Great Mother Goddess: Astarte is one of her many fragments. Poe's historical moment presents readers with the culmination of inherited patriarchal revisions of the Mother Goddess that attempted to regulate socially acceptable mores for human females. Poe presents Eulalie as a woman unable to reject completely this diabolical facet of her womanhood, thereby aligning her with a culturally complicit reading of Woman as always in danger of committing a religious and sociocultural trespass. This chapter analyzes Poe's use of allusions to the Mother Goddess and her imagery in "Catholic Hymn" and "Morella" to uncover the Mother Goddess's subversive presence, a subversion unintended by Poe, yet typical of texts that use Her inherited symbolic revisions.[8]

In contrast to readings proposed by Arthur Hobson Quinn and Álvaro Salas Chacón, the composition of "Catholic Hymn" is unlikely a manifestation of Poe's personal devotion to the Virgin Mary.[9] Due to Morella's dubious character, her invocation of Mary does not mirror Poe's own perspective on the Virgin. Since no extant letter or essay exists that articulates Poe's attitude regarding the Mother of God, one alternative is to plumb his historical moment.

In "Culture," Stephen Greenblatt argues that readers can learn about a culture by looking at "the kinds of literature that are explicitly engaged in attack and celebration: satire and panegyric."[10] Greenblatt provides a heuristic to guide interpretation. This analysis focuses on two of his six questions:

1. Why might readers at a particular time and place find this work compelling?
2. What are the larger social structures with which these particular acts of praise or blame might be connected?[11]

To derive to answer for the first question, the second question must be addressed, and to do so, one must investigate antebellum America's relation to Catholicism. Poe's time period witnessed a resurgence of Marian debates, which resulted in Protestants alleging Mariolatry against the Catholics. The Catholics appeared to resolve the Mary "problem" in 1854, five years after Poe's death, with the acceptance of the Immaculate Conception as dogma.[12] Mary's "problem" status arose many centuries prior to the nineteenth century. As David Kinsley reports in *The Goddesses' Mirror*, "In their enthusiasm and devotion to Mary, many Christians in effect have elevated Mary to a position equal to, or superior to, that of Jesus."[13] The issue at stake not only involved Mary's status but also what Franchot terms the "alternative family structures" of the Church.[14] The convents, run by the Mother Superiors, were viewed by Protestants as the conflation of Mary the divine with Mother Superior the human. Franchot recounts the Ursuline Convent riots, in which the Mother Superior had to defend herself against charges that she mandated that her novitiates worship her. As Franchot reports, the Mother Superior asserted that the nuns referred to her as "mother," "president," and "ma mère" (or "my mother") but never as "divine mother."[15] In addition to the scrutiny the Mother Superiors received from the Protestants, the Catholic periodicals attempted to debunk the Protestant vitriol against Mary as an ignoble way to oppose Catholics. For instance, a letter to the editor in an 1843 issue of *The Catholic Telegraph* asks, "Can there be anything in this world of woe worse, than offering insults to the ever blessed Mother of our Lord!"[16]

Poe's initial exposure to the Mary controversy may have occurred during his early years when he attended the Monumental Episcopal Church in Richmond under the leadership of Rev. Richard Channing Moore. As a man who held to the "evangelical system of doctrine," Bishop Moore had a Low Church approach to the worship service. According to the Episcopal Diocese of Southwestern Virginia, Moore and others were "unsympathetic to the high church influence of the Tractarians and the Oxford Movement."[17] Thus, the

Virgin Mary was probably not exalted in Moore's church. "Morella" demonstrates the unlikelihood of Poe's endorsement of any type of Mary worship, even though he includes a prayer to her in the first version of the tale. By contextualizing the poem within the story's development, his intent to malign the Virgin becomes apparent.

Unlike Leslie Fiedler's and James W. Gargano's readings of Morella's transmogrification, as well as in contrast to the way in which Poe most likely intended, Morella's refusal to die can be read as a moment of empowerment rather than terror.[18] To accomplish this interpretation, Morella must be read from the outset as a supernatural being rather than a human aberration. From this perspective, Morella does not destroy her child but transports her soul/intellect from one body to the next. In "Animatopoeia: Morella as Siren of the Self," Martin Bickman refers to this event as "Morella's sense of transpersonal identity."[19] However, Catholics in particular can read this moment as one that parallels the Holy Ghost's role in the Virgin birth—the agent that moves God from one form to another. From the Catholic perspective, the Holy Ghost is part of the Trinity, along with God and Jesus. According to the Gospel of Luke, God, in the form of the Holy Spirit, descends upon Mary to beget Jesus.[20] Jesus, as God, is also the Holy Spirit. Therefore, the transference of the essence of God in the birth of Jesus functions similarly to the movement of Morella's essence.

However, a female deity, especially one on the level with the One True God, is not permitted in Catholicism, or in any branch of Christianity. If one views Morella as a Mother Goddess figure attempting to accomplish a similar feat as the Christian Father God, the debacle in the church, witnessed by Poe's narrator, demonstrates a clear victory of patriarchy over matriarchy. During the sacrament/ritual of baptism, the narrator attempts to name the Goddess/daughter in the patriarchal Catholic Church. However, he (re)names her using the Goddess's signifier (i.e., Morella) rather than claiming her for patriarchy via a deliberate speech act in which the father bestows his own name upon his child. He speaks aloud Her name in the sacred space of the Father God, and the Goddess is abashed, which is shown through her subsequent—and second—corporal death.

In order to understand why Poe's readers would find this work compelling, the uncanny resemblance between Morella and the Virgin Mary must be further investigated. Within the early nineteenth-century context, many Protestants viewed Mary not as a Christian figure but as a pagan remnant. Therefore, when Morella alludes to the cypress tree after the *Sancta Maria*, an antebellum Protestant would probably recognize the pagan symbol due to its close juxtaposition to the prayer. Although Thomas O. Mabbott's textual note connects the cypress with Dis, the cypress tree is also an icon for Artemis.[21] In *The Cult of the Virgin Mary*, Michael P. Carroll notes the phenomenon of "one goddess under many names."[22] He asserts that "adding the Virgin Mary to the list" of Minerva, Venus, Diana, Proserpine, Ceres, and Isis does "not change the basic hypothesis that . . . all these goddesses are in some sense the same goddess."[23] Artemis, a moon goddess, is equated with Diana. Diana is linked directly to the Virgin Mary, which the Catholic Church was quite aware of when it held the Council of Ephesus in 431 CE. In *The Myth of the Goddess: Evolution of an Image*, Anne Baring and Jules Cashford explain that the location for the Council was not a mere coincidence:

> Ephesus was, significantly, the very place where the great temple to Artemis, or Diana as she was called in Roman times, had stood for many centuries. The cult of Artemis or Diana had been repressed in AD 380 by the Emperor Theodosius, and the people, deprived of their goddess, readily turned to Mary instead.[24]

The metamorphoses of various goddesses from one to the next over time (what Andrew Greeley, a Catholic priest, refers to as "the eternal feminine") parallels Morella's replacement of her daughter's essence with her own.[25] When she declares that this is a day "more fair for the daughters of heaven and death," readers should ask, why are daughters placed above sons? (228). At the moment of the birth/death scene, the rainbow, a symbol of Iris, "from the firmament had surely fallen" (227). This line can be interpreted as an exchange between the sacred and the earthly, thereby reinforcing a reading of Morella as an earthly embodiment of a goddess, in addition to Morella's emphasis on "Earth and Life" rather than a focus on heaven (2:228). The moon, which is implied in the line "a warm glow upon the waters," further sets the scene for the Goddess's presence (227). The water, according to Rachel Pollack in *The Body of the Goddess*, relates to "a baby growing in its mother's womb" and how it "floats in a sac of liquid."[26] As the location for the beginning of life, the sea is viewed as a Great Mother.[27] The collusion of all these symbols is used by Poe to signal a fateful moment, but he uses them to reinscribe the patriarchal portrayal of the Goddess as a force to fear rather than to invite. In other words, the description of the setting is intended to enhance the narrator's distraught state of mind rather than to convey any positive feeling about Morella's identity.

Poe's tactics resemble those used in the Old Testament to rewrite the Goddess as an idol. For example, in Judges 2:12–14, the King James Version of the Bible reads:

> 12 And they forsook the Lord God of their fathers, which brought them out of the land of Egypt, and followed other gods, of the gods of the people that were round about them, and bowed themselves unto them, and provoked the Lord to anger. 13 And they forsook the Lord, and served Baal and Ashtaroth. 14 And the anger of the Lord was hot against Israel, and he delivered them into the

hands of spoilers that spoiled them, and he sold them into the hands of their enemies round about, so that they could not any longer stand before their enemies.

Rather than link Morella explicitly to Baal and Ashtaroth, Poe cites a location. When Morella is close to death, she mentions a place long associated with Mother Goddess worship: "For the hours of thy happiness are over; and joy is not gathered twice in a life, as the roses of Paestum twice in a year" (233). Although Mabbott's edition glosses that this is an allusion to Paesti in Virgil's *Georgics*, the site itself has ties to the Mother Goddess and was (re)discovered during the nineteenth century. During Poe's time, the ruins at Paestum were, for the most part, thought to be dedicated to Neptune by the Romans after they conquered Poseidonia.[28] In this one allusion, Poe deftly cites a Roman location to elicit Catholic idolatry in the minds of his Protestant readers, reminding them, as Franchot argues, of the insidious link between paganism and Catholicism. She writes, "'Romanism' functioned as metaphoric construct and surrogate for the Roman Catholicism. That construct embraced not only the Roman Catholic church as a historical institution in nineteenth-century America but also the conflicted political, aesthetic, and gender issues surrounding its troubled reception."[29]

In this case, the beauty of the ruins, which drew many nineteenth-century American travelers, as well as the facility with which Roman society and religion accommodated, or in this case appropriated, female symbols of power, relate to Poe's tale. "Morella" alludes to this pagan ritualistic site to make the point of the rarity of happiness in life and to align her with Romanism. Moreover, he selects a locality that serves as an admonition to Protestants. One nineteenth-century writer explained the fall of Paestum as "a gross darkness which fell upon the people who 'refused to retain God in their knowledge,' and who multiplied their idols, until, to use the saying of one of their philosophers, it was easier in some of their cities to find a god than a man."[30] His assessment is intentionally ambiguous in order to convey this author's contempt for the Catholic faith; he deliberately implies all the saints in Roman Catholicism, along with the pantheon of the ancient Romans.

The conflicted gender issues in the Church are also apparent in "Morella." The distrust of women in power, particularly in the family, becomes more overt as the narrator comes closer to the realization that his daughter is his wife. Poe's narrator, in his initial disavowals of his own daughter as "*her* child," mirrors the relationship between Mary and Joseph while she is pregnant with Jesus. Joseph, her betrothed, had to be reassured of Mary's fidelity by means of a dream in order to accept the task of raising a child that was neither his own nor fully human. Indeed, this sacrifice of the immediate family for an alternative family structure is a facet of Catholicism that Protestants outright rejected. Franchot presents the antebellum Protestant view as follows:

> Roman Catholics, having betrayed their own domestic allegiances by pledging filial obedience to their father in Rome and to their priest in the confessional while urging their daughters to lives of cloistered chastity rather than marriage and motherhood, then sought to disrupt the naturalized structures of Protestant family life and replace them with the mazelike structures of priestly hierarchy, confessional, and conventual living.[31]

In effect, Joseph is displaced by the Holy Spirit as the father figure. Yet, as if in some sort of gentleman's agreement, Matthew 1:18–25 tells of how the Lord sends an angel to explain the situation to him and reassure Joseph that Mary did not elect to take control of her sexuality through infidelity. Once this is revealed to him, he realizes that his nuclear family is not threatened by a promiscuous wife.

According to the Protestants, however, the Catholics complicated the role of women in that they "both elevated and oppressed women."[32] By including Mary, along with many female saints, in the hierarchy of their faith, Catholics allowed select women authority that actively countered the discreet female influence of the Protestant family construct, what Franchot describes as "maternal authority, credited by Catharine Beecher and Harriet Beecher Stowe with redemptive spiritual and (indirectly) political power, [which] operated through promptings, not commands, its authority indicated precisely by its invisibility."[33] The possibility of strong female figures disrupted the Protestant view on family, and Morella's "Catholic Hymn" aligns her with the perverse notion of female empowerment when, at her death, she invokes the Virgin rather than the Father.

In light of the descriptions and allusions Poe employs in the tale on either side of the inset poem, the prayer to Mary accrues significant meanings within the tale rather than if it were read in isolation. Here is the invocation in its entirety:

> Sancta Maria! Turn thine eyes
> Upon the sinner's sacrifice
> Of fervent prayer, and humble love,
> From thy holy throne above.
>
> At morn, at noon, at twilight dim
> Maria! Thou hast heard my hymn:
> In Joy and Woe—in Good and Ill
> Mother of God! Be with us still.
>
> When my hours flew gently by,
> And no storms were in the sky,
> My soul—lest it should truant be—

> Thy love did guide to thine and thee.
>
> Now—when clouds of Fate oe'rcast
> All my Present, and my Past,
> Let my Future radiant shine
> With sweet hopes of thee and thine. (227–28)

When Morella refers to "thine and thee" and then to "thee and thine" in lines 12 and 16 of "Catholic Hymn," the referents may not be to Mary and Jesus, Joseph, or any other saints, such as Elizabeth or John, but to the line of goddesses of which she is one of the most recent manifestations. By using the epithet "Mother of God," Morella invokes the Virgin as well as previous female deities who were known by the same title, including Hestia and Rhea, who were praised in Orphic hymns using this identical appellation.[34] The list of the Mothers of God(s) also includes Aditi; Anat and Isis; Danu; Cybele; and Frigg.[35]

When we read Morella's prayer within its historical context, Poe's personal relationship to her becomes ancillary to how his Protestant audience would read this prayer. Poe's prayer would probably not have been read by his audiences as a panegyric but as an attack on the Mother Goddess, in this case the Virgin Mary, due to its placement in the mouth of a woman whom the tale has characterized as monstrous. As Protestants suspected, the Catholic doctrine that allowed for the honoring of Mary seemed dangerously close to a return to an all-powerful female deity worship. Mary could be viewed as the latest incarnation in a chain of many pagan reincarnations, which Poe capitalized on when he showed Morella reincarnate herself through the birth of a daughter, to whom Morella refers to as a "daughter of Heaven" (232).[36] Moreover, in this portrayal, Poe's story continues to support patriarchal demonization of the Goddess. The tale itself is framed as a trauma narrative, which is evident when the narrator says,

> What demon urged me to breathe that sound, which, in its very recollection, was wont to make ebb the purple blood in torrents from the temples to the heart? What fiend spoke from the recesses of my soul, when, amid those dim aisles, and in the silence of the night, I whispered within the ears of the holy man the syllables—Morella? (235).

Once the narrator speaks her name, she replies not with "I AM" (i.e., the name of God) but similarly with "I am here!" (235). Yet the Goddess's appearance results in the narrator's madness rather than his salvation. The narrator finishes his tale by declaring, "I laughed with a long and bitter laugh as I found no traces of the first, in the charnel where I laid the second—Morella" (236). In contrast to the jubilant rejoicing by Mary Magdalene, Joanna, and Mary the mother of James upon discovering Jesus's ascension (corporal and spiritual) from his tomb, Morella's widower admits that he felt "bitter," while also revealing that he may be slightly mad upon his discovery of Morella's similar resurrection. His opposite reaction can be attributed to his lack of belief in Morella as a divine being. Although he describes his relationship with her in terms similar to those found in biblical descriptions of the relationship between the disciples and Jesus, he never acknowledges her divinity. At their first encounter, he readily confesses his inability to pinpoint the exact type of "fires" he felt when they first met. He explains, "Thrown by accident into her society many years ago, my soul, from our first meeting, burned with fires it had never known. But the fires were not of Eros—and bitter and tormenting to my eager spirit was the gradual conviction that I could in no manner define their unusual meaning, or regulate their vague intensity" (229). Again, using the word "bitter," the narrator betrays that his negative feelings toward Morella stem from his inability to categorize their relationship rationally.

His powerlessness to comprehend fully her role in his life recalls accounts in the New Testament, particularly instances of those who encounter Jesus as he teaches. For instance, in Mark 1:22, "The people were spellbound by his teaching." This "amazement" is echoed at Pentecost. The tongues of fire descend upon each apostle, and those Jews who hear the apostles speaking are struck by their ability to hear each in his or her own tongue. Yet this demonstration of Jesus's divine powers is not readily accepted, and, as told in Acts 2:14–41, Peter pleads for the sobriety of the apostles and urges the Jews assembled to seek baptism. In addition to the link between incomprehensibility in the presence of God, in Hebrews 1:7, the alignment of fire with discipleship is made: "He makes his angels spirits, and his servants flames of fire." Also, in Hebrews 12:29, the use of fire as a metaphor for the love of the Divine is expressed: "God is a consuming fire." These references, and many more, align fire not with *eros* but with *agape*, the unconditional love for the divine being. However, the narrator cannot name it as *agape* love, for he feels it in relation to the divine feminine rather than for the culturally appropriate focus, the Almighty Father.

After learning the story's resolution, on subsequent readings readers can register the foreshadowed elements of Morella's nature with ease. In addition, they can perceive how Poe uses this literary device to encode her as malevolent rather than beneficent. For example, the story's epigram, translated "Itself–alone by itself—eternally one and single," points to Morella's supernatural configuration as one that repeats *ad infinitum* (229 epigraph). The phrase "eternally one and single" subverts the Holy Trinity. Since Catholics believe in a God in three persons, Morella's devotion to the Virgin Mary is an overdetermined symbol of her refusal to accept Mary's relegated status. Morella's invocation and reincarnation seem to signify that she views the eternal single as a reference to the all-powerful Mother Goddess.

However, rather than endorse the goodness and positivity of the Mother Goddess in his work, Poe inherits Her as a displaced figure assigned to the realm of black magic, which Mabbott indicates in his note on Morella's "Presburg education" (229).[37] Poe's narrator describes her impression upon him as one that induced a "most singular affection" (229). He also defines her as strange, freakishly so: "Her talents were of no common order—her powers of mind were gigantic" (229), which in turn adversely affects the narrator, who claims that he "grew pale, and shuddered inwardly at those too unearthly tones" (230). Her strangeness disturbs him even more as she nears death. He believes that "the mystery of my wife's manner oppressed me as a spell" (231), which reminds the reader of the narrator's earlier description of Morella "poring over forbidden pages" (230). While "rak[ing] up from the ashes of a dead philosophy some low, singular words," apparently found in her book of spells, her husband claims to have "felt a forbidden spirit enkindling within [him]" (230).

Although Poe's text implies this spirit may be akin to demon possession, one wonders whether this spirit may be more closely related to a form of the Holy Spirit. As the potential harbinger for the Mother Goddess, the narrator labels it as "forbidden," which explains why he recoils from Morella's attempts to initiate, or confirm, him, in a sacramental sense, into her alternative religion. As a nominal Christian, apparent through his (deferred) decision to seek baptism for his daughter, he cannot help but recoil from Morella's proselytizing, and he labels the experience as one in which "joy suddenly faded into horror, and the most beautiful became the most hideous, as Hinnon became Ge-Henna" (230). His revulsion peaks when he looks upon her as she dies: "I met the glance of her meaning eyes, and then my soul sickened and became giddy with the giddiness of one who gazes downward into some dreary and unfathomable abyss" (231–32). Yet, "her meaning eyes" can be plumbed beyond this one woman's will to live, for she does not merely reincarnate; she replicates. As his daughter grows, the narrator remarks upon the "too perfect *identity*" between mother and daughter (234, Poe's emphasis). He purports that "as years rolled away, and I gazed, day after day, upon her holy, and mild, and eloquent face, and pored over her maturing form, day after day did I discover new points of resemblance in the child to her mother, the melancholy and the dead" (234). The raptness with which he observes his daughter relies on words of idol worship to convey the degree to which he is transfixed: "gazed" and "pored." The adjectives "holy" and "mild" couple the daughter/Morella with Mary, who is described in Luke 1:39–56 as "blessed" and "humble." Despite her unthreatening demeanor, the narrator insists that "hourly, grew darker these shadows of similitude, and more full, and more definite, and more perplexing, and more hideously terrible in their aspect" (234). Repeating the process by which he had vilified her mother, the narrator now views the daughter as aberrant, testifying that "she grew strangely in stature and intelligence. Strange indeed was her rapid increase in bodily size—but terrible, oh!" (234).

By the end of the tale, he is totally confounded by the situation and can only view his lack of understanding in terms of the grotesque: "I found food for consuming thought and horror—for a worm that *would* not die" (235, Poe's emphasis). The narrator likens his unceasing wife to a worm, which symbolizes perpetual corruption. The narrator's emphasis on the corporal rather than spiritual fate of the deceased once again indicates that he turns away from Christian doctrine while in his daughter's/Morella's presence.

His wife's ability to defy bodily deterioration proves her mastery of "the wild Pantheism of Fichte; the modified Paliggenedia of the Pythagoreans; and, above all, the doctrines of *Identity* as urged by Schelling" (230–31).[38] In Morella's characterization, Poe portrays a woman who wills herself to be godlike. Indeed, she discovers the way in which to become one with the divinity—not with God but with the Goddess—through intense study of Ficthe's, Schelling's, and Pythagoras's works. When the narrator claims, regarding her reading materials, "These for what reasons I could not imagine, were her favorite and constant study," his incapacity to figure out the link between Morella and the divine seems a willful act. He only allows for the possibility of witchcraft as an explanation (229).

He also cannot imagine a world in which the endurance of a *female* spirit could be construed as positive. He is terrified of the turn of events related to his daughter, for he sees the mother taking shape in his daughter and cannot help but experience her company as a haunting, one aggravated by her impending second death. He says, "I kept no reckoning of time or place; and the stars of my fate faded from heaven; and, therefore, the earth grew dark, and its figures passed by me like flitting shadows, and among them all I beheld only—Morella. The winds of the firmament breathed but one sound within my ears, and the ripples upon the sea murmured evermore—Morella" (236). The personification of the elements of air and water, which the narrator interprets as ominous reminders of his first loss, could be interpreted more accurately as a reclamation of their Goddess.

Also, it is noteworthy that the narrator has no valid reason to fear the reincarnation of Morella (other than its affiliation with the abnormal) because she never posed any danger to him. In fact, she had always treated the narrator with patience, kindness, and understanding. Although James Gargano argues for the interpretation of the name "Morella" as both referring to "little death" and "nightshade," his final conclusion about the significance of her name fits best with the ending. He asserts that "Morella refines herself into a spirit or disembodied name eternally and pervasively existing, according to the rhythm of nature, in wind and water—and in the mind of man."[39] However, the "mind of man" (at least the narrator's) experiences her "pervasive existence" as a terrifying haunt. In a typically Romantic move, Poe writes nature in sympathy with *man*, thereby allowing his narrator to project his anthropocentric view on nature, which then reflects back to him his own fears. By doing so, Poe repeats his own society's repudiation of a positive iteration of a powerful Mother Goddess as a possibility. She, at best, can resurface in spurts as a demon of sorts that frightens men and is then dispelled. Yet, as noted before, in this case, Morella has given no sign that she is to be feared.

In conclusion, we return to Greenblatt's query: "Why might readers at a particular time and place find this work compelling?" For readers today, the use of the Mother Goddess images in "Morella" and "Catholic Hymn" can be decoded in a way most likely unintended by Poe and inaccessible to the majority of his readers, who were steeped in a patriarchal Protestant culture. The Mother Goddess began as an all-powerful, dominant figure and then was gradually overwritten by male-dominated theologies. Poe inherits these revisions. However, she continues to cling to her former glory through gaps in texts, religious and otherwise. One of her epithets, the Queen of Heaven, lives on in the Virgin Mary, although her powers are now greatly reduced. As Elisabeth Benard and Beverly Moon write, "Not a warrior, not a lover, Mary rules as a mother of the king of peace."[40] In a sense, Mary is the domesticated version of the Mother Goddess. Despite Protestant outcries of her seeming authority within the Catholic Church, she has relatively little power. She retains her position due to an attempt by the early church to provide a feminine complement, albeit relegated, to the rampant masculinity in Christian doctrine. In Bickman's interpretation of "Morella," he argues that the narrator seeks unification with his "anima" and that this impulse is rooted "in the narrator's own psyche."[41] The union of anima and animus is a long-standing archetype in mythologies, including Christianity.

Before patriarchy erased a feminine equal, Astarte/Ishtar had been "the consort of YHWH," but the Christian God now stands alone as a He.[42] His closest female consort is a fully human virgin who miraculously gives birth through circumventing the sin of physicality outside of marriage. Unlike the multifaceted goddesses of the past, no human woman can emulate the paradox that is the Virgin Mary. Yet Poe's patriarchal culture had effectively endorsed and realized a culture of women who strove to be the virgin-mother. Perhaps, by refusing to elevate her as the Catholics do, the Protestant implication is that Mary's piety and obedience is attainable for any woman. As "Eulalie" hints at and "Morella" illustrates, long before science "dragged Diana from her car" (as Poe writes in "Sonnet—To Science"), patriarchal religions had demonized and dethroned the Goddess in an attempt to control her sexuality and, by extension, her autonomy. Due to this centuries-old patriarchal refashioning, Poe inherited an array of Mother Goddess imagery that he could use in his tales and poems as literary shorthand to craft a mood of terror tailored precisely for his Protestant audience.

NOTES

Thanks to Autumn Athey for her research assistance on this project and to Rev. Edward Chapman, Dr. James R. Walker, and Dr. Amy Amendt-Raduege for their comments, as well as the audience members at the Powerful Women session for the Third International Edgar Allan Poe Conference: The Bicentennial.

1. Edgar A. Poe, *The Collected Works of Edgar Allan Poe,* vols. 1–2, ed. Thomas Olive Mabbott (Cambridge, MA: Belknap Press, 1978). Further references to Poe's texts are from this edition and noted parenthetically in the text.
2. Sandra Gilbert and Susan Gubar, *The Madwoman in the Attic* (New Haven, CT: Yale University Press, 2000), 16–44.
3. Miriam Robbins Dexter, *Whence the Goddess: A Source Book* (New York: Teachers College Press, 1990), 161.
4. *Oxford English Dictionary*, s.v. "Chastity."
5. Carleton Mabee, "Patriarchy," in *The American Leonardo: A Life of Samuel F. B. Morse* (New York: Knopf, 1957), 354–66.
6. Jenny Franchot, *Roads to Rome* (Berkeley: University of California Press, 1994), 111.
7. Astarte refers to a Semitic goddess of fertility and sexuality, among many other roles, and is indicated in the Old Testament by the name Ashtoreth. For an example, see 1 Samuel 12.
8. Although Poe eventually excised "Catholic Hymn" from "Morella," I will discuss it within the context of the story for which he initially composed it.
9. See Arthur Hobson Quinn, *Edgar Allan Poe: A Critical Biography* (New York: Appleton-Century-Crofts, 1941; rpt. Baltimore: Johns Hopkins University Press, 1998), 213–14; Alvaro Salas Chacón, "Allusions to the Virgin Mary in Edgar A. Poe and Robert Lowell: An Unconscious Oedipal Process," *Káñina* 22, no. 2 (1998): 73–78.
10. Stephen Greenblatt, "Culture," in *Critical Terms for Literary Study,* ed. Frank Lentricchia and Thomas McLaughlin (Chicago: University of Chicago Press, 1995), 226.
11. Ibid.
12. Carl Olson, *The Book of the Goddess: Past and Present* (New York: Crossroad, 1983), 85.
13. David Kinsley, *The Goddesses' Mirror* (Albany: State University of New York Press, 1989), 236.
14. Franchot, *Roads to Rome*, 117.
15. Ibid., 143.
16. P. McL., "Mariolatry or the Idolatry of Mary," *Catholic Telegraph,* November 25, 1843, 347.
17. Katharine L. Brown, "A Historical Sketch of the Diocese of Southwestern Virginia," The Episcopal Diocese of Southwestern Virginia, accessed March 31, 2010, http://www.dioswva.org/about/our_history.html.
18. See Leslie Fiedler, *Love and Death in the American Novel* (New York: Anchor Books, 1966), 415; James W. Gargano, "Poe's 'Morella': A Note on Her Name," *American Literature* 47, no. 2 (May 1975): 259–64.
19. Martin Bickman, "Animatopoeia: Morella as Siren of the Self," *Poe Studies* 8, no. 2 (December 1975): 30.
20. Luke 1:26–38.
21. Mabbott, *Collected Works*, 237.
22. Michael P. Carroll, *The Cult of the Virgin Mary* (Princeton, NJ: Princeton University Press, 1986), 32.
23. Ibid.
24. Anne Baring and Jules Cashford, *The Myth of the Goddess: Evolutions of an Image* (London: Arkana, 1993), 550.
25. Qtd. in Olson, *The Book of the Goddess*, 93.
26. Rachel Pollack, *The Body of the Goddess* (Shaftesbury, UK: Element, 1997), 20.
27. Ibid., 21.

28. Depending on the source, educated guesses included a temple ("The Three Temples of Paestum," *American Farmer*, May 6, 1825, 54); a temple to Neptune ("Intelligence," *United States Literary Gazette*, December 15, 1824, 268); or "a court," "royal residence," or "an exchange and marketplace" ("Paestum," *American Magazine of Useful and Entertaining Knowledge,* October 1836, 33). One poet queries: "Whose was this shrine, this towering monument / This proud memento of a golden clime?"; the conclusion he reaches is that it belongs to "Oblivion" ("Paestum," *Philadelphia Album and Ladies Literary Gazette,* June 13, 1827, 13). The temples are now known to have been dedicated to the Greek goddesses Hera and Athena before the Roman takeover. Yet, the persistence of the site as a male deity's temple persists. As late as 1975, J. J. Coulton is compelled to note "Poseidon" in a parenthetical phrase following the identification of the temple with Hera. See J. J. Coulton, "The Second Temple of Hera at Paestum and the Pronaos Problem," *Journal of Hellenic Studies* 95 (1975): 13.

29. Franchot, *Roads to Rome*, xviii.

30. "Extracts from Bruen's Essays," *Western Luminary,* July 28, 1824, 41.

31. Franchot, *Roads to Rome*, 128.

32. Ibid., 117.

33. Ibid., 130.

34. Asphodel P. Long, *In a Chariot Drawn by Lions* (Freedom, CA: Crossing Press, 1993), 62, 211.

35. Like the Virgin Mary today, Cybele had been associated with virginity (Carroll, *The Cult of the Virgin Mary*, 96).

36. Franchot notes that "by 1835 anti-Catholicism had become a moneymaking venture that many entered into with entrepreneurial gusto" (106). Poe published "Morella" in the *Southern Literary Messenger* for April 1835. Franchot also devotes a portion of *Roads to Rome* to an analysis of Poe's "The Pit and the Pendulum" as an anti-Catholic tale (165–71).

37. Mabbott, *Collected Works*, 236.

38. Ibid., n. 236–37.

39. Gargano, "Poe's 'Morella,'" 264.

40. Elizabeth Benard and Beverly Moon, *Goddesses Who Rule* (New York: Oxford University Press, 2000), 80.

41. Bickman, "Animatopoeia," 29, 31.

42. Long, *In a Chariot Drawn by Lions*, 125.

Chapter Four

Poe's 1845 Boston Lyceum Appearance Reconsidered

Philip Edward Phillips

Until as recently as the 2009 bicentennial celebrations of his birth, Edgar Allan Poe was best known to most students, general readers, and aficionados as a son of Baltimore, Philadelphia, Richmond, New York, and even Sullivan's Island, but usually not of Boston. Even now, when Poe is associated with the city of his birth, it is usually because of the "bad reputation" that he earned as a result of his one-sided war of words with Henry Wadsworth Longfellow and his subsequent October 16, 1845, appearance before the Boston Lyceum, an event that drew mixed reviews but whose aftermath tainted Poe's professional and personal reputation. According to Major Mordecai Manuel Noah of *The Sunday Times* and *Messenger*,

> Mr. Poe was invited to deliver a poem before the Boston Lyceum, which he did to a large and distinguished audience. It was, to use the language of an intelligent hearer, "an elegant and classic production, based on the right principle; containing the essence of true poetry, mingled with a gorgeous imagination, exquisite painting, every charm of metre, and graceful delivery." And yet the papers abused him, and the audience were [*sic*] fidgety—made their exit one by one, and did not at all appreciate the efforts of a man of admitted ability, whom they had invited to deliver a poem before them. The poem was called the "Messenger Star." We presume Mr. Poe will not accept another invitation to recite poetry, original or selected, in that section of the Union. [1]

This event, which took place at the pinnacle of "The Raven's" *annus mirabilis*, was a well-documented "disaster" for Poe,[2] but not entirely, as I will suggest, for the reasons usually cited. While I would not go so far as to say, as Sidney Moss asserts in *Poe's Literary Battles*, that this incident, combined with some others, "cause[d] Poe's downfall as a critic,"[3] I would argue that it brought to the surface Poe's conflicting feelings about the city of his birth. Rather than confirming Poe's animosity toward the city of Boston, its authors, and its institutions, the event instead reveals Poe's desire not only to appear before a Boston audience but also to be accepted by that audience as a Bostonian. When Poe's motivations and anxieties are taken into consideration, the Boston Lyceum appearance reveals Poe's desire to reclaim his birthright.

If Major Noah's account had been the final word on the incident, Poe's Boston Lyceum lecture would have attracted little attention thereafter. However, according to Poe's *post facto* account in the *Broadway Journal*, his poem, "Al Aaraaf," renamed "The Messenger Star" for the occasion, was intended as a "hoax," or "quiz," on the Bostonians. According to Cornelia Wells Walter of the *Boston Evening Transcript,* Poe's performance was an absolute "failure"; according to later biographers, the event revealed Poe's "sad inability to cope any longer with the affairs of this world,"[4] and it served as yet another example of the "Imp of the Perverse," in which Poe was seeking simultaneously to please and to irritate his audience.[5] By other accounts, it constituted a "public relations fiasco" that "damaged his already eroding reputation" by trying "to launch another literary war of words, like the Longfellow episode."[6] While these critical assessments attest to Poe's professional failure on this occasion, I would like to consider his personal failure: that is, Poe's failure to attain what he most desired that evening—acceptance in the city of his birth by an audience of Bostonians.

Poe's Boston Lyceum *appearance* was not itself disastrous, despite the assertions of reviewers, including Walter, who zealously "poh"ed Poe's performance, and others, such as Thomas Dunn English, who berated him for accepting the Boston Lyceum's money and insulting his distinguished audience by delivering a "mass of ridiculous stuff" when his "want of ability" prevented him from delivering a new poem as expected.[7] What was disastrous for Poe was his reaction to his critics in the first issue in his new capacity of editor and proprietor of *The Broadway Journal*, in which he admits to having prefaced his reading with "an apology for not 'delivering,' as is usual in such cases, a didactic poem: a didactic poem, in our opinion, being precisely no poem at all. After some farther words—still of apology—for the 'indefiniteness' and 'general imbecility' of what we had to offer—all so unworthy of a *Bostonian* audience,"[8] remarks aimed both at the poetry of Longfellow and the followers of Ralph Waldo Emerson. Poe noted furthermore that his poem was well received, more so than the lengthy discourse of Mr. Caleb Cushing, but that, before the evening concluded, he was prevailed upon to accept the invitation to deliver "The Raven," which he did to more applause. As if it were not already enough, Poe launched into a diatribe on Boston and the "soul-less" Bostonians:

> We like Boston. We were born there—and perhaps it is just as well not to mention that we are heartily ashamed of the fact. The Bostonians are very well in their way. Their hotels are bad. Their pumpkin pies are delicious. Their poetry is not so good. Their common is no common thing—and the duck pond might answer—if its answer could be heard for the frogs.[9]

Poe would subsequently take the disingenuous position that he substituted "Al Aaraaf" as a "hoax" upon an audience that could not appreciate one who had magnanimously "enlightened" them on the poetry of Longfellow and whose aims were Beauty, not Truth.

Poe's published account is a mixture of fact and fiction, more especially of hyperbole intended to draw more attention to the incident and to bait his readers to respond. Poe confesses to a "hoax," which undermines his own credibility, and he fabricates details about his poem, such as its date of composition, claiming that it was written when he was scarcely ten years old, when in fact it was written while he was serving as an enlisted soldier in the U.S. Army. Poe writes that he does not consider the poem "a remarkably good one," but he clarifies this statement to suggest that Transcendentalists would not consider it to be a "good" poem.[10] Though uneven, Poe's poem is a serious composition written in an epic style that includes lyrical passages, such as the song "Ligeia," which impressed several members of his audience that evening, most notably the young Thomas Wentworth Higginson, then an undergraduate at Harvard College. Higginson recorded his memories in more than one publication, later recalling the poem in a testimonial he sent to the organizers of the 1876 Baltimore monument committee, and including the selection below in his chapter on Poe in his *Short Studies in American Authors*:

> Ligeia! Ligeia,
> My beautiful one!
> Whose harshest idea
> Will to melody run,
> Oh! is it thy will
> On the breezes to toss?
> Or capriciously still
> Like the lone albatross
> Incumbent on night
> (As she on the air)
> To keep watch with delight
> On the harmony there?[11]

Higginson gives a full account of that evening and notes that "it was not then generally known, nor was it established for a long time thereafter—even when he had himself asserted it,—that the poet himself was born in Boston; and no one can now tell, perhaps, what was the real feeling behind the apparently sycophantic attitude" that Poe expressed in his introductory remarks, in which he anticipated "criticism of the Boston public."[12] However, concerning Poe's recitation of the lines above, Higginson wrote that "[Poe's] voice seemed attenuated to the finest golden thread; the audience became hushed, and, as it were breathless; there seemed no life in the hall but his; and every syllable was accentuated with such delicacy, and sustained with such sweetness, as I never heard equalled by other lips."[13] He concludes his account with the admission that on the way back to Cambridge from Boston, Higginson and his classmates felt they had been "under the spell of some wizard."[14]

Poe's professed "shame" over having been born in the city and his dismissive estimation of his "juvenile" poem and its inappropriateness for this audience do more to raise questions than to produce answers. Ottavio Casale convincingly notes that just as Poe's enemies effectively had "trivialized" Poe's Lyceum appearance, more importantly, Poe himself trivialized his selection of "Al Aaraaf": indeed, "Instead of being a perverse choice, the reading of 'Al Aaraaf' was probably a deliberate attempt to impress" his audience.[15] Furthermore, Daniel Hoffman argues, "'Al Aaraaf' is very ambitious. It is Poe's most ambitious failure."[16] Although it contains epic qualities that Poe would attack in "The Philosophy of Composition," it is what Hoffman calls "the best he ever did in the line of Jumbo Productions."[17] It is a poem, moreover, that draws seriously upon the poetry of both Percy Bysshe Shelley and John Milton in an effort to create a mythological place "out of space, out of time," a realm beyond this world of suffering, that only the *vates*, or poet-prophet, can imagine and relate to his audience. The epic scope of Poe's youthful vision in "Al Aaraaf" would not be seen again until the publication in 1848 of his prose-poem *Eureka*. Nevertheless, Poe was prepared for the worst: if the poem should go unappreciated, as it apparently did, then Poe could, and would, call attention to its having been a "juvenile" poem, even going so far as to claim that he had written it earlier than he had in order to save face by having been a child prodigy and to ridicule a "cultured" audience for not having been able to recognize the poem as that of a child.

What has probably *not* been misread is Poe's self-destructive, even "perverse," reaction to the event, which did little to enhance his reputation even as it sold magazines (though not enough to save *The Broadway Journal* from folding in less than a year). Any unconscious desire Poe may have had to win the approbation of the Bostonians was irrevocably dashed as a result of this episode. But why would Poe sabotage himself in such a colossal way on this occasion? What could have contributed to his strange behavior that evening and his "perverse" reaction to his critics in the wake of his performance?

Already having delivered a lecture earlier that year on "The Poets and Poetry of America" before the New York Historical Society in which he criticized the didacticism of such revered New England writers as Longfellow and Charles Sprague, Poe knew to anticipate a chilly reception in Boston. That he was unable also to compose a new poem for the occasion, as expected by the Boston Lyceum planning committee, surely added to Poe's anxiety. Nevertheless, Poe wanted to come to Boston. Although he does not mention the fact in his own account of the lecture, Poe, in 1844, had actively sought the influence of his then friend James Russell Lowell to secure an invitation from the Boston Lyceum to appear on one of that year's programs. The chairman was unable to grant Lowell's request at the time, but he assured Lowell that an invitation could be extended to Poe during the following year. Poe went out of his way to mention publicly that he had been "invited" to "deliver" a poem, and he was very likely honored finally to have received the invitation from this respectable institution. However, Poe was featured second on the program, following the Honorable Caleb Cushing, former four-term representative from Massachusetts and late ambassador to China. While both speakers were expected to draw sizable crowds, Cushing was better known to the general public and therefore given top billing that evening, with his name appearing above Poe's in the local papers. As was increasingly commonplace in Lyceum series by the 1840s, one speaker would provide the primary "substance" while the other would provide the "entertainment." One can only speculate as to how Poe would have regarded his status that evening.

Cushing's lecture, which began at 7:30 p.m., lasted for more than two hours without intermission, and so Poe's "delivery" was delayed until at least 9:30 or 10:00 p.m. It is therefore understandable that some people began to leave the auditorium midway through Poe's delivery, especially considering that Poe began with a "preface" in which he rehashed old complaints about didacticism in American literature and "apologized" that his poem was not sufficiently didactic for the tastes of Bostonians, before commencing his reading of "Al Aaraaf." Even if Poe believed "Al Aaraaf" to be a worthy poem (based on his own estimation and that of Lowell and John Neal, critics for whom Poe had considerable respect), as it seems clear that he did, it is remarkable given the late hour and Poe's "preface" that the majority of the audience remained in their seats to the bitter end. Had Poe not taken the bait of his critics and had he not attempted to bait them in return, had he let his "delivery" stand on its own merits, the Boston Lyceum incident would probably take up no more than a paragraph in Poe biography, at the most, and a footnote, at the least. That they had been edified by Cushing's political observations and exotic anecdotes and entertained by "The Raven" himself, who was prevailed upon eventually to recite his signature poem, would have been enough to convince most of the audience that the evening had been well worth the cost of admission. The problem, though, was that Poe did not like to be regarded as "second fiddle" or, worse, as the "sideshow."

Why would this consideration matter to Poe, who was used to the cutthroat world of early nineteenth-century American print culture? Why would it matter to one who believed that almost any publicity is good publicity, even when one's own character is damaged? Perhaps his pride was wounded when he was selected as second to Cushing, when perhaps Ralph Waldo Emerson, a favorite of the Boston Lyceum planning committee, would not have been. But Poe had managed to obviate any perceived advantage that Cushing had over him (at least in his own mind) by stating publicly that his performance had received more applause than the former ambassador's. Perhaps Poe was hoping to make a name for himself in the city that prided itself on its considerable literary and intellectual talent of such writers as Longfellow, Emerson, and Margaret Fuller, or perhaps he was hoping, finally, to break in to the center of American literary culture and to expose the cliques that seemed to have a monopoly on the production and promotion of American literature. Perhaps Boston was home to the Muses and to their favorite sons and daughters, but Boston was *his* home, too; it was Edgar Poe's birthplace. This consideration, that Poe was a Bostonian and even saw himself as such on some level, I believe to be the most significant and the least appreciated piece of the puzzle.

Boston was the city where Poe's parents, David and Elizabeth Poe, had performed on stage. It was, more importantly, the city that his mother, Eliza, had commended to Poe, as recorded by Marie Louis Shrew Houghton in her journal, on the back of a watercolor she left to him upon her death: "For my little son Edgar, who should ever love Boston, the place of his birth, and where his mother found her best, and most sympathetic friends."[18] Indeed, Poe cherished this watercolor, titled "Boston Harbour, morning, 1808," along with the few other items left to him by his mother, until his death. Poe also valued the miniature that she left to him and a copy of the novel *Charlotte Temple*, despite its sentimentality, because it had once belonged to her.[19] Given Eliza Poe's feeling about the city of Boston, it is especially significant that the Odeon, where Poe delivered his poem to the Boston Lyceum, was originally the Boston Theatre, where his parents had performed when they lived in Boston from 1806 to 1809 and where his mother continued to perform until the time of Poe's birth.

According to the Boston Athenaeum Theater History Database, the building—which was located on the corner of Federal and Franklin Streets and designed by the noted architect Charles Bulfinch—opened its doors on February 3, 1794. Although the original Federal Street Theatre burned down four years later, it was quickly rebuilt, served as a theater until 1835, and was converted to a public hall, which was renamed the Odeon. Figure 4.1 shows the Boston Theatre—also known as the Federal Street Theatre—as it looked in the early nineteenth century. It was at this theater that Poe's parents performed at the time of Poe's birth in 1809. Figure 4.2 shows the same building, renamed the Odeon, as it looked between 1834 and 1852, when Poe delivered his Boston Lyceum lecture there in 1845. The hall had been remodeled and leased for a period of years by the Boston Academy of Music,[20] and it later served as a popular venue for such events as the Boston Lyceum lecture series until it was reopened as a playhouse under its old name in 1846. The building was demolished in 1852.[21] Thus, Poe delivered his poem on the very stage on which his mother had performed to great acclaim.[22] Of all of Poe's biographers, only Mary E. Phillips notes that "the Odeon was one of several later names given Old Federal Street Theatre, upon which stage Poe's parents played so often and the last time during the spring of 1809," but neither she nor later biographers have pursued the potential implications of this fascinating connection.[23]

Geddeth Smith writes that the Federal Street Theatre was the first stage upon which the young Eliza Poe performed as a girl when she came to America with her mother (Poe's grandmother),[24] the English actress Elizabeth Arnold, and it was the stage where Eliza and David Poe would perform together until David's disappearance from Eliza's life and the lives of their children. It was also the last stage upon which Eliza performed in Boston prior to Edgar Poe's birth, which means that Edgar was on that stage *in utero* even before he was born. Because of the watercolor left to him and the knowledge that his mother (indeed, his parents and his grandmother) had

Figure 4.1. Boston Theatre, Federal Street, c.1824. The image is reproduced with permission of the Boston Athenæum.

Figure 4.2. Odeon, from *Bowen's Picture of Boston*, 3rd ed. (Boston, 1838). The image is reproduced with permission of the Boston Athenæum.

performed regularly there, Poe would have associated Boston with his mother, her successes, her struggles, and her love for the city. Poe expresses his love for his mother in the following tribute, included in one of his theater reviews:

> The actor of talent is poor at heart, indeed, if he do[es] not look with contempt upon the mediocrity even of a king. The writer of this article is himself the son of an actress—has invariably made it his boast—and no earl was ever prouder of his earldom than he of his descent from a woman who, although well born, hesitated not to consecrate to the drama her brief career of genius and of beauty.[25]

When Poe left the household of John and Frances Allan for the final time in 1827, it makes sense that he would have traveled to Boston to become a published poet, not only because Boston was a major publishing center but also because it was where his parents' theatrical career had flourished (or floundered, as the case may be), and in spite of John Allan's outspoken dismissal of Poe's poetic aspirations and the unrespectable career of his "real" parents. One can only speculate, as Arthur Hobson Quinn does in his authoritative critical biography, that it is likely that Poe would have sought out opportunities to join an acting troupe in the city.[26] As enticing, though unsubstantiated, as that prospect may be, it seems very likely that the young Poe at least would have sought out some of the venues, or former venues, associated with his parents when he was in Boston. Poe was employed as a clerk in Boston's wharf district, and his first book, *Tamerlane and Other Poems, By a Bostonian*, was published by Calvin F. S. Thomas on 70 Washington Street, which was within easy walking distance of the theatre district. While Poe's failure to achieve fame and financial security eluded him, leading him to enlist in the U.S. Army under the name of Edgar A. Perry at Fort Independence in Boston Harbor, his self-identification as "a Bostonian" is significant in my view, not only for what it would have meant to him in 1827 but also for what it would have meant to him in 1845 when he was invited to deliver a poem to the Boston Lyceum. Though he may not have known beforehand that the particular venue would be the auditorium formerly known as the Federal Street Theatre, when the venue was announced or when he actually arrived in Boston he surely would have realized that this was, indeed, the very stage upon which his mother had performed before an adoring crowd. That he could not expect the same degree of affection or adoration from his Bostonian audience would have been a profound source of anxiety for one who openly despised but inwardly desired Boston's approval. That anxiety would likely have grown more acute the longer he waited for Caleb Cushing's oration to conclude and for his own turn on stage to arrive.

Poe has been charged with having contempt for the city of Boston, largely based upon his overblown rhetoric in the aftermath of his 1845 Lyceum lecture, thus contributing to his "bad reputation." It is true that Poe identified Boston with writers who embodied the literary establishment, but his notion of the literary establishment extended beyond Boston more broadly to New England as well. His so-called hatred of Boston has taken on undue proportions, I think, based upon the documentation associated with the Boston Lyceum incident. However, Poe had enough vitriol to go around; Boston was simply the most conspicuous target for his critical tomahawk. By taking Poe's hyperbolic statements about Boston at face value (a dangerous thing to do, as anyone familiar with Poe's exaggerations and prevarications can attest), we run the risk of undervaluing Boston's significance to Poe, both professionally and personally. Poe takes such an extreme position toward the city of his birth in his journalistic writing because it *does* matter to him: it was his mother's city, the city that he should love, the city that was the

"Athens of America," and in an ideal sense, the place that *should* recognize and promote real literary merit. However, it is "Frogpondia" according to Poe's public persona, a place where critics are too loudly croaking to hear themselves croak and croaking to praise the works of their friends. But Boston was not alone: New York, Philadelphia, Baltimore, and even Richmond were all guilty of this, and the kind of "puffery" that Poe denounced in others (and was, at times, himself guilty of producing), was the practice that was preventing American literature from rising to the heights of which it was capable. Poe denounced Longfellow more because he viewed his work as derivative than because he thought his literary borrowing, or downright plagiarism, to be the mark of Cain. Poe saw the possibility of originality in American letters in a way that his contemporaries could not, and he "clear[ed] the GROUND" for it, as William Carlos Williams would later write,[27] in his own creative and critical work. A century later, Williams convincingly observed, "Poe gives the sense, for the first time in America, that literature is *serious*, not a matter of courtesy but of truth."[28] At the same time, though, Poe undermined his own project by placing himself above others, by picking unworthy and unnecessary battles in New England and elsewhere around the country, and in the case of Boston, by failing to realize that the "home" that he sought, the final end that was his beginning, the Boston that his mother Eliza had loved so well, never was and never would be the Boston of his imagination. Poe's Boston remained as elusive as the dark beauty of his elegiac verse, as dim and distant as "Al Aaraaf."

NOTES

The author would like to thank the Boston Athenæum for a 2008–2009 Mary Catherine Mooney Research Fellowship to support his research on Poe and Boston and the College Graduate Studies of Middle Tennessee State University for a Scholarly Dissemination Grant to cover the costs of photo reproductions and permissions.

1. *The Sunday Times and Messenger*, October 26, 1845.
2. For the most recent critical perspectives on Poe's Boston Lyceum appearance, see Katherine Hemple Brown, "The Cavalier and the Syren: Edgar Allan Poe, Cornelia Wells Walter, and the Boston Lyceum Incident," *New England Quarterly* 66, no. 1 (March 1993): 110–23; Kent P. Ljungquist, "Poe's 'Al Aaraaf' and the Boston Lyceum Contributions to Primary and Secondary Bibliography," *Victorian Periodicals Review* 28, no. 3 (Fall 1995): 199–216; Kent P. Ljungquist, "'Valdemar' and the 'Frogpondians': The Aftermath of Poe's Boston Lyceum Appearance," *Emersonian Circles: Essays in Honor of Joel Myerson*, ed. Wesley T. Mott and Robert E. Burkholder (Rochester, NY: University of Rochester Press, 1997), 181–206; and Eric Carlson, "Poe's Ten-Year Frogpondian War," *Edgar Allan Poe Review* 3, no. 2 (2002): 37–51.
3. Sidney P. Moss, *Poe's Literary Battles: The Critic in the Context of his Literary Milieu* (Durham, NC: Duke University Press, 1963), 190.
4. Hervey Allen, *Israfel: The Life and Times of Edgar Allan Poe* (New York: George H. Doran Co., 1926), 2:662.

5. Kenneth Silverman, *Edgar A. Poe: Mournful and Never-Ending Remembrance* (New York: HarperCollins, 1991), 267.
6. James M. Hutchisson, *Poe* (Jackson: University of Mississippi Press, 2005), 184–85.
7. From *The Evening Mirror* (1846); qtd. in Allen, *Israfel*, 664.
8. *The Broadway Journal*, November 1, 1845, 2:261R–262R, in *The Collected Writings of Edgar Allan Poe*, vol. 3, ed. Burton R. Pollin (New York: Gordian Press, 1986), 297–99.
9. Ibid.
10. Interestingly, Poe resisted Transcendentalism while simultaneously sharing some of its central concerns. In "Naysayers: Poe, Hawthorne, and Melville" (in *The Oxford Handbook of Transcendentalism*, ed. Joel Myerson et al. [Oxford: Oxford University Press, 2010], 597–613), Richard Kopley identifies Poe, Hawthorne, and Melville as "naysayers" who set themselves in opposition to the "prelapsarian vision" of Emersonian Transcendentalism by offering a "postlapsarian corrective" that more fully acknowledges the "darker side of humanity" (597). According to Kopley, Poe criticized Transcendentalism for its "verbal obscurity, its naïve reformism, and its inadequacy"; although Poe was interested in the Transcendent, "'Frogpondian' (or Bostonian) Transcendence could be, in his view, problematic" (597). Kopley concludes that Poe "evidently believed in a balance regarding the condition of humanity, a view that shaped his judgment of the Transcendentalists' faith in utopian achievement" (599).
11. From Edgar Allan Poe, "Al Aaraaf," qtd. by Thomas Wentworth Higginson in *Short Studies of American Authors* (Boston: Lee and Shepard, 1880), 14.
12. Ibid., 13.
13. Ibid., 14.
14. Ibid., 15. Apparently, Poe cast a lasting spell on Higginson, who nearly thirty-five years later adds, "Indeed, I feel much the same in retrospect, to this day" (15).
15. Ottavio M. Casale, "The Battle of Boston: A Revaluation of Poe's Lyceum Appearance," *American Literature* 45, no. 3 (November 1973): 423.
16. Daniel Hoffman, *Poe Poe Poe Poe Poe Poe Poe* (Garden City, NY: Doubleday, 1972), 36.
17. Ibid., 37.
18. Qtd. in John Carl Miller, *Building Poe Biography* (Baton Rouge: Louisiana State University Press, 1977), 121.
19. Kevin J. Hayes, "More Books from Poe's Library," *Notes and Queries* 55 (December 2008): 457.
20. See Abel Bowen, *Bowen's Picture of Boston, or the Citizen's and Stranger's Guide to the Metropolis of Massachusetts, and Its Environs*, 3rd ed. (Boston: Otis, Broaders and Company, 1838), 71–73 and 187–93. I would like to express my sincere appreciation to Catharina Slautterback, Curator of Prints and Photographs, Boston Athenaeum, for her expert assistance in locating images of the various façades of the Boston Theatre, later the Odeon, located on Federal Street. The representation of the "Odeon" printed in *Bowen's Picture of Boston* (opposite p. 188) is the only image of which she is aware that shows the building's façade as it looked between 1834 and 1852, when it was razed.
21. For the best short history of the Boston, or Federal Street, Theatre, see the Boston Athenaeum Theater History Database, created by Rebecka Persson, Rare Material Cataloger, Boston Athenaeum, at http://www.bostonathenaeum.org/node/224.
22. On the cultural implications of the fact that Poe's Lyceum lecture took place on the stage where his parents had performed, see Paul Lewis and Dan Currie, "The Raven in the Frog Pond: Edgar Allan Poe and the City of Boston," an exhibition at the Boston Public Library, December 17–March 31, 2010. While I consider how an awareness of the connection could have affected Poe's anxiety level at the time, Lewis and Currie emphasize the connection between anti-theater Puritan laws and highbrow Frogpondian aesthetic views in their exhibition.
23. Mary E. Phillips, *Edgar Allan Poe: The Man* (Chicago: John C. Winston Co., 1926), 2:1054.
24. Geddeth Smith, *The Brief Career of Eliza Poe* (Rutherford, Madison, and Teaneck, NJ: Fairleigh Dickinson University Press, 1988), 85.

25. *The Broadway Journal*, July 19, 1845, 2:29L, in *The Collected Writings of Edgar Allan Poe*, ed. Burton R. Pollin (New York: Gordian Press, 1986), 3:176; qtd. in Smith, 133.

26. Arthur Hobson Quinn, *Edgar Allan Poe: A Critical Biography* (New York: Appleton-Century-Crofts, 1941; Rpt. Baltimore: Johns Hopkins University Press, 1998), 118.

27. William Carlos Williams, "Edgar Allan Poe," from *In the American Grain* (New York: New Directions, 1956), 216.

28. Ibid.

Chapter Five

"Torture[d] into aught of the sublime"

Poe's Fall of the House of Burke, Ussher, and Kant

Sean Moreland

Baudelaire once observed that each of Poe's "opening paragraphs draws the reader in without violence—like a whirlpool,"[1] describing what can be termed the *sublimity* of Poe's greatest tales, their power to affect, to absorb, even to enrapture generations of readers. The simile itself is apt, as it reflects an image that is ubiquitous throughout Poe's fictions,[2] that of a figure perched precariously on the lip of a precipice, drawn irrevocably into the terrific involutions of an abyssal vortex. Psychoanalytic critic Marie Bonaparte argued for the centrality of this figure to any understanding of Poe's writings, as many of his tales feature a male narrator/character who is "drawn into a vast whirlpool—which, for all its terror, fatally attracts him." Following Freudian reason to its ineluctable conclusion, Bonaparte tirelessly insisted that this figure "expresses a version of the return-to-the-womb phantasy."[3] I would like to resituate this observation in terms of the historical discourse on the sublime, by suggesting that the image of the vortex[4] throughout Poe's fictions can be read as emblematic of Poe's conception of sublimity, an affective state thought to combine wondrous attraction with overwhelming terror, and one that was also thought to result in an absorption of the mind of the reader into that of the author, via the medium of the sublime text.

If Poe's tales trace the return to the womb, as Bonaparte insisted, it is finally a textual matrix, a Poetic vor*text*, to which they return and to which they invite their readers to return. This involution, and the attendant dissolution of the distinction between reading subject, writing subject, and text, was considered, from *Peri Hypsous* on, to be the sine non qua of literary sublimity. While Poe's engagement with the discourse on the sublime is "omniprevalent" throughout his writings,[5] this essay focuses specifically on "The Fall of the House of Usher," since, as critics including Kent Ljungquist and Jack G. Voller have observed, it is this tale which offers Poe's most sustained fictional engagement with and simultaneous disengagement from the discourse on the sublime.

In effect, the tale performs a dramatic negation of the architecture of sublime theorizations Poe inherited from European intellectuals, including Edmund Burke, James Ussher, and Immanuel Kant, each of whom produced definitive contributions to the discourse on the sublime, in part by their conceptual circumscription of the affect of terror. Such circumscription lent itself to the formation of a moral teleology and a literary hierarchy in popular aesthetics, both of which Poe was determined to overturn. While Poe ultimately rejected the theories of Burke, Ussher, and Kant,[6] "Usher" testifies to the degree to which he refigured, rather than entirely abandoning, their concepts. The tale's negative sublimity also evidences the degree to which Poe's investment in the discourse on the sublime led to his critical revision of a number of contemporaneously prevalent philosophical and aesthetic binaries, including Burke's distinction between beauty and sublimity, Samuel Taylor Coleridge's distinction between fancy and the imagination, and Anne Radcliffe's distinction between terror and horror. These interconnected aesthetic hierarchies are figured by Usher's overdetermined house, with its generic Gothic ancestry and unstable architecture, and their radical revision by Poe is finally figured by the revelatory collapse of the house itself.

While generally concurring with Voller, who argues that with "Usher" Poe is "writing a tale directed against established theories of sublimity,"[7] I would like to refine and add to some of his arguments, especially by considering the potential relevance of James Ussher's 1767 treatise *Clio* to the tale. *Clio* has been notably absent from prior discussions of the tale's pre-texts; this absence is understandable insofar as there appear to be no direct references to *Clio* in Poe's letters or critical writings. Nevertheless, *Clio*'s influence on the late eighteenth- and early nineteenth-century British discourse on the sublime[8], and Poe's keen interest in this discourse, make it likely that Poe would have had at least a passing familiarity with Ussher and the basic thrust of *Clio*'s arguments. Moreover, the degree to which many of *Clio*'s central themes, and even its specific phrases, are echoed throughout Poe's tale reinforces the probability that James Ussher's name is a partial source for the tale's patronym.

There are two things about Ussher's conception of the sublime in *Clio* that particularly illuminate Poe's revision of the sublime with "Usher." *Clio* expounds a conception of the sublime that first, drawing heavily on Burke's *Enquiry*, is far more piously theistic, and which carefully circumscribes the role that terror plays in the experience of the sublime. This is a circumscription that Poe's "Usher" goes to great lengths to explode. Second, *Clio*'s conception of the role of the object in the psychology of the sublime contradicts Burke's theory in a way that Poe's critical writings echo, and this contradiction is dramatized by the narrative of "Usher." As Ashfield and de Bolla observe, Ussher's account opposes Burke's delineation of the specific qualities of sublime objects, emphasizing instead that "the object of the sublime is vacant,"[9] much like the "eye-like" windows of the tale's central architectural image. In this respect, "Usher," like Ussher, breaks from Burke's object-based theory.

Before returning to these issues, some of the structural, symbolic, and phrasal continuities between *Clio* and "Usher" bear explication. *Clio*'s narrator attributes his pontifications on the sublime to an "old friend," "a genius" who, like Roderick, dwells in an isolated locale, surrounded by wilderness: "He had withdrawn himself from the trifling bustle of the little world, to converse with his own heart, and end a stormy life in obscure quiet."[10] This mediated narrative structure, itself owing something to Johnson's *Rasselas*, anticipates the structure of Poe's tale. *Clio*, described as "an enthusiastic gentleman's" (132) rhapsody on taste, sets up an opposition to the skepticism of Hobbes, Locke, and Mandeville, arguing that the power to recognize beauty and sublimity inheres in a "universal spirit," an idea proximate to Kant's later notion of a *sensus communis*. Ussher claims that "the sublime, by an authority which the soul is utterly unable to resist, takes possession of our attention, and of all of our faculties, and absorbs them in astonishment. The passion it inspires us with is evidently a mixture of terror, curiosity, and exultation: but they are stamped with a majesty that bestows on them a different air and character from those passions on any other occasion" (102). Ussher goes to great lengths to contain the terror that Burke had more openly identified as the "common stock of everything which is sublime," a containment that will also characterize Kant's revision of the sublime encounter in the *Critique of Judgment*'s "Analytic of the Sublime" (1790), a text that Poe was less likely to have read.[11] Ussher claims that:

> the combination of passions in the sublime, renders the idea of it obscure. No doubt the sensation of fear is very distinct in it; but it is equally obvious, that there is something in the sublime more than this abject passion. In all other terrors, the soul loses its dignity, and as it were shrinks below its usual size: but at the presence of the sublime, although it be always awful, the soul of man seems to be raised out of a trance; it assumes an unknown grandeur (103).

Ussher restates this central point later, writing that "we must carefully distinguish between common accidental fear, and this noble sensation that elevates while it overawes" (117). The distinction Ussher makes here between abject terror and elevated terror is one that is echoed by Anne Radcliffe's later differentiation of the sublime affect of terror from the repulsive affect of horror. In a dramatic dialogical essay titled "On the Supernatural in Poetry," first penned in 1798 and later republished as part of her late novel *Gaston de Blondeville*, Radcliffe placed a distinction in the mouth of one of her characters between terror and horror, which "are so far opposite, that the first expands the soul, and awakens the faculties to a high degree of life," whereas "the other contracts, freezes, and nearly annihilates them."[12]

As Radcliffe's readers would have immediately recognized, this description of terror paralleled Burke's account of the sublime affect in the *Enquiry* closely. While Burke had made no clear distinction between "terror" and "horror" in the *Enquiry*, Radcliffe's amanuensis viewed this as a terminological oversight; "while I apprehend, that neither Shakespeare nor Milton by their fictions, nor Mr. Burke by his reasoning, anywhere looked to positive horror as a source of the sublime, . . . they all agree that terror is a very high one."[13] This distinction, while to some degree founded on the etymology of each word, was also clearly designed to serve Radcliffe's aesthetic-political agenda. First penned shortly after she read Matthew Lewis's scandalous Gothic novel *The Monk* (1796), which he openly admitted had been inspired by her own *Mysteries of Udolpho* (1794), it gave her an opportunity to create a distinction between Lewis's frenetic, transgressive novel and her own more restrained and rationalistic fiction. Thus, like Ussher, Radcliffe hierarchizes both affect and literary style, elevating terror above horror by associating the former, but never the latter, with the grandeur of divinity.

In *Clio*, Ussher goes on to claim that "the Greeks, the fathers of thought and sublime knowledge, always nicely observed the difference between the native powers of the mind over its stock of sensible ideas, and the sublime influence to which it was passive" (122).

Ussher's account identifies precisely that element of the sublime that made Enlightenment thinkers so uncomfortable. Sublimity was thought to possess the power to, in Burke's formulation, "anticipate our reasonings" and "hurry us onward" even in opposition to them. As Hume's skepticism had already postulated, reason, understood as merely "a calm determination of the passions," could not be an adequate goad to moral behavior in the face of more extreme determinations of the passions, such as those experienced during a moment of sublime *ekstasis*.

The power of the sublime to inspire action independent of rational consideration was something that would be wrestled with both by the later Burke and by Kant. As Voller has shown, however, "The Fall of the House of Usher" implicitly rejects the resolutions presented by both theories. The tale's engagement with and transformation of the Burkean sublime is signaled in its vortex-like opening paragraphs by its reference to and refusal of "that half-pleasurable, because poetic, sentiment, with which the mind usually receives even the sternest natural images of the desolate or terrible."[14] This negative invocation of that "pleasurable, because poetic sentiment" implies the narrator's familiarity with the discourse on the sublime, and also highlights his vain expectation of experiencing such poetic affects. He is, in this regard, a literary confrere of both the travelogue-addicted Arthur Gordon Pym and Jane Austen's quixotic Catherine Morland, whose experience of reality is mediated by her enthusiasm for Radcliffean Gothic fictions.

To the narrator's apparent disappointment, neither the rapturous transports of Radcliffe's novels nor the tortuous arguments and definitive distinctions of Burke's and Kant's theories seem to apply to his experience. As Paul de Man explains, "The initial effect of the sublime, of a sudden encounter with colossal natural entities such as cataracts, abysses, and towering mountains, is one of shock, or says Kant, astonishment that borders upon terror. . . . By a play, a trick of the imagination, this terror is transformed into a feeling of tranquil superiority."[15] This second movement of the Kantian sublime's cognitive symphony is notably absent here. As Voller puts it, "The mind's ability to resist the power of sublime objects, to regard them as 'without any dominion over us and our personality' is shown by Poe to be an illusion. . . . 'Usher' flatly rejects Kant's easy confidence in the mind's superiority over nature."[16] Instead of the delightful terror of the sublime, the narrator experiences "an iciness, a sinking, a sickening of the heart—an unredeemed dreariness of thought which no goading of the imagination could torture into aught of the sublime." (*TS* 397).

This allusive and sibilant phrasing signals both the tale's rejection of prior theories of the sublime, and following Dennis Pahl, Poe's adaptation of "Burke's notion of sublime 'effects' to his own materialist aesthetics, an aesthetics that emphasizes, among other things, the sensory-emotional effects of language and sounds on human subjectivity."[17] With its emphasis on the feeling of "sinking," the narrator's phrase both foreshadows the tale's conclusion and invokes Pope's *Peri Bathos, or On the Art of Sinking in Literature*, itself a satiric stab at the profusion of imitative literature produced in the eighteenth century in response to the popularity of Longinus's treatise. The narrator's description also effectively revises both Burke's physiological account of the sublime experience and Radcliffe's strategic distinction between terror and horror. The sensations of iciness, sinking, and sickening were sensations Radcliffe claimed were produced by the affect of *horror*, rather than *terror*, which by her formulation is alone associated with both Burke's sublime, and less explicitly, her own Gothic productions.

The narrator questions his own affective response to the house as he draws closer, asking, "What was it that so unnerved me in the contemplation of the House of Usher? It was a mystery all insoluble; nor could I grapple with the shadowy fancies that crowded upon me as I pondered" (*TS* 397–98). The word *fancy*, more or less synonymous with *imagination* throughout the eighteenth century, became semantically demoted by Coleridge's influential distinction in *Biographia Literaria* between mere fancy and revered imagination. Poe notably rejected Coleridge's distinction in one of his reviews:

> 'Fancy,' says the author of 'Aids to Reflection,' (who aided Reflection to much better purpose in his 'Genevieve')—'Fancy combines—Imagination creates.' This was intended and has been received, as a distinction, but it is a distinction without a difference—without even a difference of degree. The Fancy as nearly creates as the imagination, and neither at all. Novel conceptions are merely unusual combinations. The mind of man can imagine nothing which does not exist.[18]

Alexander Schlutz has persuasively shown that, for all Poe's debts to Coleridge, he is "far from completing the philosophical structure that Coleridge had attempted to build, and if he inhabits it, he does so not as a headstone in its supporting arch, but rather as a threat to its desired foundations."[19]

Poe's rejection of Coleridge's distinction also notably represents a return to Burke's sensationist psychology, as it echoes Burke's claim that:

> [the] mind of man possesses a sort of creative power of its own; either in representing at pleasure the images of things in the order and manner in which they were received by the senses, or in combining those images in a new manner, and according to a different order. This power is called imagination. . . . But it must be observed, that this power of the imagination is incapable of producing any thing absolutely new; it can only vary the disposition of those ideas which it has received from the senses.[20]

Further dramatizing this rejection of Coleridge in "Usher," Poe repeatedly deploys not only the term *fancy* (it appears eight times in the tale) but also a number of its etymological siblings, phantasmagoric, fantasias, fantastic, and phantasm, chiefly in describing the artistic productions of Roderick, and the affective states they embody.

Each of these usages suggests the tremendous power Usher's "unusual combinations" can have on those who experience them, further undermining Coleridge's distinction. Similarly, the delusions fostered by the affective power of Usher's art, and the consequences these delusions have for both the unfortunate narrator and the Usher siblings, must be recognized as a direct challenge to the theories of both Kant and Ussher. For both these thinkers, as for most eighteenth-century commentators on the sublime, what saved the concept from a dangerous, enthusiastic amorality was the anchoring of its power in some transcendent moral order. Where Kant employs the notion of moral reason in this place, Ussher emphasizes the concept of divine authority. In *Clio* he states, "I know no reason for our perception of absolute eternal beauty in the virtues I have mentioned, but by supposing, that the Father of being, who is eternal truth and goodness, and the original standard of grandeur and beauty, has stamped on our minds a sense of those absolute and eternal perfections" (12). Further, Ussher emphasizes that the sublime had its source in the divine well before Longinus wrote his tract, since the Greeks "traced the [sublime] through its various appearances, and never failed to attribute it to divine power; sometimes to the Muses, sometimes to Apollo, to the Furies, to Pan, to the Sylvan deities, and to the genius of the place" (152).

This sacred anchorage is notably absent[21] from the phrasing of Poe's "Usher." But Ussher's attribution of an irresistible sublime influence to "the genius of the place" is important to "Usher," since the entirety of the tale depends upon a recognition of the coextensive nature of the pathological "genius" of Roderick Usher and the "genius" of the house and its environs, a genius which (like that described by the narrator of Poe's "The Imp of the Perverse") inexorably affects all in its presence, drawing them into its vortex. *Clio* valorizes the aristocratic aesthete as the agent of the sublime, as Ussher instructs his reader to "observe the few of a higher station, who by their fortunes are disengaged from wretchedness and poverty, who vegetate freely, and take the bias of the unfettered human genius. You see their taste soon distinguish them from the crowd, they assume a more elevated character" (40). Once again, Roderick Usher, with his theory of "the sentience of all vegetable things" provides a dark reflection of James Ussher's expression. Roderick, the quintessential Romantic genius, can be readily recognized as an embodiment of Ussher's ideal, but also as its ultimate subversion, as his elevation is merely the prelude to his, and his lineage's, final collapse. Thus Poe's "Usher" both echoes James Ussher's conception of genius and subverts it by anticipating Max Nordau's later linkage of genius with degeneracy and madness. For Ussher, nothing could be further from the sublime than madness. He writes that:

> of all the objects of discord and confusion, no other is so shocking as the human soul in madness. When we see the principle of thought and beauty disordered, the horror is too high, like that of a massacre committed before our eyes, to suffer the mind to make any reflex act on the god-like traces of pity that distinguish our species; and we feel no sensations but those of dismay and terror (174).

Poe's tale, on the contrary, presents a movement from sublimity to madness, through Roderick's genius and art, and from pity to madness, through the narrator's unnatural affinities for Usher. The narrative's presentation of Roderick's elevation (genius) and descent (madness) is also one of its many ludic allusions to the etymology of the word *sublime*, as it emphasizes the fact that, in the two-dimensional world of the text, depth is always illusory, and height and depth are ultimately relative characteristics; thus, in contradiction to Ussher's sublime, an *elevated* character is ultimately indistinguishable from a *fallen* character.

The detailed description of the house's exterior reinforces its critical figuration of Burke/Ussher/Kant's sublime, as "there appeared to be a wild inconsistency between its still perfect adaptation of parts, and the crumbling condition of the individual stones" (*TS* 400). While these theories of the sublime seem potent when taken as totalities, "Usher" implies that each, when its elements are scrutinized closely, presents only a "specious totality," riven by "a barely perceptible fissure." This fissure, whose expansion is coterminous with the tale's progression, is inclusive of Burke's artificial isolation of beauty from sublimity, Ussher's understatement of the role of terror in the sublime, and both Ussher's and Kant's containment of terror within a moral teleology.

The tale's critical perspective on this subordination of terror to an abstract moral system is particularly important when considering the role played by Roderick Usher's art. As Philip Shaw explains, "In the 'Analytic of the Sublime,' Kant links the beautiful with the bounded. A beautiful object has clear outlines and distinct form, whereas the sublime is found in formlessness,"[22] and it is just this formlessness that the narrator claims gives Usher's art its terrible potency. Usher's paintings, like his features and those of the house, force the narrator to "the unsatisfactory conclusion" that their "power lies among considerations beyond our depth" (*TS* 398), mirroring Ussher's claim that art often has its most powerful effect on those who do not comprehend how it achieves this effect, as "a fine picture charms and transports a spectator who has no idea of painting" (3). As the narrator finally confesses, his attempts to interpret these seeming ciphers are in vain, as are his attempts to interpret Roderick's physiognomy: "I could not, even with effort, connect its Arabesque expression with any idea of simple humanity" (*TS* 402).

It was his recognition of the sustained opposition established throughout Poe's writings between the ornate involutions of the arabesque and the "idea of simple humanity" that led Baudelaire to write of Poe's title *Tales of the Grotesque and Arabesque* that it is "remarkable and deliberately chosen," "for the grotesque and arabesque ornaments thrust aside the human figure."[23] This recognition in turn informs David Ketterer's argument that "the arabesque designs are active symbols of Poe's efforts to melt away the rigid pattern that is imposed by man's reason."[24] Following this logic, it can be recognized that Usher's "arabesque expression" is meant to "melt" such "rigid patterns," including these influential rationalizations of the sublime.

Poe's emphasis on the link between Roderick's unreadable features and his indefinite works of art also mirrors *Clio*, in which Ussher observes that "if grace has any fixed throne, it is in the face, the residence of the soul" (52) and that "the countenance is the very palace in which it takes up its residence" (54).This statement may well underlie Poe's framed poem, "The Haunted Palace," which the narrator includes because, he claims, it reveals "a full consciousness on the part of Usher, of the tottering of his lofty reason upon her throne" (*TS* 406). No mere parergon, "The Haunted Palace" is another example of Usher's art's indefinite ability to escape the limitations of any imposed frame, spreading, like the crack in the house's foundations, throughout the entire tale. The poem expands the equivocal use of the word *expression* on which much of the story's effect depends, revealing Roderick's own facial expressions in both his musical expressions and in the expression of his ancestral estate, and it grotesquely literalizes James Ussher's claim that we "look as well as speak our minds" (75). Similarly, the narrator's inability to read this relationship reflects Ussher's insistence that "we can no more account for the relation between the passions of the mind and a set of features, than we can account for the relation between the sounds of music and the passions" (76).

It must also be noted that Poe's use of the term *arabesque* in describing Usher's expression was almost certainly influenced by one of the chief champions of the arabesque in painting, Friedrich Schlegel,[25] who was also an important influence on Coleridge. Winfried Meninghaus explains that "for Friedrich Schlegel the arabesque was 'the original form of painting' and also 'the genuine mother, the embryo of all of modern painting.' . . . But Schlegel went further than this. He declared the arabesque to be indeed 'the oldest and original form of human fantasy.'"[26] Schlegel's conception informs the dark whorls of Usher's paintings, which even at their most representational, partake of a "formlessness" and "abstraction" that signals their negative sublimity, their "thrilling vaguenesses." The narrator's account links the influence of these abstract spectacles to the roles of both Usher and the narrator in Madeline's premature interment (a prefiguration of which appears to be the subject of one of these paintings), exploding both Usher's and Kant's insistence on the necessary connection between the apprehension of the aesthetic sublime and the influence of, respectively, divine authority or moral reason.

It is perhaps no coincidence that both Ussher's *Clio* and Poe's "Usher" finally situate themselves with the staging of an act of reading by their respective narrators. Ussher's amanuensis produces his most telling comments on the sublime following a "reading [of] Homer on our way to the seaside. When we sat down, our conversation turned on the strange power of the sublime" (106). This is mirrored in Poe's tale when the narrator reads Roderick "The Mad Trist," a poem full of clangorous rhetorical effects that deliberately parodies the poetic devices Longinus iterated as productive of sublimity in *Peri Hypsous.* The poem's title provides a wry comment on the conflation of the narrator's identity with that of Usher, as they are joined together throughout the tale in a kind of textual-affective conjugation. This perversely reflects Longinus's claim that "the mind is naturally elevated by the true sublime, and so sensibly affected with its lively strokes, that it swells in transport and an inward pride, as if what was only heard had been the product of its own invention."[27] In other words, the mind that apprehends the literary sublime seems to lose itself in the mind that created the sublime text, and ultimately, author, reader, and text become indistinguishable, inter-involved, and utterly confused.

Burke's *Enquiry* disseminated a similar notion, arguing that in the apprehension of the sublime, the mind is "always claiming to itself some part of the dignity and importance of the things which it contemplates."[28] This absorption parallels the vertigo that Baudelaire experienced upon his discovery of Poe's tales, and it also influenced Poe's own conception of authorial propriety in a manner most pertinent to his inconsistent attitude concerning plagiarism. Echoing Longinus and Burke (unconsciously or otherwise), Poe claimed that the poetic sentiment "implies a peculiarly, perhaps an abnormally keen appreciation of the beautiful, with a longing for its assimilation, or absorption, into the poetic identity. What the poet intensely admires, becomes thus, in very fact, although only partially, a portion of his own intellect."[29] As Meredith McGill has pointed out, "What is perhaps most striking about this defense of plagiarism is the utter passivity of the offending poet. He is not only fully possessed by another's thought in the act of reading, he is subject to a kind of hair-trigger reproduction of his thought."[30] This passivity reflects the Longinian/Burkean conception of the reader's response to a work of the sublime.

Thus, while I agree with Voller's argument that, through "Usher," Poe reveals the degree to which earlier theorizations of the sublime fail to competently explain or account for the importance and vitality of terror, I do not agree that this constitutes Poe's wholesale rejection of the discourse on the sublime, as the tale's depiction of an intersubjective contagion experienced during the act of reading is heavily influenced by many of these earlier writers on the sublime, as, apparently, is Poe's "own" theory of authorship and inspiration. As Dennis Pahl has recently argued, despite Poe's apparent rejections of Burke's *Enquiry*,[31] Poe's writing continued to adapt, if in an altered form, Burke's theory of language, and "Usher" offers much to support this interpretation.[32]

In addition, the sublimity of Roderick and his art presents a problem for the more allegorical dimensions of Voller's approach to the tale, as Voller claims that "the lure of the imaginative, the nonrational, is embodied (not surprisingly for Poe) in the story's only female character."[33] Voller's allegorization of Madeline is largely founded on a desire to see Kant's theory of the sublime dramatized in the tale, and as far as that goes, it is productive. Despite the likelihood of Poe's not having read the *Critique of Judgment*, Madeline's parallels with the imagination—which, in Kant's conception, is sacrificially lain at the altar of moral reason—remain striking. Yet this allegorical generalization is unsatisfactory insofar as it excludes the relationship that obviously exists between Usher, the archetypical mad genius, and Poe's conception of the imagination; and it also fails to account for the other conceptual binaries that the House of Usher's collapse effectively overturns through Madeline, who can as readily be read as personifying Burke's attempt to subordinate the feminized beautiful to the masculinized sublime, and Coleridge's attempt to subordinate the feminized fancy to the masculinized imagination. The tale suggests that, like Madeline, Burke's denatured conception of beauty, separated from the vitality of terror, and Coleridge's conception of fancy, denying the power of creativity, have been prematurely buried, and thus must be made to return to life.

However, keeping in mind Poe's suspicion of allegory and his monomaniacal penchant for literary one-upmanship, it is clear that a degree of both caution and humor is called for in such interpretations of "Usher," whose symbolic fluidity and occultation of causal relations are among its greatest strengths. It may be more apt to read this dramatization as a kind of elaborate parodic play, meant to trap readers who are, in Poe's phrase, "theory mad beyond redemption."[34] This is especially true since, for all its sophisticated critical engagements with the discourse on sublimity, the story's status as a work of and not merely on the sublime is ultimately dependent on the inadequacy of theoretical interpretations that seek to define or restrict its meanings.

In praising the sublimity of Milton's evocation of Death, Burke wrote that "in this description all is dark, uncertain, confused, terrible, and sublime to the last degree,"[35] emphasizing that uncertainty is an exigent ingredient of effective sublimity. Considering the power of music, Poe echoed this sentiment in terms redolent of both Burke's and Ussher's, arguing that "indefiniteness" is the key to evoking "sensations which bewilder while they enthral—and which would *not so* enthral if they did not so bewilder."[36] This commingled bewilderment and enthralment, characteristic of sublimity, is what underlies the image of the vortex, the "whirlwind," with its "rushing sound as of a thousand waters" (*TS* 417), with which "The Fall of the House of Usher," like many of Poe's tales, closes. It is a testament to the unity of the tale's sublime effect that it continues to bewilder while it enthrals, reinforcing its status as a work both on and of the sublime.

NOTES

1. Charles Baudelaire, "Edgar Allan Poe: His Life and Works," in *The Painter of Modern Life and Other Essays*, trans. Jonathan Mayne (London: Phaidon, 1995), 90.

2. Examples include "MS Found in a Bottle," "Metzengerstein," "A Descent into the Maelstrom," "The Pit and the Pendulum," and "The Imp of the Perverse," to name a few.

3. Marie Bonaparte, *The Life and Works of Edgar Allan Poe: A Psychoanalytic Interpretation*, trans. John Rodker (London: Imago, 1949), 353.

4. Poe's numerous references to vortices synthesize a variety of potential meanings. One of the most important for understanding the vortex as the emblem of Poe's aesthetic practice is the Cartesian theory, which posited that vortices accounted for the origins and behavior of the material universe—an idea that had been largely discredited by Poe's time. For example, in his 1833 *Table Talk*, Coleridge stated that "Descartes' vortices were not a hypothesis: they rested on no facts at all." Poe was clearly aware of this, as he recommended the book in his "Notice of Coleridge's *Table Talk*" for the *Baltimore American*, July 22, 1835, yet he would revisit, and revise, the Cartesian vortical theory in his own way in *Eureka* (1848).

5. Poe's extensive interest in the sublime is readily evidenced by J. Lasley Dameron's identification of thirty-eight usages of the term *sublime* in Poe's critical writings alone. Citing Dameron, Kent Ljungquist suggests that Poe's familiarity with the sublime may have arisen largely from his familiarity with Burke's *Enquiry*, to which there are "several references" in Poe's works. See Kent Ljungquist, *The Grand and the Fair: Poe's Landscape Aesthetics and Pictorial Techniques* (Potomac, MA: Scripta Humanistica, 1984), 48.

6. Readers interested in the eighteenth- and nineteenth-century discourse on the sublime should consult James Kirwan, *Sublimity: The Non-Rational and the Irrational in the History of Aesthetics* (New York: Routledge, 2005); Andrew Ashfield and Peter de Bolla, *The Sublime: A Reader in Eighteenth-Century Aesthetic Theory* (Cambridge: Cambridge University Press, 1996); and Philip Shaw, *The Sublime* (New York: Routledge, 2006).

7. Jack G. Voller, "The Power of Terror: Burke and Kant in the House of Usher," *Poe Studies* 21, no. 2 (1988): 27–35. Voller places his arguments in a wider context in his book *The Supernatural Sublime: The Metaphysics of Terror in Anglo-American Romanticism* (DeKalb: Northern Illinois University Press, 1994).

8. See, for example, Andrew Ashfield and Peter de Bolla, "Irish Perspectives," in *The Sublime: A Reader in Eighteenth-Century Aesthetic Theory*, 131–157.

9. Ashfield and de Bolla, *The Sublime*, 128.

10. James Ussher, *Clio: Or, a Discourse on Taste. Addressed to a Young Lady, The Fourth Edition, with Large Additions* (London, 1778), 105–6. Eighteenth-Century Collections Online. Accessed October 13, 2012. Accessed September 5, 2012. http://gdc.gale.com/products/eighteenth-century-collections-online/.

11. For more on Poe's (lack of) knowledge of Kant and other German writers, see Thomas S. Hansen with Burton R. Pollin, *The German Face of Edgar Allan Poe: A Study of Literary References in His Works* (Columbia, SC: Camden House, 1995).

12. Anne Radcliffe, "On the Supernatural in Poetry," qtd. in E. J. Clery and Robert Miles, *Gothic Documents: A Sourcebook 1700–1820* (Manchester, UK: Manchester University Press, 2000), 166.

13. Radcliffe, "On the Supernatural in Poetry," 167.

14. Poe, "The Fall of the House of Usher," in Edgar Allan Poe, *Tales and Sketches, Volume I: 1831–1842*, ed. Thomas Olive Mabbott (Urbana: University of Illinois Press, 2000), 397. Hereafter cited in text as *TS*.

15. Paul de Man, "Phenomenality and Materiality in Kant," in *The Textual Sublime: Deconstruction and Its Differences*, ed. Hugh Silverman (Albany: State University of New York Press, 1990), 102.

16. Voller, "Burke and Kant in the House of Usher," 29.

17. Dennis Pahl, "Sounding the Sublime: Poe, Burke, and the (Non)sense of Language," *Poe Studies/Dark Romanticism* 42 (2009): 41–60, 44.

18. Edgar Allan Poe, "American Prose Writers, No. 2: N. P. Willis" (Text-02), *Broadway Journal* 1, no. 3 (January 18, 1845): 37–38. Accessed September 5, 2012. http://www.eapoe.org/works/criticsm/bj45wn01.htm.

19. Alexander Schlutz, "'Purloined Voices': Edgar Allan Poe Reading Samuel Taylor Coleridge," *Studies in Romanticism* 47, no. 2 (Summer 2008): 195.

20. Edmund Burke, *A Philosophical Enquiry into the Origin of Our Ideas of the Sublime and Beautiful*, ed. James T. Boulton (London: Routledge, 1967), 17.

21. The story clearly does employ biblical phraseology and rhetoric, but I would argue that, in keeping with the tale's Schlegelian irony, this only serves to reinforce its displacement of the power of the sublime from a theistic moral center. On this point I concur with Voller's statement that Poe's "greatest value is in the sense of horror that accrues from the realization that the romance . . . can uncover the emptiness not only in reality but in our schemes to rise above reality." Voller, *The Supernatural Sublime*, 225.

22. Philip Shaw, *The Sublime*, 117.

23. Baudelaire, "Edgar Allan Poe," 78.

24. David Ketterer, *The Rationale of Deception in Poe* (Baton Rouge: Louisiana State University Press, 1979), 36.

25. Readers interested in Schlegel's importance for Poe should consult G. R. Thompson, *Poe's Fiction: Romantic Irony in the Gothic Tales* (New York: Madison, 1973).

26. Winfried Meninghaus, *In Praise of Nonsense: Kant and Bluebeard*, trans. Henry Pickford (Stanford, CA: Stanford University Press, 1999), 85.

27. Ashfield and de Bolla, "Introduction," *The Sublime*, 23.

28. Burke, *Philosophical Enquiry*, 51.

29. Edgar Allan Poe, "Plagiarisim—Imitation—Postscript," from the *Broadway Journal*, April 5, 1845. Accessed September 5, 2012. http://www.eapoe.org/works/criticsm/bj45lh07.htm.

30. Meredith McGill, "Poe, Literary Nationalism, and Authorial Identity," in *The American Face of Edgar Allan Poe*, ed. Shawn Rosenheim and Stephen Rachman (Baltimore: Johns Hopkins University Press, 1995), 297. Of course, as it is situated in the epistolary-editorial feud known as "The Longfellow War," this conception serves Poe as a defense against accusations of plagiarism made in the wake of his own accusations against Longfellow. For more on this subject, see also Stephen Rachman, "Es Lässt Sich Nicht Schreiben: Plagiarism and 'The Man of the Crowd,'" 49–91, in the same volume.

31. For example, in his "Notice of Coleridge's *Table Talk*," from the *Baltimore American*, July 22, 1835, Poe cites approvingly Coleridge's statement that "Burke's Essay on the Sublime and Beautiful seems to me a poor thing; and what he says upon Taste is neither profound nor accurate."

32. Pahl, "Sounding the Sublime." 41.

33. Voller, "Burke and Kant in the House of Usher," 29.

34. Edgar Allan Poe, "The Poetic Principle," *Critical Theory: The Major Documents*, ed. Stuart and Susan F. Levine (Urbana: University of Illinois Press, 2009), 186.

35. Burke, *Philosophical Enquiry*, 115.

36. Edgar Allan Poe, "Marginalia [part XIII]," Southern Literary Messenger (April 1849): 218. Accessed September 5, 2012. http://www.eapoe.org/works/misc/mar0449.htm.

Chapter Six

Poe and Perversity

Daniel Fineman

The first sentence of "The Man of the Crowd" seems almost self-reflexive: "It was well said of a certain German book that "*er lässt sich nicht lesen*"—it does not permit itself to be read."[1] Such a sentiment might be the motto too of much of Poe's own work that presents motives, causes, and purposes that remain inscrutable even after the tale's final period. But the quotation also offers a hint at—if not a solution to—the philosophical ambiance from which this tale and its obscurity might have come: the German idealism of Schlegel, Schiller, Tieck, Novalis, and Hegel. Behind them, one finds the echoes of their shared philosophical heritage reaching back, first to Spinoza and, further yet, to Lucretius.

In *De rerum natura*, we find the potential origin of a darker tradition than that of science, of straight rational explanation. This is a philosophy not based primarily on Platonic form or Aristotelian order. In part, Lucretius takes exception to the predominant concepts of reason, explanation, and linear causality. Famously, we find in his work the concept of the *clinamen*, nature's unjustified "swerve" of becoming from the line of unerring sameness. This difference comes not from exterior cause but through an autonomic variation, a spontaneous deviation.

For Poe, this insistent turn is not just a physical theory, though it appears as a governing material principle in *Eureka*, but also the underlying force for his compositional technique. His is a narrative practice that deconstructs its initially ordered material to leave a consequent supernal "effect" in its stead. This too is the secret ingredient that makes understandable the apparent inconsistency between his compositional formality and his persistent practice of decomposing the subjects and objects that formed his settings and characters.

As his story "The Imp of the Perverse" makes clear, he views the human swerve from the rational course not as a purely aleatory exception or an inexplicable madness but as one of the *"prima mobilia* of the human soul."[2] Thus his tendency toward obscurity, humor, puzzle, prank, and the grotesque are not reverse proofs, as in Aristotle's *Poetics,* of order out its comic or tragic inversion. Instead, his works are celebrations of a necessary, natural, and desirable deviation toward a paradoxically constructive dissolution and cosmic reconstitution. This celebration of free change explains evil and the death instinct as the epiphenomena of a cosmic tendency to undo every particular entity, the endless tumult of "a novel Universe swelling into existence, and then subsiding into nothingness, at every throb of the Heart Divine."[3]

To theorize this swerving perversity, this chapter will at moments employ vocabularies and insights reminiscent of twentieth-century French theory. However, these thinkers of difference are not impositions but the latest manifestation of the darker metaphysical tradition that began with the philosophical father of Lucretius, Epicurus. In these Greeks, one finds the same trajectory from which Poe derives his disposition. Indeed, the accusations of Germanic influence that Poe mentioned in the preface to the *Tales of the Grotesque and Arabesque,* was not one of literature alone. As Poe's essays make clear time after time, his concept of literature was formulated against the debates engendered out of the philosophical milieu of Kant, Hegel, and the less well remembered figures of the Enlightenment and its enemies. Behind these, especially at the start of the nineteenth century, we find that instigator who so valued Lucretius and who excited early American romanticism, Baruch Spinoza.

The crux most at issue here is stated famously in Lucretius's *On the Nature of the Universe*:

> When the atoms are travelling straight down through empty space by their own weight, at quite indeterminate times and places they swerve ever so little from their course, just so much that you can call it a change of direction. If it were not for this swerve, everything would fall downwards like rain-drops through the abyss of space. . . . Thus nature would never have created anything. (1219)

For Lucretius, as for Poe, deviation is the precondition of creation without which nothing is conceivable: invariant sameness is sterile and disallows both creation and creativity. In both the world and in writing, deviation in becoming is what makes becoming possible. Difference or differencing is not a stable quality internal to ontology but its determining aspect, its constitutive internal agitation that forms the underlying motivation of his fictional plots and even the narrative poems, most famously "The Raven."

While Lucretius was content in his radical materialism to understand difference as genetic, Hegel wanted to put difference to work for progress through contradiction and sublation. This version of undoing seems nearer to Poe's time and his practice. For Hegel, each entity found itself fulfilled in its other, a kind of figure/ground complementarity. For Hegel, every definition of an entity itself was found necessarily outside itself, a kind of apophatic realization. In this Hegel was affirming a Christian version of knowledge through negation, the *via negativa* of the Pseudo-Dionysius. Indeed, even earlier Erigena could write in his *Periphyseon*: "The creative nature permits nothing outside itself because outside of it nothing can be."[4] In short, the individual is an emanation of the divine whose individuation is illusory and whose real existence is wholly in the corpus of God. Thus the perversity of mortification is the sensible exchange of the hubris of selfhood for the reincorporation in the body of divinity. This is the philosophical and religious context of Poe's perverse, a seeming perversity only from the perspective of the scientifically secular and not of the dark supernal.

For Poe, as he makes clearest at the conclusion of *Eureka*, man has two identities and so two frames of reference for thought, and these diverge. The normal or rational supplies the usual criterion for evaluation and deviation, but that is because it judges by its own lower standard. Still, men are of two minds and therefore are double thinking, "conscious, first, of a proper identity; conscious secondly and by faint indeterminate glimpses, of an identity with the Divine Being of whom we speak."[5] Individual identity is always already for Poe a swerving away from the totality that cannot be identified. That holism cannot fall under a name or representation since it forms the productive heterogenesis that is the whole cosmic ontology. This is the arena that Poe would have us reach—not as rational comprehension, since that would be oxymoronic, but in the disorientation of the centered subject, the protagonist, and in the sublime elevation of the reader.

His mastery of ratiocination—demonstrated through his detective, Dupin—and of taxonomy as in *The Conchologist's First Book*—was but just the ground for deviation, for swerving. Order is then not his highest end but the presentation of a structure created for cancellation, for a nonprogressive cancellation into the nonparticular. This is not Hegelian sublation, for it postulates an eternal return, a universal cyclicality that always antagonizes the particulars it overcomes. But how is this inversion to be accomplished with language, a structure given to sameness and identity?

His aesthetics supplies a path. In "The Philosophy of Composition" he states his method: "I prefer commencing with the consideration of an *effect*."[6] Art, for Poe, is neither an end in itself nor a didactic opportunity; he sought to neither please nor instruct, as both traditional functions pandered to the self he wished to ablate. He wanted not an Apollonian but a Dionysian art, whose consciousness was nonsense to the logical and rational. This becoming different he could represent in transitional states that qualified the concept of discrete personhood: drunkenness, drugged intoxication, illness, and love. But how could verbal art perform these functions, those not found in theories of language as speech act: absent in Austin, Searle, or even Butler? These theories of verbal performance all depend—more or less—on models of analytic self-possession that Plotinus saw kept one from divine unification. For Plotinus, as for Poe, the dissolution of individual identity is a positive activity, since the fragmentation that is the self alone is ecologically dead: "We cannot break life into parts: if the total was Life, the fragment is not."[7] However, the *Enneads* imply that the best path to reunification is contemplative wisdom, while Poe's way swerves to cancellation and dissolution—a violent undoing that finds its image in death. How is literature to accomplish this cancelling deviation from its own normative character and yet remain intelligible?

The tale for Poe is a transitional process, the object of which is to undo the very elements that make it manifest and in this very disassembly to instill an apprehension in spite of its nominal constituents. Like a rocket that burns itself to nothing in its attainment of height, his tales dissolve their own materials. Poe states in "The Poetic Principle:" "Through the attainment of a truth we are led to perceive a harmony where none was apparent before, we experience at once the true poetic effect but this effect is referable to the harmony alone, and not in the least degree to the truth that merely served to render the harmony manifest."[8] Harmony for Poe is the musical analogy of a destructive sublation that de-individuates artistic elements for their swerving apotheosis.

Edmund Burke, perhaps, offers a model of an aesthetic based on the apprehension of destruction. In his *Inquiry* (1757), he produces an affective theory of art that suggests a function for art that is similar to Poe's abiding concern with reader response. For Burke, the greatest art astonishes so that the participant is transported in an ecstasy that exceeds rational capacity. This irrational sublimity was—for Kant—one of the central concerns of the third *Critique* (1790), but for Burke it suggests an affective functionality antagonistic to the demands of the understanding. What the perverse writer wants is the opposite of the purgative catharsis of Aristotle's *Poetics*. Instead, literary *clinamen* is a cathexis to affect. Here, unlike classical tragedy, unwarranted events are not cancelled as proof of the inevitable return of order. Rather, order's particular manifestation is revealed as contingent and temporary. Only out of the perverse threat to the order of identity can art accomplish feelings of the highest rank. Burke states that the sublime is "that state of the soul, in which all of its notions are suspended, with some degree of horror."[9]

Unlike Poe in *Eureka*, Burke could not explain why threats to the "body" should raise "the mind."[10] However, he could offer a reason why an apparently uncongenial medium like language—which has superficially only a medial relation to sensation—should be affecting, since "by words we have it in our power to make such *combinations* as we cannot possibly do otherwise."[11] Words—like harmony in music—allow us to mix entities in a swerving from their quotidian identities as separate and integral selves. Literature then is an excellent medium for the oxymoron of affect, a constructive deconstruction of the constituents of composition. Here we can now trace this operation of destructive sublation in the "Imp of the Perverse."

This very short story follows a pattern familiar in Poe's tales but exaggerated here. The narrator's initial discourse appears in a form appositional to the last: a path from academic distance to personal threat. Indeed, the first presentments are those of a scholastic essay by a disinterested third party and not a biographic confession of murder. The story begins:

> In the consideration of the faculties and impulses—of the *prima mobilia* of the human soul, the phrenologists have failed to make room for a propensity which, although obviously existing as a radical, primitive, irreducible sentiment, has been equally overlooked by all the moralists who have preceded them. In the pure arrogance of the reason, we have overlooked it. [Poe's emphasis, 1219]

The text has already begun to set up the swerve it will constitute or enact.

The language dissembles its own apparent order to undertake a narrative deviation and sublation not only of its nominal fields—science and morality, the alpha and omega of knowledge—but of its own medium. The repetition of "overlook" in the quotation echoes the map trick in "The Purloined Letter," the sense that it is the ubiquitous that is invisible: the universality of difference is hidden in the open. While the slight joke—"make room" on the skull—already hints at the autoimmune disorder that is to be the destruction of this first posture; it is the passage's style that forms the straight man from which the grotesque of perversity will depart.

The sentences are wrought with an almost ironic allegiance to pedantry. The syntactic constructions are long, complex, compound, periodic, and involuted. The lexicon is Latinate, polysyllabic, effete, self-satisfied, and ostentatious. The net effect then seemingly capitulates discursively with the very structures under criticism by a person, we are later to learn, whose experience and current position are antithetical to the mode and the implied institutions of logical regulation. Perhaps this is parodic, an extended trope in which the work is a double or—like William Wilson—a Doppelgänger of its ostensible identity. Such a possibility, always inherent in parody, suggests a connotative deviation without difference, a constitutive swerve, or as Schlegel said, a "permanent parabasis." Still, the small but central mark of the coming destructive sublation is found in the first pronominal usage.

The text at first favors "we." This seems calculated to give some normative impression of sensible collectivity later to be undone. The first person plural hints here at a community of centered subjects that share a common concept of science and morality even as the text brings these into question. "We" is a collection of individuals who share rationality, convictions of causality, and sufficient reason. We are not perverse.

In this frame, the reader receives the ensuing discussion of perversity. The disembodied narrative voice defines perversity as "a mobile without a motive. . . . Through its promptings we act without comprehensible object; or, if this shall be understood as a contradiction in terms; we may so far modify the proposition as to say, that through its promptings we act, for the reason we should not. In theory, no reason can be more unreasonable" (1220). The previous implicit assurances of the "we" now threaten, for they catch the implied audience in a universal move of difference, in an ontology of deviation without norm. The pronoun no longer identifies a collection of rational beings but the opposite, where we are caught up in a maelstrom of uncontrollable impulse.

The text changes from a rational discussion of irrationality contained within institutional rhetoric to a lived instance of expressive insanity. The sentences become short and active, and our inclusion is now an irresistible participation in a narrated flow of compulsion. "We have a task before us which must be speedily performed. We know that it will be ruinous to make delay. . . . We struggle in vain" (1222). Procrastination is but a mild but pervasive perversity that substantiates the universality of its contradiction of rational behavior. The principle of the perverse is not speculative or objective, a scientific symptom for calm study, but our own self-annihilating tendency, our unstoppable swerve that overcomes the order of reason with emotion: "We perpetrate [perversity] . . . because we feel we should *not*" (1223). Short, terse, emotive, the text can again change registers, from the collective to the personal, from the abstract to the active, from the discussion of morality to the commitment of immorality.

Again, the undoing is marked by a pronominal shift: "I have said this much, that in some measure I may answer your question—that I may explain to you why I am here . . . wearing these fetters, for my tenanting this cell of the condemned" (1223–1224). This has been then a narrative bait and switch: rather than a community of scientific moralists, the reader finds herself or himself as the intimate friend of a murderer and thief. We are the confidants of the irrational, engaged in a tête-à-tête that we asked for. Quickly we learn the facts: our dialectical other committed the perfect crime by poisoning an inveterate night reader's candle, another undone—like us—by thinking language only supplied light. He has remained uncaught, and he is safe until he thinks: "If I be not fool enough to make open confession!" (1225).

Immediately, he is assailed by perversity against his own rational interest. He is in the fit and cannot resist: "I became blind, and deaf, and giddy. . . . The long-imprisoned secret burst forth from my soul. They say I spoke with a distinct enunciation, but with marked emphasis and passionate hurry, as if in dread of interruption before concluding the brief but pregnant sentences that consigned me to the hangman and to hell" (1226). Again, the progress of perversity is marked with a pronominal variation. He is now an "I" only in the eyes and the ears of others. At that moment he can only recall himself in the narrative of others. He is decentered and finds his distal image himself only in the crowd's disoriented and disassociated retrospect. "They say" marks now not a community to which the narrator belongs since they are still part of the delusion of the rational "we." "They" are now his opposite from which he only appears to himself as the object of their narration. His speech was not that of his own rational subjectivity but that of another self that did not share his narrow instinct for preservation. Thus his most critical moment was not the quintessence of his personal identity but its opposite, an impersonal difference.

Finally, the tale ends not with the abstraction and distance that since Aristotle has signaled the summing up, the resolution of loose ends, but with the immediate, the personal, and the empirical. But the swerve of the perverse has done its work, and all these sense certainties are undone. "But why shall I say more? To-day I wear these chains, and am *here*! To-morrow I shall be fetterless!—*but where*?" (1226). What were answers or even givens—the taken-for-granted elements of rational discourse—are now more than problems. The pronominal shifters—we, I, they—now become completely destabilized in space-time, the here and now. These indexical and referential terms are deconstructed not just for the narrator but also for the reader, whose hubris and sense of identity also swerve away from previous certainty. We enter instead the sublimity of perversity, the swerve to a differencing unregulated by the metrics of the rational.

NOTES

1. Edgar A. Poe, *The Collected Works of Edgar Allan Poe*, ed. Thomas Olive Mabbott (Cambridge, MA: Belknap, 1978), 2:506.

2. Mabbott, *Collected Works*, 3:1219. Further references to Poe's texts are from this edition and are noted parenthetically in the text.

3. Lucretius, *On the Nature of the Universe*, trans. R. E. Latham (Baltimore: Penguin Books, 1976), 66.

4. John Scotus Erigena, *Periphyseon: Division of Nature*, trans. I. P. Sheldon-Williams and John J. O'Meara (New York: Dumbarton Oaks, 1987), 675.

5. Edgar Allan Poe, *Eureka,* in *Edgar Allan Poe: Poetry and Tales* (New York: Library of America, 1984), 1358.

6. Edgar Allan Poe, "The Philosophy of Composition," in *Edgar Allan Poe: Essays and Reviews*, ed. G. R. Thompson (New York: Library of America, 1984), 13.

7. Plotinus, *The Six Enneads*, trans. Stephen MacKenna and B. S. Page (New York: Kessinger, 2004), 632.

8. Edgar Allan Poe, "The Poetic Principle," in *Edgar Allan Poe: Essays and Reviews*, 93.

9. Edmund Burke, *A Philosophical Enquiry into the Origin of our Ideas of the Sublime and Beautiful*, ed. Adam Phillips (New York: Oxford University Press, 1998), 53.

10. Ibid., 117.

11. Ibid., 158.

Chapter Seven

From the Romantic to the Textual Sublime

Poesque Sublimities, Romantic Irony, and Deconstruction

Stephanie Sommerfeld

In his essay on the Dupin trilogy, Peter Thoms detects that the three stories exhibit a "narrative unrest that sustains the possibility of both order and disorder."[1] He illustrates that Dupin does not only act as the agent of order and justice who is solely dedicated to solving the case but is also "fond of manufacturing the very anxiety he is supposed to soothe."[2] Thoms explains that "fashioning moments that astonish and shock others appeals to the detective's aesthetic sensibility and appetite for power."[3] Acting like the "skilful literary artist"[4] of Poe's famous review of Hawthorne's *Twice-Told Tales*, Dupin thus employs his craft to achieve a "preconceived effect"[5] and to evoke certain affects in his audience. In the case of "The Purloined Letter," he elaborately delays the revelation of the letter and thus succeeds in making the story's narrator and the Prefect feel astonishment: "I was astounded. The Prefect appeared absolutely thunderstricken. For some minutes he remained speechless and motionless, looking incredulously at my friend with open mouth, and eyes that seemed starting from their sockets."[6] While Thoms uses terms like "power and subjection"[7] to describe the dynamics at work in this passage, the signals for sublimity should not be overlooked. Especially the word "astounded" and the Prefect's motion—and speechlessness—point to the Burkean sublime, where astonishment is defined as "that state of the soul, in which all its motions are suspended, with some degree of horror" and is considered "the effect of the sublime in its highest degree."[8] The Prefect's speechlessness repeats the "kind of temporary aphasia," the "lapsing out of discourse" that the moment of the sublime entails according to Weiskel.[9] Furthermore, the fact that the Prefect is "thunderstricken" nods to the locus classicus of *Peri Hypsous*:

> For the effect of genius is not to persuade the audience but rather to transport them out of themselves. Invariably what inspires wonder, with its power of amazing us, always prevails over what is merely convincing and pleasing. For our persuasions are usually under our own control, while these things exercise an irresistible power and mastery, and get the better of every listener. . . . A *well-timed flash of sublimity* shatters everything *like a bolt of lightning* and reveals the full power of the speaker at a single stroke.[10] [emphasis added]

In Longinus as in "The Purloined Letter," the listener's control is shattered while the speaker's "irresistible power and mastery" is asserted. The effect "to be wrought out"[11] is one of enjoyable ecstasy: The addressee loses his previous state of control and is confronted with the addresser's artistic mastery. Like the Longinian orator, Dupin has good timing when it comes to generating his effects, as Thoms observes: "Dupin carefully shapes the unfolding action so that his revelation springs most unexpectedly upon his audience."[12] "At a single stroke," he succeeds in revealing his "full power," leaving behind a flabbergasted audience struck by thunder and lightning, whose control of language and body has been shattered.

In addition to taking up the rhetoric of Burkean and Longinian sublimity in the above quotation, Poe also refers us to another of his own renderings of an individual who deliberately seeks the thrills of sublimity. The Prefect's eyes, which seem "starting from their sockets," are reminiscent of Psyche Zenobia's eyes that—literally—are "absolutely starting from their sockets"[13] in "A Predicament." This intertextual reference stresses the (bodily) disintegration of those who experience sublimity.

Dupin thus deliberately produces effects of sublimity that force his audience to lose control. However, the even more interesting part of the dynamics of power and subjection—which are, as I have shown, in fact the dynamics of the sublime—is their transmission to the extradiegetic levels. Thoms offers the following account of this transmission:

> The tension between power and subjection is eventually channeled into the relationships between storyteller and audience: between Dupin and the companion-narrator, and the companion-narrator and the reader. In the final relationship, however, the submissive party (now the reader) willingly chooses to acquiesce to the powerful party (the teller), trusting that the infliction of suffering (the nervousness engendered by the story) can paradoxically bring pleasure.[14]

I will try to account for this transmission by exploring the interplay of Kantian- and Burkean-infused, diegetic sublimity on the one hand and a textual sublimity that is indebted to Longinian rhetorical sublimity to a certain degree, on the other hand. Poe's Burke- and Kant-based romantic sublimity on the diegetic level, as it manifests itself, for example, in the sublimity of Dupin that I have described above, shifts from one character or object to another only to be transmitted to the narration itself. While for Thoms, the ultimate powerful party is the "teller" (i.e., Dupin, who takes over the narration),[15] his friend the narrator is also a carrier of sublimity, who then passes his capacity of producing sublime effects on to Dupin, who, in turn, loses his sublimity when he becomes just another agent in the diegetic shifting of letters, power, and sublimity. In my reading, the "powerful party" in the "final relationship" is the narration itself, which ends up producing the same power relations vis-à-vis its audience that we know from Dupin.

Poe thus takes the diegetic game of shifting sublimity to a different level by having the demise of romantic sublimity prepare the ground for the narration's textual sublimity. The latter casts the implied reader in the same role as Dupin's "companion-narrator" and the Prefect, as Thoms outlines in the above quotation. The reader willingly subjects himself to the narration's domination and sublime effects, trusting that his "suffering"—that is, his pain, or rather pains, to control the narration and establish order—will afford pleasure. Vainly trying to master the text, the reader will experience the text's sublime effects and consequently become an astonished witness experiencing a "perfect agony of joy"[16] —that is, a Burkean mixture of pain and pleasure.

Before we trace the steps of the way from diegetic to textual sublimity in "The Purloined Letter," let me dwell on the general significance of Poe's concept of textual sublimity. Investigating the deferral of sublimity and the nature of Poe's textual sublimity may help us to exceed somewhat vague (or even esoteric) notions of genius-created textual magic,[17] which tend to foreground the author's extraordinary capacities. Commenting on what T. S. Eliot calls Poe's "magic of verse,"[18] Shoshana Felman suggests that the effect of Poe's language is "unaccountably insidious, exceeding the control, the will, and the awareness of those who are subjected to it."[19] Felman's account of an "irresistible"[20] textual power overpowering the reader's understanding and provoking the latter's ensuing loss of control strikingly resembles the sublime of Longinus's *Peri Hypsous* and simultaneously mirrors the power struggle and "negative" moments in experiencing the sublime. This illustrates that, by writing a textual sublimity into existence, Poe develops a striking alternative to traditional (e.g., Emersonian) models of romantic sublimity[21] and its function in the communication between reader and text: He refuses to invite the reader to immerse himself or herself in successful diegetic encounters with the sublime and to partake in the characters' transcendence.

In "The Purloined Letter," the power struggle between Queen, King, Minister, detective, narrator, and reader, revolving around the question of who will be potentate and who will be subjected, is a fight about the mastery of the letter. The letter functions as a sublime object for all the above; it is the unfathomable object they are obsessed with. If one applies Thomas Weiskel's terms, the letter definitely exhibits the "excess of the signified"[22] of the Kantian dynamic sublime. It is the obscure and magnificent object whose power all characters are trying to make their own. Instead of relinquishing its power, the letter only triggers a process of transmission of power and of the capacity to produce sublime effects, which ends when the latter capacity is bestowed upon the text itself.

With his transfigurations of the romantic sublime into textual sublimity, Poe triggers a transformation within the discourse of the sublime itself: While Samuel H. Monk provides us with a narrative that describes the history of the sublime as successfully turning from Longinian rhetoric to the aesthetics of the romantic sublime,[23] Poe's tales, I will argue, successfully reverse this apparently teleological transmutation, redirecting the course of the sublime's conceptual history from the "aesthetics of optimism"[24] that are at the core of the Emersonian romantic sublime toward the sublimity of literary language. This is an aspect that makes Poe somewhat of a precursor of postmodern notions of literary sublimity, as found in Thomas Pynchon,[25] which focus on intricate textual, or, more generally, semiotic structures. Situating Poe's transfigurations within the discursive framework of the romantic sublime will simultaneously allow us to trace the roots of Poe's (post)modernism in further detail. I will argue that those who find traces of Derridaen *différance* in his work (e.g., in "The Purloined Letter") succeed in doing so because of Poe's original use of romanticist concepts. Moving from one object/character to another, from aesthetics to textuality, and from the diegesis to the extradiegetic levels of communication, Poe's transfigurations of the sublime consist of the circular process of creating, destroying, and renewing sublimity. This circular structure may certainly leave the addressee of the final textual sublimity in doubt about the latter's endurance. Transformation is a defining feature of the Poesque sublime, and its constant state of becoming simultaneously constitutes the answer to the compulsory question about its metaphysical potential. In Poe, the romantic sublime's transcendental potential lies in its demise. Only through its destruction is it able to transcend its former state of existence. Instead of those who experience sublime effects, it is the sublime itself that takes a new shape. As the stability of its identity is undermined, it becomes clear that its potential for transcendence lies in its constant renewal, in the circular process of rising and falling.

The basic structure of creation and de-creation is a shared characteristic of Derrida's *différance* and Schlegel's concept of romantic irony.[26] The romantic ironist embraces the universe's constant state of "becoming" (as opposed to static being) by affirming indissoluble contrasts and constantly practicing self-parody.[27] Anne K. Mellor summarizes Schlegel's concept as follows:

> Having ironically acknowledged the fictiveness of his own patternings of human experience, [the romantic ironist] romantically engages in the creative process of life by eagerly constructing new forms, new myths. And these new fictions and self-concepts bear with them the seeds of their own destruction. . . . The resultant artistic mode that alone can properly be called romantic irony must therefore be a form or structure that simultaneously creates and de-creates itself.[28]

This self-creative process that, in very Poesque manner, always already contains the germ of its own inevitable annihilation, to appropriate the phrase taken from *Eureka*,[29] is at play in the interactions between subject and object within the diegesis, between narrator and narratee, and ultimately even confronts the implied reader.

In "The Purloined Letter," all characters that function as carriers of sublimity at one point in the story exhibit a conspicuous overconfidence: In the first two paragraphs, the narrator starts to tell the story with a firm hold on the process of narration, providing us with the setting that finds Dupin and the narrator in the usual seclusion in his friend's "little back library, or book-closet"[30] —which, of course, already indicates that this story will also be "a story of reading and writing."[31] He introduces Dupin as "[his] friend,"[32] which, together with the intimacy of the "book-closet" and the emphasis on their shared past, reveals that he also establishes a firm hold on Dupin. This proves premature, as soon as the tale has Dupin take narrative control and succeed in "astound[ing]" the narrator. The Minister's presumptuous assumption of being able to carry out his evil scheme is obvious, and Dupin's overconfidence[33] is betrayed in his desire to not only solve the letter's mystery and come up with a "well-timed" plot of his own to stun his audience but also to make the last word of the diegetic power struggle and of the whole narration his own. The narrator, the Minister, and Dupin all expect to emerge as beneficiaries of the letter, the sublime and powerful object. This overconfidence ironically acknowledges the futility of these characters' "patternings." The reader may conclude that this kind of attempt to appropriate sublimity necessarily entails its dissolution. This might also work as a useful hint for the reader's own expectations regarding the appropriation of "The Purloined Letter" (i.e., the ultimate sublime object), as its deferral of closure and sublimity only leads to the reader's confrontation with the pose of literature's mastery, leaving him in awe without allowing for self-empowerment.

If we accept Thoms's notion of Dupin as the "teller" who finally reveals his elaborate plot, which enables sublime effects, we can read Dupin as the prototypical Poe "narrator" who practices romantic irony by conspicuously revealing himself as the shaping force of the action while at the same time mocking and undermining his own creation. His romantic irony can thus be labeled with Schlegel's term "transcendental buffoonery."[34] Like the *buffo* in the commedia dell'arte, who controls and simultaneously mocks the play,[35] Poe's prototypical narrator—some obvious examples can be found in "William Wilson," "Ligeia," or "The Tell-Tale Heart"—practices "irony as permanent parabasis,"[36] as the eternal interplay of the creation and breaking of illusion.

Both on the level of story and on the level of discourse, the processes of romantic irony thus undermine any stable order and resist easy epistemological appropriation, which may help account for Thoms's notion of "narrative unrest that sustains the possibility of both order and disorder"[37] in "The Purloined Letter." While stable meaning is deferred, the text itself assumes the power of the sublime and self-reflexively exhibits its power of simulation, which is how the effects of Poesque textual sublimity are transmitted to the implied reader.

As I have hinted at before, the romantic irony at play on the levels of story and discourse resembles Derrida's *différance*, and the structural similarities between deconstruction and romantic irony can help illuminate that whenever we unveil a poststructuralist Poe, we are simultaneously unveiling a Poe deeply rooted in romanticist traditions. Although Poe's romanticism might seem self-evident, I suggest that we may attempt to put deconstructivist readings of Poe on more solid foundations by confronting them with the texts' romanticist contexts. Grounding poststructuralist analyses in cultural history may allow us to realize that deconstruction is by no means original in its reaction to the unattainability of a metaphysical absolute, its questioning of established notions of reality. Deconstruction is as much of an answer to the condition of the modern self as romantic irony or Poe's self-reflexive fictions that critically and productively engage with the dissolving belief in a reliable metaphysical order. This is not to devalue deconstruction, but merely to say that the complex creations and de-creations of Poe's fictions not only foreground the power of simulated reality when read against the backdrop of Derrida's concepts but succeed in outdoing reality and replacing it with self-conscious fictions of sublimity[38] by drawing from theories of the sublime and Schlegelian romantic irony. To put it in a nutshell, the common ground between Poe's version of the romantic sublime, romantic irony, and deconstruction consists in the following shared structural features: The interaction of subject and object is marked by simultaneous creation and dissolution, which results in an indecisive hovering between opposites, and results in a self-reflexive deferral of meaning. These processes betray an epistemological and metaphysical skepticism that insists on the truth of the simulacrum and celebrates the sublimity of the literary artifact itself.

The common ground between deconstruction and Poe's textual sublime is the obsession with the signifier. To understand this parallel and grasp its connection to the romantic sublime, we shortly need to turn to the semiotics of one of the vital foundations of the romantic sublime, to the Kantian mathematical and dynamic sublime, which are arguably as much foregrounded by Poe as by Thomas Weiskel and Paul de Man. Poe's tales bespeak his acute awareness of the parallel structures between the processes at work in the Kantian sublimities and in language. De Man points at the ruptures in the *Critique of Judgment* and claims that it "depends on a linguistic structure (language as a performative as well as a cognitive system) that is not itself accessible to the powers of transcendental philosophy."[39] Reading the mathematical sublime as the "pseudo-cognition of tropes"[40] and equating the dynamic sublime with language as performance, he unveils that Kant implicitly describes the linguistic structure of the sublime. While Burke analyzes how "words have as considerable a share in exciting ideas of beauty and of the sublime as [natural objects, painting or architecture], and sometimes a much greater than any of them,"[41] Kant looks at the semiotic structures of the sublime experience itself. As the scope of this paper does not allow me to explore the implications of de Man's analysis in further detail, suffice it to say that de Man's take on Kant uncovers structures similar to those in Thomas Weiskel's identification of the dynamic sublime with an "excess of the signified" and the mathematical sublime as the "excess of 'substance' in the signifier."[42]

The transformation from diegetic romantic into textual sublimity in Poe's tales can be traced back to the semiotic undercurrents of Kantian sublimity that Poe, like Weiskel or de Man, unveils. Poe, however, uses the dynamics of the sublime within his narrated worlds to tease out its semiotics.

To explore the interplay of romantic irony, romantic and textual sublimity, and the semiotics of the sublime at work in "The Purloined Letter," it helps to turn back to the conspicuous doubling of Dupin in its predecessor "The Murders in the Rue Morgue," where the narrator "amuse[s] [him]self with the fancy of a double Dupin—the creative and the resolvent."[43] The double operations of romantic irony and the aforementioned coexistence of opposites manifest themselves in the shape of the double Dupin, who exists simultaneously as creator and resolver. In "The Purloined Letter," this Janus-like figure is, as is well known, again doubled by its likewise doubled antagonist, the Minister, who fulfills the roles of creator and resolver by being both poet and mathematician. Both Dupin and Minister D. are conspicuously obsessed with the letter, which is significant as both object and sign, and doubled by its fac-simile. Inasmuch as the signified resolves the signifier in the Saussurrean sense, the original letter exists as the resolver of the fac-simile. This doubling thus creates a hall of mirrors (see Figure 7.1) that causes constant creation and resolution or dissolution, destabilizes identities and, particularly in the case of the fake letter, insists that the simulacrum has a truth of its own.

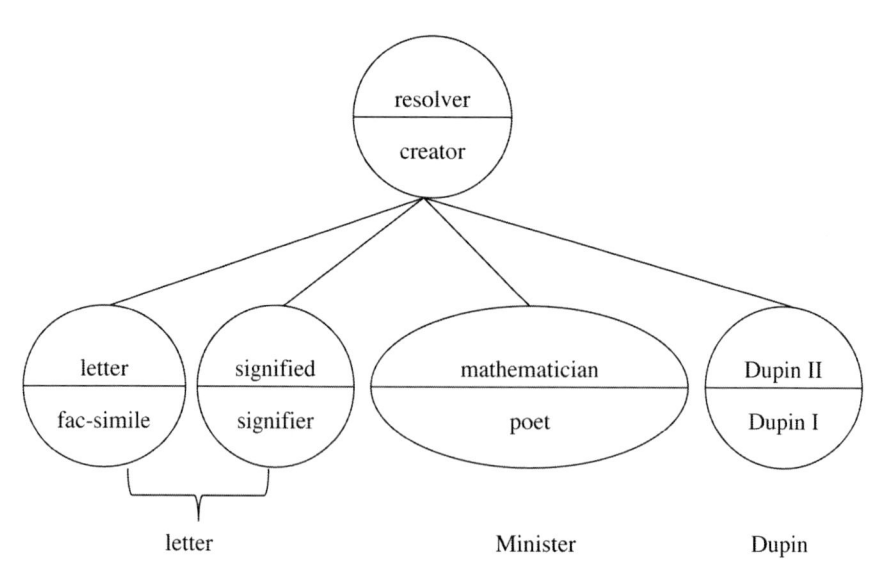

Figure 7.1. Diagram I

In the same way that the fac-simile, the simulacrum conspicuously bearing the fingerprint of its creator in good romantic ironist fashion, traces the steps of the original letter, Dupin becomes obsessed with mimicking the Minister.[44] In the same manner, the narrator becomes obsessed with the unfathomable Dupin. Subsequently, the narratee and also the implied reader become preoccupied with trying to follow the steps of the plot and grasping the complex narration with its simultaneous creations and dissolutions (see Figure 7.2).

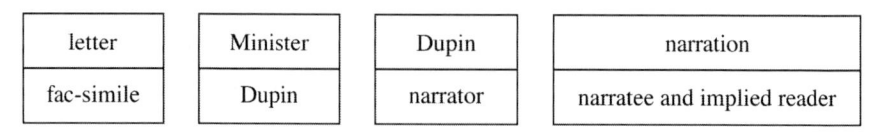

letter	Minister	Dupin	narration
fac-simile	Dupin	narrator	narratee and implied reader

Figure 7.2. Diagram II

The romantic sublime transcends its diegetic boundaries and metamorphoses into textual sublimity when the implied reader is confronted with the process of constant deferral and the lack of "positive" moments in the romantic sublime. The romantic sublime's emphasis on the signified becomes dubious as it is applied to ever new objects. It is from this instability that the textual sublime with its stress of the signifier grows. The sublimity thus moves from the letter to the Minister, then to Dupin, and ultimately to the narration itself. Especially in the last transfiguration, one can observe that the textual sublimity increases to the same extent that Dupin's sublimity decreases. If we appropriate Lacan's analytical tools and adopt his triangular notion of the position of the blind, the unaware seer, and the perspicacious profiteer,[45] we may realize that the text acquires its final instability and epistemological unfathomability as soon as Dupin moves to the position of the unaware seer and as the analyst who becomes the perspicacious profiteer realizes that he might easily end up or already be in the position of the unaware seer (see Table 7.1).[46]

Table 7.1. Diagram III

blind	unaware seer	perspicacious profiteer
1. King	Queen	Minister
2. Queen	Minister	Dupin
3. Minister	Dupin	Analyst (Lacan)

The processes at work in this and other Poe tales with their simultaneous articulation of opposing ideas and the simultaneous creation and destruction of sublime scenarios slowly dissolve the "aesthetics of optimism" that are built on a belief in Hegelian sublation, on epistemological confidence, and a belief in stable boundaries between original and simulacrum. On the levels of story and discourse, these processes that draw from romantic irony, rewrite the romantic sublime on Poesque terms, and anticipate deconstructivist thought, emphasize the fluidity of identity, the transfiguration of sublimity, and the existence of a textual sublimity that increases with the growing deferral of meaning. It might thus be in his creation of a textual sublime that foregrounds the primacy of the signifier while at the same time playing with the power of sublime simulation that Poe is both most advanced and most conventionally romantic.

NOTES

1. Peter Thoms, "Poe's Dupin and the Power of Detection," in *The Cambridge Companion to Edgar Allan Poe*, ed. Kevin J. Hayes (Cambridge: Cambridge University Press, 2002), 145.
2. Ibid., 143.
3. Ibid.
4. Edgar Allan Poe, *Essays and Reviews,* ed. G. R. Thompson (New York: Library of America, 1984), 572.
5. Ibid.

6. Edgar Allan Poe, *Poetry and Tales*, ed. G. R. Thompson (New York: Library of America, 1984), 688.
7. Thoms, "Power of Detection," 145.
8. Edmund Burke, *A Philosophical Enquiry into the Origin of Our Ideas of the Sublime and Beautiful,* ed. Adam Phillips (Oxford: Oxford University Press, 1990), 53.
9. Thomas Weiskel, *The Romantic Sublime: Studies in the Structure and Psychology of Transcendence* (Baltimore: Johns Hopkins University Press, 1976), 30.
10. Longinus, *On the Sublime,* trans. W. H. Fyfe, in Aristotle, *Poetics*, Longinus, *On the Sublime*, Demetrius, *On Style*, rev. Donald A. Russell (Cambridge, MA: Harvard University Press, 1995), 164–65.
11. Poe, *Essays and Reviews*, 572.
12. Thoms, "Power of Detection," 144.
13. Poe, *Poetry and Tales*, 294.
14. Thoms, "Power of Detection," 145.
15. See Thoms, "Power of Detection," 134.
16. Poe, *Poetry and Tales*, 688.
17. Shoshana Felman provides some examples of such notions in "On Reading Poetry: Reflections on the Limits and Possibilities of Psychoanalytical Approaches," in *The Purloined Poe: Lacan, Derrida and Psychoanalytical Reading*, ed. John P. Muller and William J. Richardson (Baltimore: Johns Hopkins University Press, 1988), 134.
18. T. S. Eliot, "From Poe to Valéry," in *The Recognition of Edgar Allan Poe: Selected Criticism since 1829*, ed. E. W. Carlson (Ann Arbor: University of Michigan Press, 1966), 209.
19. Felman, "On Reading Poetry," 135.
20. Ibid., 137.
21. When I use the term "romantic sublime," I am referring to literary embodiments of sublimity in American romanticism that are heavily influenced by the Burkean and Kantian sublime. While I merely focus on Poe's literary sublimities here, it is significant that his renderings of romantic sublimity are constructed in opposition to the Emersonian concept of a self-aggrandizing sublime, i.e., the nineteenth-century American embodiment of the "optimistic" notion of a "linear . . . experience that terminates benignly if not affirmatively," to quote from Jack G. Voller, "The Power of Terror: Burke and Kant in the House of Usher," *Poe Studies* 21, no. 2 (1988): 27. For an account of how Poe disenchants the self-empowering Emersonian sublime in "The Domain of Arnheim," see Stephanie Sommerfeld, "The Sublime's Invasion of Ellisonland," in *Edgar Allan Poe: Doscientos años después*, ed. Beatriz González-Moreno and Margarita Rigal-Aragón (Cuenca, Spain: Ediciones de la Universidad de Castilla–La Mancha, 2010), 141–54.
22. Weiskel, *The Romantic Sublime*, 26.
23. Cf. Samuel H. Monk, *The Sublime: A Study of Critical Theories in XVIII-Century England* (Ann Arbor: University of Michigan Press, 1960).
24. Voller, "The Power of Terror," 27.
25. For Kantian and Lyotardian sublimity in Pynchon, cf. Zofia Kolbuszewska, "Pynchon, Kant, Lyotard, and the Sublime," in *Approaches to Teaching Pynchon's* The Crying of Lot 49 *and Other Works,* ed. Thomas H. Schaub (New York: MLA, 2008), 163–68.
26. In the following I will merely refer to Anne K. Mellor's (rather optimistic) version of Schlegelian romantic irony. The landmark study on romantic irony in Poe's texts, G. R. Thompson's *Poe's Fiction: Romantic Irony in the Gothic Tales* (Madison: University of Wisconsin Press, 1973), provides illuminating observations on the German roots of Poe's romantic irony. However, its aim of "reading Poe as an ironist instead of a completely serious Gothicist" (xi) ties the project to the comic-satiric vs. serious Gothic dichotomy, which keeps Thompson from analyzing the more subtle occurrences of romantic irony in the tales of ratiocination.
27. Cf. Anne K. Mellor, *English Romantic Irony* (Cambridge, MA: Harvard University Press, 1980), 12.
28. Ibid., 5.
29. Poe, *Poetry and Tales*, 1261.
30. Ibid., 680.

From the Romantic to the Textual Sublime 85

31. Thoms, "Power of Detection," 134. While Thoms does not mention Jacques Derrida's reading of the tale, he echoes the latter's notion that, in essence, "The Purloined Letter" is "an affair of writing, and of writing adrift"; cf. "The Purveyor of Truth," trans. Alan Bass, *The Purloined Poe*, 199.

32. Poe, *Poetry and Tales*, 680.

33. For a reading of Dupin's hubris and function as "divine author," cf. Frank Kelleter, "Zusammen-Fall und Aufhebung: Edgar Allan Poe und das spätromantische Todesbild," in *Die Moderne und der Tod: Das Todesmotiv in moderner Literatur, untersucht am Beispiel Edgar Allan Poes, T.S. Eliots und Samuel Becketts* (Frankfurt a. M: Peter Lang, 1997), 208–26.

34. Friedrich Schlegel, "Critical Fragments," trans. Peter Firchow, in *Friedrich Schlegel's Lucinde and the Fragments* (Minneapolis: University of Minnesota Press, 1971), 148.

35. Cf. Mellor, *English Romantic Irony*, 17.

36. Ibid.

37. Thoms, "Power of Detection," 145.

38. For an intriguing discussion of Poesque simulations, cf. Frank Kelleter, "Zusammen-Fall und Aufhebung,"157–292.

39. Paul de Man, "Phenomenality and Materiality," in *The Textual Sublime: Deconstruction and Its Differences,* ed. Hugh J. Silverman and Gary E. Aylesworth (Albany: State University of New York Press, 1990), 97. In this collection of essays, Silverman vaguely defines the *textual sublime* as the "marking of alternatives within the operations of the text itself" (xiii) but admits that his volume does not offer a consistent concept of textual sublimity (cf. xii). While the "textual sublime" of Silverman and Aylesworth's volume is thus a deconstructivist concept, my own notion of "textual sublimity" does not carry Derridean overtones but describes the operation of highlighting the literary text's status as a powerful agent vis-à-vis the reader—in other words, as the reader's sublime object of fascination.

40. Ibid., 96.

41. Burke, *A Philosophical Enquiry*, 149.

42. Weiskel, *The Romantic Sublime*, 26.

43. Poe, *Poetry and Tales*, 402.

44. The Minister himself not only exists as a Janus-faced character like Dupin but also appears in other twin constellations with the detective, e.g., in the final pairing of "Atrée" and "Thyeste" (Poe, *Poetry and Tales*, 698). Especially, the phrase "D—cipher" (ibid., 696) is targeted at preventing the adept reader from reading "Dupin" and "D—" as anything other than two sides of the same coin.

45. Cf. Jacques Lacan's description of the three different kinds of glances in "Seminar on 'The Purloined Letter,'" trans. Jeffrey Mehlman, in The *Purloined Poe*, 32. Felman provides a triangular visualization of Lacan's analysis (cf. Felman, "On Reading Poetry," 145).

46. The numerals "1," "2," and "3" refer to the three scenes Lacan identifies (cf. Lacan, "Seminar on 'The Purloined Letter,'" 30).

Chapter Eight

The Armchair *Flâneur*

Tim Towslee

Not unlike today's twenty-first-century media consumers, the American readership that grew from the emergence of the penny press in the 1830s sought entertainment rather than information. In efforts to feed that desire, publishers of the New York penny papers ran stories of railroad accidents, steamboat explosions, human oddities, and most of all, sensational stories of rape, murder, and incest. In July of 1841, the body of the "Beautiful Cigar Girl" Mary Rogers washed up on the banks of the Hudson River, and a frenzy in the headlines of these penny papers ensued. Recognizing the urban public's desires for voyeurism and modernity, Edgar Allan Poe saw the inflated attention Mary Rogers's case received in the media as an opportunity to exploit this phenomenon in what he hoped would profitably combine the media spectacle with high-art literature in "The Mystery of Marie Rogêt." By providing his readership with a window into the "horrible details" and "further particulars" of the Mary Rogers case, Poe hoped to demonstrate his ratiocinative and literary skills by having his fictional detective Monsieur C. Auguste Dupin solve the real mystery behind Rogers's case before the police, through careful examination of the newspaper articles about her.

Although Poe sandwiches the story between "The Murders in the Rue Morgue" and "The Purloined Letter," the tales for which he is credited with defining the detective fiction genre, "The Mystery of Marie Rogêt" is not a work of detective fiction in the sense that his other Dupin tales are. Unlike his other detective tales, in which Poe has his detective analyze the milieu of the crime scenes and then solve those crimes based on superior intellect and intuition (planting the seeds for Arthur Conan Doyle's Sherlock Holmes stories and thereby solidifying the genre's position in popular literature[1]), in "The Mystery of Marie Rogêt," Dupin never leaves his apartment—not to find and scrutinize any clues, not to compile a list of suspects based on said scrutiny or at least anything more concrete than guesswork, not to do any detective work at all. Even though the tale does follow mystery fiction's convention of offering information that allows the reader to attempt solutions to the crime along with the protagonist, the tale is better aligned with Poe's earlier urban spectator tale and essay "The Man of the Crowd" and "The Philosophy of Furniture." By extending the device of the latter, in which Poe reflects that the cultural phenomenon of Moving Day brought the private parlor into the public urban milieu, turning things inside out, one is able to read furniture like the former story's unnamed narrator is able to read people by their appearance and actions.[2] Similarly to the ways Moving Day turns the urban environment inside out, through the penny papers of the day, Dupin brings the object of his gaze into his parlor. While "Marie Rogêt" was less successful than the other Dupin tales, we cannot dismiss it as a poor story; rather, by blending fact and fiction through newspaper voyeurism and armchair *flânerie*, Poe invents a new archetype altogether: detective fiction's antisocial, sedentary cousin the armchair detective, whose stories are based in secondhand particulars of true crime, but written to entertain by allowing the media to do the detective's legwork, and solved (or in Poe's case, not solved) by pure intellect and intuition. Through this paradoxical variant of his detective established in "The Murders in the Rue Morgue," Poe anticipates the ugly nature of the mass media wherein the audience substitutes what he sees on the page for worldly experience and interactions with text for firsthand knowledge.

Before we can effectively analyze Poe's tale as the emergence of the armchair detective, we must first look at a brief history of crime in the media in the late eighteenth and early nineteenth centuries because it is instrumental to crime fiction's existence. In 1829, a federal copyright decision made a clear distinction between books and newspapers, deeming newspapers free from copyright restraints because of their ephemeral character.[3] This decision opened the floodgates of mass media, creating the first information age in America between 1830 and 1840 with the emergence of the penny press. Where eighteenth-century print culture "had been the providence of gentlemen and clergymen, new printed matter had now begun to appeal to the masses, men and women."[4] The deluge of newly available, inexpensive print matter led to increased literacy rates in American cities and further served as a democratizing agent. With an increasing readership, penny papers like the *New York Sun* and the *New York Herald* sought to provide the people with "stories about ordinary working people doing ordinary and sometimes embarrassing things."[5] Unfortunately, this approach didn't sell papers, but the spectacle—primarily gruesome accounts of murder and the occasional train wreck—did.

The stories that filled the pages of the *Sun* and the *Herald* were certainly not the first appearances of crime in print. In seventeenth- and eighteenth-century America, execution sermons, tales of public hangings, and lurid criminal confessions were very popular, but their purposes were more didactic—morality lessons for church folk, urging them to keep on the right side of the law and the Lord. By the mid-1830s, a different breed of crime story had replaced these tales of the pillory. These criminal accounts in the penny papers often mocked the inefficient police force of the day, creating a pointed journalism that appealed to a working-class audience that fancied itself as an alternative, and potentially more effective, police force. This is the same convention that Poe would adopt in "The Mystery of Marie Rogêt."

Perhaps the most well-known of these criminal accounts are those of the bloody murder of Helen Jewett. In April of 1836, the well-to-do Richard P. Robinson of a prosperous Connecticut family brutally murdered the pretty young prostitute by bashing in her skull with a hatchet and then lit her room on fire in an attempt to destroy the evidence of his crime. Immediately, the penny press editors battled for scoops and new information to run about what Andie Tucher calls the "hot local story loaded with moral meaning, full of sex, gore, intrigue, and sin."[6] The Jewett murder generated news stories for months with coverage of the investigation, eyewitness accounts, public scandals, and condemnations of prostitutes (not so much of murderers)—before Robinson's trial had even begun. If the news wasn't quite sensational enough, editors took it upon themselves to embellish the story or to invent one, so that it sold. Tucher, again:

> The "horrible and melancholy affair," the "cold-blooded, atrocious" way in which the young woman was "horribly butchered," inspired page after page of baroque prose, lurid melodramatic scenes, dark innuendoes, blatant partisanship, obvious inconsistencies, vicious personal attacks on other editors as well as suspects in the crime, and accusations of blackmail against virtually everyone involved. . . . Day to day, the "facts" varied wildly, and the whole story was fraught with exaggeration, inconsistency, illogic, speculation and bias. Any attempt to discover, from the penny papers alone, exactly what happened on Thomas Street snarls into an insoluble knot of contradictions and confusion.[7]

This confusion sold more and more papers, as readers not so patiently read each day in hopes of making sense of this and other "lively human interest stories [that] center on sex, crime, and above all, sex crime."[8] Five years after the Jewett spectacle, Mary Rogers's death filled the pages of the dailies in a way that would outlive Jewett's story through its inspiration of Poe's second Dupin tale. Just as the penny press had been a product of the city, for the city, so had Mary Rogers. The new modernity of the urban milieu gave Mary the opportunity to leave the home and the true cult of womanhood and enter the marketplace. Mary was well known to the newsmen of the penny press, since she lived with her mother in a house located at 126 Nassau Street, among the buildings where the *Tribune* and the *Herald* kept their offices. Surely she became the object of their gaze as she walked to and from work at Anderson's cigar shop each day. She was popular among other city dwellers as well, having gained notoriety behind the counter. The shop's clientele included the likes of Washington Irving, James Fennimore Cooper, and possibly Poe himself.

In the early nineteenth century, a beautiful young woman certainly did not have a proper place among the businessmen and gamblers of the tobacco shop; the implication that she might have been a prostitute, or at the very least promiscuous, was not missed by the locals or those who read about her in the papers. The image of a young woman handling phallus-shaped cigars for the men of New York on a daily basis surely further supported this implication. However, if Mary's moral character and chastity was questionable when she was living, it was even more so after her body was found floating in the Hudson River on that Wednesday in July of 1841.

Rogers was last seen alive in the company of a dark-complexioned man on Sunday, July 25, at Nick Moore's House, an inn and tavern run by Mrs. Frederika Loss. The newspapers ran varying descriptions of the state of Mary's body when it was pulled from the river, and scores of scenarios that could have led to her death, all of them verging on pornographic. Some papers had Mary raped and murdered by her gentleman companion, others had her raped multiple times and murdered by one of New York's many street gangs, still others had her the victim of a botched abortion. Any of these speculative scenarios challenged Mary's chastity and virtue, and therefore meant profits for the penny papers. Accounts of these brutal events were paired with descriptions indicating signs of struggle in the thicket near the river where Mary's clothing and personal effects were found. The descriptions of these effects were no less lurid than the accounts of her rape and murder, with vivid descriptions of her petticoats and garters, all eye candy for the voyeuristic reader. Perhaps most sensational, and also inconsistent, were the reports from various medical examiners, either factual or embellished, that treated Mary's body as though she had presented it to the readers for their scrutiny. Engravings of Mary's body, scantily clad and bosomy, often accompanied and contrasted with the violent descriptions of her corpse; in woodcuts, she appears, as Amy Srebnick describes, "a poetic, sleeping beauty, ready to be awakened."[9]

By "sensationalizing the more or less taboo subjects of sex and violence and selling them as 'news,' the penny press caught and held the eye, as well as the purse, of the public."[10] The accounts of Mary Rogers's death varied in so many ways that it was next to impossible to discern anything credible or consistent from the majority of the accounts. Nevertheless, Poe saw these stories as a convergence of three tropes of nineteenth-century culture: the taboo of femininity in the marketplace, the mystery of death, and the enigma of the urban milieu. Furthermore, since Mary Rogers was beautiful, and dead, she fit the mold of Poe's perfect heroine.

With his story already laid out for him by the press, Poe seized the opportunity to bring the conflicting reports of Mary's death into his closet via the newspaper and to use his own brand of pseudoscience to attempt to solve the real mystery of the beautiful cigar girl, through his fictional detective, C. Auguste Dupin. Given the popularity of the penny press among the urban masses, Poe was able to recreate the mystery of Mary Rogers as "The Mystery of Marie Rogêt" by changing the names—to protect himself, though, not the innocent—and the setting in order to juxtapose it with his previous Dupin tale, "The Murders in the Rue Morgue." The then unsolved case gave Poe a backdrop for his story, in which he aimed to answer the question he and his critics posed about his previous tale: "Where is the ingenuity of unraveling a web which you yourself (the author) have woven for the express purpose of unraveling?"[11]

Through Dupin, Poe addresses the contradictory press accounts of the girl's death to emphasize that "it is the object of our newspapers rather to create a sensation—to make a point—than to further the cause of truth."[12] This rings similar to Poe's satires of sensational journalism in "The Folio Club" and "How to Write a Blackwood Article" and alludes to the uncritical masses and their gullibility. Poe doesn't hide his distrust and distaste for the masses or the mass media, particularly because of their sensationalism, but he also acknowledges that "to be appreciated you must be read, and these things are invariably sought after with avidity."[13] So, he gives in to the masses with "The Mystery of Marie Rogêt;" however, throughout the story, Poe makes it clear that he is writing with the pointed aim of repudiating the erratic, indulgent reportage of crime in the popular press. He follows through by having Dupin "solve" the case without leaving his house, making a mockery of the police and the press. Whereas Marie Rogêt's undoing is a result of her venturing out into the city, Dupin extracts the particulars of her undoing by choosing to remain inside.

Unfortunately, the story falls short of Poe's intended financial mark, because he gets caught in the same trap in which he criticizes the penny press writers of ensnaring themselves—that of the influence of popular opinion. He makes assumptions about the particulars of his case for the sake of writing a better story by focusing on the more romantic—the rape and murder of a beautiful woman—thereby missing the solution all together. He believes the "facts" that he chooses to read into the story, ignoring the allegations that Mary died as the result of a botched abortion, which would eventually come out as the actual cause of her death through the deathbed confession of Mrs. Frederika Loss: that Mary Rogers had died from complications of a "premature delivery" that took place at her tavern, where Rogers was last seen. The results of this manipulation of the press are several inconsistencies between the first two parts of Poe's tale and the conclusion, which had to be delayed a month so he could make the changes that would prevent disaster and personal failure.[14]

Poe supports his analysis of the Rogers case, saves his own reputation, and establishes his armchair detective through his use of the reenactment. His reenactments appear in the form of eyewitness accounts in fictional newspapers that he inserts in the story. This eyewitness account appears in his fabricated *Morning Paper* and provides details of a family's encounter with a gang of young men in a boat who followed them and then gagged and "brutally treated" the daughter when she returned to her own boat to retrieve her parasol. By having this family, who are obviously more trustworthy than a tavern owner, witness the presence of gangs on the Seine the day of Marie's disappearance, he corroborates the "evidence" alluding to gangs of undesirables in the vicinity and the inability of the police to catch them. Dupin points out that he includes these extracts in his analysis "chiefly to show you the extreme remissness of the police, who, as far as [he] can understand from the Prefect, have not troubled themselves, in any respect, with the examination of [Dupin's primary suspect] the naval officer" (754).

More concretely supporting Dupin's analysis, and diverting attention from the actual solution of the Rogers case, are the footnote on the first page and the infamous bracketed omission near the end, which together obscure and remove evidence from the story, respectively. Later collected publications of Poe's serial open with a footnote in which he discounts his own methods:

> The "Mystery of Marie Rogêt" was composed at a distance from the scene of the atrocity, and with no other means of investigation than the newspapers afforded. Thus much escaped the writer of which he could have availed himself had he been on the spot, and visited the localities. It may not be improper to record, nevertheless, that the confessions of *two* persons, (one of them the Madame Deluc [Frederika Loss] of the narrative) made, at different periods, long subsequent to the publication, confirmed, in full not only the general conclusion, but absolutely *all* the chief hypothetical details by which the conclusion was attained. (723)

As previously mentioned, this is the exact opposite of the truth: Loss's confession completely discredits Poe's conclusion. The other "confession," although entirely fabricated, is presumably from the naval officer. Finally, the story concludes with an omission, credited to the editors "of the magazine in which the article was originally published" but obviously carried out by Poe to cover up the errors in his solution:

> For reasons which we shall not specify, but which to many readers will appear obvious, we have taken the liberty of here omitting, from the MSS. placed in

our hands, such portion as details the *following up* of the apparently slight clew obtained by Dupin. We feel it advisable only to state, in brief, that the result desired was brought to pass; and that the Prefect fulfilled punctually although with reluctance, the terms of his compact with the Chevalier. (772)

The importance of "The Mystery of Marie Rogêt" is not Poe's ability to solve crimes (or not solve them, as was the case) by reading the newspapers, but his understanding of crime as an essential element of the urban environment through the city's representation as "a place of violence and overcrowding, a polluted haven for criminal gangs which offers few gratifications to Dupin's refined taste,"[15] and then bring that environment into the parlor. The city is more than a mere backdrop for these tales; it is these very horrors of the urban events and situations that have kept Dupin and his unnamed American partner indoors, hiding from the metropolis under the cover of their research. The pages of the penny papers provide Dupin a window through which to peer out onto the seedy underbelly of Parisian society without having to leave his library. The papers bring the urban environment and all of its unpleasantry to Dupin, allowing him to conduct all of his ratiocination and *flânerie* from the comfort of his armchair. Since Dupin does not leave his house during the course of the tale, "The Mystery of Marie Rogêt" cannot be considered a detective story in the traditional sense, because Dupin does not conduct any ratiocinative work, any detecting, at the scene of the crime; he merely voyeuristically observes the work of others and analyzes his own reenactments of these accounts using his intellectual, purely mathematical "Calculus of Probabilities" (724) to "solve" the case of Mary Rogers.

As the armchair spectator, Dupin is able to project himself anywhere he wants to in the newspaper stories. By merely observing and analyzing the pages of the penny press, he is able to imagine himself simultaneously as both the detective solving the case and the "murderer" himself. He reads the newspapers much as the narrator in "The Man of the Crowd" reads the crowd and Poe himself reads the contents of peoples' houses on Moving Day in "The Philosophy of Furniture," which "encouraged parlor *flânerie* because it served to break down the barriers between exterior and interior, public and private."[16] He makes assumptions based on preconceived notions that exist nowhere outside of his own head. He sees what he wants to see. Since the narrator finds himself the *flâneur* in a dangerous, violent urban environment, it goes without saying that mystery and crime are afoot. Some critics, including Laura Saltz and David Reynolds, read "The Man of the Crowd" as a detective story, but it is a weak one at best, because there is no crime committed, no criminal, no motive, and so on. The element of mystery is created by the city itself, as it is in "The Mystery of Marie Rogêt," because the spectator and his target are individuals among the masses, they are both in danger of meeting violent fates, and they are both suspect of committing violent acts. Even if the old man "is the type and the genius of deep crime,"[17] unlike the newspapers in "Marie Rogêt," he doesn't allow himself to be read, so any such assumption is purely in the eyes and the mind of the voyeur for which the man is the object of his gaze.

Where Poe's genius is clearly evident in "The Mystery of Marie Rogêt" is in his anticipation that the masses would become so enraptured in the "horrible details" and "further particulars" of the penny press crime sensation for many years to come. The voyeurism in Poe's *flâneur* tales predicts a similar voyeurism currently seen in reality crime television and social media. The scenes depicted in the penny press and exploited in "The Mystery of Marie Rogêt" foreshadow the popularity of true crime shows such as *America's Most Wanted*, *Cops*, and the myriad of incriminating video files available on YouTube. What was true of mass culture in Poe's day is true of mass culture in the twenty-first century: people don't want to know the details of criminal activity or the social milieu so that they can protect themselves from harm, and we don't need to hear confession sermons to have morality instilled upon us. Viewers, readers, and browsers today want the "horrible details" and "further particulars" for the sheer entertainment value. We want to experience the filth, the muck, and the scum of the earth without getting dirty. We want that window that looks out at the seedy underbelly of society, but we want the view from the safety and comfort of our homes.

NOTES

1. Carl D. Malmgren, "Anatomy of Murder: Mystery, Detective, and Crime Fiction," *Journal of Popular Culture* 30, no. 4 (1997): 120.

2. Kevin J. Hayes, "The *Flâneur* in the Parlor: Poe's 'Philosophy of Furniture,'" *Prospects* 27, no. 1 (2002): 103–19. Hayes's article identifies the paradoxical variant of the stationary *flâneur* and makes connections between this variant and the detective, primarily through Walter Benjamin's study of *flânerie* in his *Arcades Project*. Benjamin discusses the similarities between the *flâneur* and the detective at length.

3. Isabelle Lehuu, *Carnival on the Page: Popular Print Media in Antebellum America* (Chapel Hill: University of North Carolina Press, 2000), 8.

4. Ibid., 15.

5. William David Sloan, *The Media in America: A History*, 5th ed. (Northport, AL: Vision Press, 2002), 127.

6. Andie Tucher, *Froth and Scum: Truth, Beauty, Goodness, and the Ax Murder in America's First Mass Medium* (Chapel Hill: University of North Carolina Press, 1994), 24.

7. Ibid., 25.

8. Mark Seltzer, "The Crime System," *Critical Inquiry* 30, no. 3 (2004): 564.

9. Amy Gilman Srebnick, *The Mysterious Death of Mary Rogers: Sex and Culture in Nineteenth-Century New York* (New York: Oxford University Press, 1995), 62.

10. Laura Saltz, "'(Horrible to Relate!)': Recovering the Body of Marie Rogêt," *The American Face of Edgar Allan Poe*, ed. Shawn Rosenheim and Stephen Rachman (Baltimore: Johns Hopkins University Press, 1995), 243.

11. Terence Whalen, *Edgar Allan Poe and the Masses: The Political Economy of Literature in Antebellum America* (Princeton, NJ: Princeton University Press, 1999), 226.

12. Edgar Allan Poe, "The Mystery of Marie Rogêt," in Edgar A. Poe, *The Collected Works of Edgar Allan Poe*, ed. Thomas Olive Mabbott (Cambridge, MA: Belknap, 1978), 3:738. Further references to Poe's texts are from this edition and noted parenthetically in the text.

13. David S. Reynolds, *Beneath the American Renaissance: The Subversive Imagination in the Age of Emerson and Melville* (Cambridge, MA: Harvard University Press, 1989), 226.

14. W. K. Wimsatt Jr., "Poe and the Mystery of Mary Rogers," *PMLA* 56, no. 1 (1941): 245.

15. Whalen, *Edgar Allan Poe and the Masses*, 230.

16. Hayes, "The *Flâneur* in the Parlor," 105.

17. "The Man of the Crowd," in Mabbott, *Complete Tales*, 2:515.

Chapter Nine

No Kidding

"The Gold-Bug" Is True to Its Title

Henri Justin

The title of a tale is the only part of it for which the writer must take unmediated responsibility. Poe is not Legrand, is not Jupiter, is not even the unnamed narrator; the whole textual body is a matter of subtle mediations—but not the title. And yet, here is a title that cannot be taken at face value. Living bugs are not made of gold, and the one in the tale is only accidentally ancillary to the plot proper. The title could be a hoax,[1] but my contention is that it is not. I intend to show that it points to the dual structure of the tale. Indeed, as a rare linguistic "bivalve"[2] hinged on its hyphen, it is an emblem of Poe's art itself.

On a first reading, the discovery of the beetle starts the whole story, but when Legrand, having lent it, wants to draw it for the benefit of his friend the narrator, he does so on a scrap of something found in his pocket—and the narrator sees a death's head. The differences and the strange similarities between the two drawings generate some misunderstanding. In Legrand's mind, there soon occurs a transfer of interest from the *Scarabaeus* to what he finally understands as a piece of parchment marked with the well-known pirates' emblem. At this point, very early on, the treasure hunt has started, and the beetle has nothing to do with it. But narrator and reader are kept in the dark.

A month later, Jupiter comes to town to buy a scythe and three spades, and to hand the narrator a letter from Legrand asking him to "come over" (813). We know Jupiter already, and the value he attaches to the bug—a bug of solid gold, in his view (809). Now, being alone with the narrator, he explains to him that his master has fallen into a gold craze, which he, Jupiter, can only account for in terms of the bug.[3] So the reader is kept suspended between two interpretive stances: Jupiter's, which is very vocal but irrational; and Legrand's, which is rational but kept secret. Indeed, Legrand, pretending to go along with his servant's fantasy, dangles the beetle at the end of a piece of whip-cord, and off they go, an improbable trio, till the whole venture, somewhat surprisingly, proves a success. At this point, Legrand offers the narrator a detailed explanation. It develops as a skillfully concatenated sequence, from the beetle to the parchment, to the marks on it, to its message as a line of coded characters, to the common alphabet and the division into words, to the further division into consecutive semantic units, to the route to the treasure. What is brought to light is a series of contiguities, from one thing to the next, each new step making the previous one obsolete, and all ending with the treasure. But then the narrator poses two further questions. The first one concerns the role Legrand gave the beetle in the treasure hunt. Answer: he used it for "a little bit of sober mystification" (844). And because the reader is told this only now, he has been mystified too. At this point, the title appears clearly as a mere false clue, and Legrand's triumph seems complete. He is the hero of the tale, and the text should conclude on his reinstatement in his family possessions, the restoration of his identity as a Louisiana aristocrat. Toni Morrison, in that case, would be right; Poe could be characterized by his "pretensions to the planter class"[4] and the reader would leave the hero bathing in "Southern comfort."

But then comes the ultimate question about the presence of skeletons on top of the pirate's chest. The obvious answer is given, and then, there emerges the absolutely new—an extra sentence, unasked for, and not clearly addressed. Legrand is now speaking to himself: "Perhaps a couple of blows with a mattock were sufficient, while his coadjutors were busy in the pit; perhaps it required a dozen—who shall tell?" (844). Read as Legrand's personal musing, the question gives a frightening depth to his character. Legrand is suddenly far from the present time, blind to his splendid future, sunk back, in fact, into a past situation—Kidd's, ostensibly, but his own too, surely, at some point. The reading *rebounds* on these last words; the reader feels he must retrace his steps. What, in fact, was said of Legrand when, the treasure chest having been opened, *he* could be tempted to do away with his "coadjutors"? One reads that he "appeared exhausted with excitement, and spoke very few words" (826). He *appeared* exhausted. In fact, we now understand, he was in the grip of a murderous trance. The narrator actually had to "arouse" him from it (826). And the words that were then suppressed come out at the very end of the tale, when they are innocuous, though not innocent. They come out in disguise, bringing along a lexical term that is utterly new in the text, and so, begs interpretation: Legrand imagines Kidd's instrument for the murders to have been a "mattock." Now, a mattock has a long handle with, at one end, a double tool: on one side a pick, and on the other an adze. Such a tool appears as a conflation of the large Spanish knife found alongside the two skeletons and probably used by Kidd to stab his victims, and the spade Legrand had at his disposal; the two words had even come into close contact in the sentence: "One or two strokes of a spade upturned the blade of a large Spanish knife" (825). Legrand's unconscious is at work here. Deep down, he shares Kidd's criminality. Like Dupin, he has a "Bi-Part" psyche,[5] half brilliant analytic intellect, half murderous drives. But *this* he cannot read.

Legrand cannot read duality. He can recognize *coded* equivalence, as when he understands the death's head on the parchment as the emblem of the pirates, or the kid as the "punning or hieroglyphical" signature of Captain Kidd (833). Such identifying logos point in one direction. They suit Legrand's intellectual tendency, which is overwhelmingly toward linear concatenation. In his account of his first interview with the narrator, he insists on his amazement at the "similarity" between the two drawings.[6] It is a "singularity" he can make nothing of (829). One sees how Poe is playing with the conflicting notions of *equivalence* and *contiguity* at the expense of his character. In such cases, Legrand concludes, "the mind struggles to establish a connexion—a sequence of cause and effect—and, being unable to do so, suffers a species of temporary paralysis" (829). Legrand shakes it off, as he goes on explaining, by recalling the circumstances of his coming by this scrap of "paper." Then, he concludes, "I had already established a kind of *connexion* [emphasizing the word]. I had put together two links of a great chain" (831)—and again, Dupin-like: "My steps were sure, and could afford but a single result" (831). Indeed, Legrand can afford but a single meaning; he cannot read symbolic values and see into the far depths of his brilliant intellect, where *gold* is equated with *murder*. Reading the decoded message, he narrows "the bishop's hostel" down to "the devil's seat," with no sense of the latter as part of the former. The local imagination had given the devil a seat in the residence of the man of God, but Legrand does not take the symbolic hint. He is blind to that logic, which is Poe's.

So the tables are now turned on Legrand, the reader sensing that Jupiter and his "goole-bug" could well be the key to deeper meaning. The whole thing started when Jupiter picked up the scrap of parchment to wrap the beetle in it, making the unrecognized parchment work as an indifferent envelope to the precious beetle, and unwittingly bringing beetle and death's head into contact. After this moment of potential revelation, beetle and parchment go into different pockets! The second moment is when the two drawings appear to Legrand, back to back, but then again, only the clear switch from one to the other can start the treasure hunt that, after all, gives the tale its storyline, the more visible part of its plot. But now that we are on the alert for duplications, we see more of them. To mention a main one right now, we see that the chest, as it appears during the telling pause, is an inflated image of the bug: the two skeletons answer the suggestion of a human skull on the bug's back; the mineralization of the chest corresponds to the metallic aspect of the bug; its heaviness recalls the abnormal weight that made Jupiter believe the bug was solid gold; lastly, the three rings of iron on each side give it six legs, insect-like. More exactly, Poe puts the six legs on, as it were, by adding that the rings could give "six persons" a firm hold of the chest (826). These six persons make no sense in terms of *contiguity*—in terms of the storyline—but they make a lot of sense in terms of *equivalence*. First, they can appear as the six pallbearers of a coffin. And then, just imagine them lifting up the chest and walking off—you see the bug on its six legs, exactly.

With this second reading, the interpretive authority has moved from Legrand to Jupiter because the latter is the one who thought it all came "of the bug" (814). Richard Hull, in his remarkable article on puns in "The Gold-Bug," sums up a trend in the interpretation of the tale when he says: "We must reject the widespread view that Legrand's way is *the* correct way to interpret. . . . We must read for meanings Legrand can't afford."[7] The key to these meanings is the bug, as Jupiter insists it is, in his way. The only thing is, one must not fall into the other extreme, now placing Jupiter on a level with Poe himself. The manumitted slave has the deep humanity of a man with the experience of suffering and death, but his language is often as one-sided as Legrand's. Although there are striking exceptions,[8] most of the puns present in his lines are not his. When he says "goole" for "gold," he does so in a stereotyped Black English that Poe bends to his own ends. Jupiter feels the duality of the bug—he is both fascinated and frightened by the strange insect—but only Poe conflates "gold" with the "ghoul," the legendary being that feeds on corpses (812–13). Or again, when Jupiter, being asked whether he *thinks* his master has been made sick by the bug's bite, answers "I don't think nothing about it—I nose it," he just means "I know it".[9] Only Poe's play on words turns this superstitious knowledge into an intuitive impression. For full effect, these words of Jupiter must not simply be decoded (as Legrand decoded the message) nor simply translated, "gold" simply replacing "goole" (even if with the gain of a touch of humor); the two must (and do) linger in the reader's consciousness as "gold" and "ghoul," echoing each other. They function very much as rhymes in a poem, creating a submerged effect, a meaning under the meaning.

As a character, Jupiter remains a humorous figure. Very human, emotional, prerational, open to superstition and myth ("I've heard about them gold-bugs before this" [813])—even open to magic, as when he feels sure the bug is of solid gold, or when he is terrorized by the insect itself, even once it is dead. Magic, confusing as it does the sign with the thing, is a failure of the sign-system; it pushes equivalence to the point of identity, and Jupiter is not immune. But by being alive to the dual quality of the insect, and so establishing it as a living and ambiguous presence in the tale, he unwittingly points to its deeper textual structure. It is in this *function*, forced on him by Poe, that he reverses the balance of interpretive power that appeared so much in favor of Legrand at first reading. It is his function as *Jupiter*, the law-giving god. One could say that, in the guise of an old uneducated servant, Olympian Jupiter keeps alive the axis of equivalence, the source of symbols.

A critical remark by Poe could well be applied to his handling of Jupiter's character. In his review of the first installments of *Barnaby Rudge* (two years previous to the publication of "The Gold-Bug"), he expresses the opinion that the ravings of the idiot young man, Barnaby, together with the croaks of his raven, "are intended to convey indistinct glimmerings of the events to be evolved"[10] —or, more precisely, of the withheld solution to the bloody riddle. And again: "Every word spoken by him [Barnaby] will be found to have an undercurrent of meaning, by paying strict attention to which the enjoyment of the imaginative reader will be infinitely heightened."[11] Typically, when Poe, now reviewing the completed *Barnaby Rudge*, found that Dickens's intentions, as he had understood them, had not been strictly carried out, he added with smiling authority that they should have. But, he went on, the *form* used by Dickens, the novel, and the serial novel at that, works against such intentions. "In tales of ordinary sequence he [Dickens] may and will long reign triumphant," but he has "no positive *genius* for *adaptation*."[12] "Adaptation," here, is the capacity to build a "plot," in the sense of a formal structure. Poe enlarged on the word when, in 1845, he came to consider "the Divine system of adaptation."[13] The beauty of it is "the complete *mutuality* of adaptation," the "reciprocity between cause and effect,"[14] or as Poe would come to express it, the "really essential symmetry" of the two opposite principles of attraction and repulsion.[15] It was in order to approach such symmetry in prose that Poe developed his own practice of the "brief prose tale," a form that he placed on "a table-land" between the poem and the novel.[16] By projecting telling equivalences onto the story line, he creates an object of special value, a value that, as he wrote to his closest correspondent, Frederick Thomas, in February 1849, he would not let go "for all the gold in California."[17]

At this point, it is worth making clear that the present study, though prompted and encouraged by a close reading of Poe's text, has been shaped, too, by a long-standing familiarity with "Linguistics and Poetics," the famous essay by Roman Jakobson.[18] The reader will remember that in this paper the great linguist offers a definition of the poetic function, using as his foundation de Saussure's diagram of the speech-act, with its *virtual* axis of selection (ruled by various degrees of *equivalence*) and its *actual* axis of combination (ruled by syntactical *contiguity*).[19] The poetic function, Jakobson argues, consists in the projection of the principle of equivalence from its own virtual axis on to the actually spoken or written line, or "on to the sequence."[20] Jakobson takes his cue from Gerard Manley Hopkins, extending the argument from rhythmic to semantic units, and then comes, secondarily, to Edgar

Allan Poe, quoting from "The Raven" and "The Philosophy of Composition." He could also have found in Poe the assertion that "equivalence" is the unique "rationale of verse"[21] (just as "ordinary sequence" can do very well for the traditional novel).[22] Poe often contrasted poetry and prose as clear opposites, the better to establish his own aesthetic of the brief prose tale, a highly artificial construct interweaving equivalence with contiguity.

This explicit interplay between the two main orientations of language was so much part of Poe's intention in "The Gold-Bug" that when he reread his story in his copy of *Tales*, sometime after 1845, he added an exchange between the narrator and Legrand that was designed, it seems to me, to heighten the reader's awareness of what was at issue in the tale. He inserted it precisely at the end of Legrand's explanation proper, just before the last two very pointed questions. "I presume," then proposes the narrator:

> I presume the fancy of the *skull*—of letting fall a bullet through the skull's-eye—was suggested to Kidd by the piratical flag. No doubt he felt a kind of poetical consistency in recovering his money through this ominous insignium. (843)

"Perhaps so," answers Legrand. As we know, Legrand can read a coded image, "an emblem" as he called it before (831). But he prefers a justification of the skull that does not belong to the axis of equivalence:

> "Perhaps so; still I cannot help thinking that common-sense had quite as much to do with the matter as poetical consistency. To be visible from the Devil's seat, it was necessary that the object, if small, should be *white*; and there is nothing like your human skull for retaining and even increasing its whiteness under exposure to all vicissitudes of weather." (843)

This addition clearly pits common sense (on the side of the one-directional chain of causality, the prose line, leading to the earthly treasure) against poetical consistency. Note how unexpected the adjective "ominous" is, in this context. To Kidd, this "insignium" could only be of *good* omen. To Legrand, the emblem of the skull (as drawn on the parchment, mentioned in the message, and confirmed in the tree) has only brought good news. But the narrator keeps alive the duality intended by Poe to the point of suggesting a symmetry of opposites in the phrase "recovering his money through this ominous insignium"—"money" being anagrammatically contained in "omin(ous)." The careful reader is now prepared for the rebound triggered by Legrand's final question to himself.

If, at long last, we turn to the title, we can see how much it is an image of the deep structure of the tale. Although Legrand is the ostensible hero of the plot, the "undercurrent of meaning" tips the balance in favor of Jupiter, whose figure then splits into old manumitted slave and lawgiver; typical of this is the distribution of the word *bug* in the text.[23] Dictionaries say that *bug* is often used in America for *beetle*, but the distinction bears another meaning in Poe's tale. A word count shows that *bug* occurs thirty-eight times and is used almost exclusively by Jupiter or in the context of Jupiter's perception of things, while *beetle*, which occurs twenty-three times, is used only by the two white friends.[24] Jupiter uses only *bug*. So the word belongs to him. It is Jupiter's, just as the whole notion of a gold bug is Jupiter's.[25] We now see that the title points, beyond Legrand, to a richer adventure than the treasure hunt. Indeed, if we add to the immediate meaning of "gold bug" the figurative meaning of "gold enthusiast," Legrand is pointed at as the comic figure of the tale. But the title does not belong to Jupiter either. By turning "goolebug" into "gold-bug," Poe clearly appropriates the phrase for his own ends. The form is totally absent from the text proper; it belongs to Poe alone, and, as such, it is well worth our close attention.

I see it as a rich locket, open, there, at the top of the page, with its two halves, its hinge, and its clasp. The open hinge is the hyphen. On each side of it, the two syllables are slightly palindromic, with initial and final "g." Fold the thing; the small "g" veers and clicks into the capital "G"—and the locket, closed, looks like the bug, with its image of a skull folded up on its gold. And so the title, with its hyphen, is a perfect emblem of the text, with its double reading hinged on its last sentence.

There can be little doubt that this hyphenated form is authorial. First, it is unusual. Gold (or golden) beetles, jewel (or jeweled) scarabs exist in nature, and if you look for them in dictionaries, you will find them without the hyphen. To be more particular, when the *Dollar Newspaper* announced, on June 14, 1843, that the tale that had been awarded the prize of $100 was Poe's, they called it "The Gold Bug," without the hyphen, confirming that it was the expected spelling. But when the first half of the tale appeared, on June 21, the hyphen was there, of course, and this original form was adhered to through the several printings by the same paper. Similarly, when publication of the tale was announced in other papers, its title was consistently printed without the hyphen, whereas after publication the practice varied.[26] Moreover, when Evert Duyckinck decided to republish the story as part of *Tales* (1845), Poe had an opportunity to introduce a few revisions, but the idiosyncratic form was respected. And it was left untouched again when he penciled in additional revisions, including the exchange quoted above, in the copy of *Tales* that Thomas O. Mabbott used as his copy text. Last but not least, on the first four occasions when Poe referred to his tale in his letters, in 1844 and 1845, he transcribed the hyphen.[27] Only in January 1848, in a long letter to a friend going over personal matters in a casual way, did he revert, typically, to the normal spelling.[28] So, gold bugs exist (and *Chrysina [plusiotis] resplendens* and *Chrysina aurigans* are of an incredibly golden yellow),[29] but there is only one "gold-bug." I have come to see it as a tiny, almost private, but insistent emblem of Poe's art.

This emblem is strictly linguistic. Another one was planted in the text—casually, as it were—in the form of an unnecessary detail. It had stuck in my memory as a version of the beetle, and yet—strictly, prosaically speaking—it is not. Indeed, the way it is proposed to the reader makes it the richest emblem of all. When Legrand and Jupiter reach their hut that first night and find the narrator waiting for them, Legrand is in one of his fits, we are told, because he "had found an unknown bivalve, forming a new genus, and, more than this, he had hunted down and secured, with Jupiter's assistance, a *scarabaeus* which he believed to be totally new, but in respect to which he wished to have my opinion on the morrow" (808). Now, as a narrative sequence, particularly by Poe's standards,[30] the text is faulty. The first find should have been a mildly interesting one, simply designed to bring in a realistic touch and serve as a springboard to the fabulous beetle. On the contrary, the balance between "unknown . . . forming a new genus" and "which he believed to be totally new" is, at best, uncertain. So much so, that the reader is liable to merge the two finds into one. Unconsciously, the bivalve, too remarkable to be simply forgotten, yet never mentioned again, will lurk in the reader's mind as a version of the "*Scarabaeus caput hominis*," the strange beetle, half gold, half death's head (810). Again, in a bold stroke of genius, equivalence has been projected onto the narrative sequence. The comparable duality of "gold-bug" and "bivalve" is striking, with the hyphen of the one as adductor muscle in the other. Each offers an image of the tale itself, with its final sentence (down to the ultimate "Who shall tell?") as the "muscle" closing and opening the text. Indeed, the literary form Poe was elaborating, tale after tale, could, in 1843, have been greeted precisely in these terms: "an unknown bivalve, forming a new genus."

NOTES

1. Like "Mesmeric Revelation," a tale in which mesmerism is only used as a fictional setting.

2. Edgar A. Poe, *Collected Works of Edgar Allan Poe*, ed. Thomas Olive Mabbott (Cambridge, MA: Belknap 1978), 3:808. Subsequent references to "The Gold-Bug" will cite this edition and be given parenthetically in the text and the notes. This seashell, found before the *Scarabaeus*, will be returned to.

3. As the narrator concludes, Jupiter's "whole intellect seemed to be absorbed by 'de bug'" (814).

4. *Playing in the Dark: Whiteness and the Literary Imagination* (Cambridge, MA: Harvard University Press, 1992), 58. I deal with Poe's attitude toward race, slavery, and democracy in *Avec Poe jusqu'au bout de la prose* (Paris: Gallimard, 2009), 149–76. Let me only insist here on Poe's meticulousness in the use of words. Morrison, having put forward the idea that Poe's imagination could accidentally escape his (white) control, writes that Jupiter "is said to whip his master" (ibid., 58). But that is inaccurate. Poe never uses the word "whip" in that context: he has Jupiter use "beat" (812) and the two white men, "flog" (812, 843). Granted, "flog" and

"whip" are near synonyms; but the instrument to be used is "a big stick" (812), "a huge stick" (813), not a *whipping* instrument. The slip might still seem trivial if the word "whip" itself never surfaced in the tale. But it does, once. Typically, it surfaces in Legrand's world—as a harmless, grammatically subordinate element in the "bit of whip-cord" on which Legrand dangles the beetle (817). Far-reaching conclusions are not in order here, except that Poe is a master—of words.

5. "The Murders in the Rue Morgue" in Mabbott, *Collected Works*, 2:533.

6. The word "similarity" occurs twice and is followed by the verb "resemble." The words "amazed" and "stupefied" are echoed by the noun "surprise" (829).

7. "Puns in 'The Gold-Bug': You Gotta Be Kidding," *Arizona Quarterly* 58 (Summer 2002): 1–18. Quotation on p. 7. This trend against Legrand as master interpreter was vigorously launched by Daniel Kempton in "The Gold/Goole/Ghoul Bug," *ESQ: A Journal of the American Renaissance* 33, no. 1 (1987): 1–19.

8. One instance when he does use the process of symbolization beautifully is when, having seen his master bitten by the beetle, he feels "certain," a month later, that he "has been bitten about the head by that gold-bug" (812—I standardize Jupiter's English). Another instance is as telling and much more moving: when Legrand asks him to find "the left eye of the skull," Jupiter expresses his horror by a conscious pun, saying: "Hum! Hoo! That's good! Why, there ain't no eye left at all" (821). That is not "stupidity," as Legrand is prompt to call it, but full humanity.

9. 813—I partly standardize Jupiter's English.

10. *Essays and Reviews*, ed. G. R. Thompson (New York: Library of America, 1984), 221.

11. Ibid., 222.

12. Ibid., 244.

13. Ibid., 366.

14. Ibid.

15. *Eureka*, ed. Stuart Levine and Susan R. Levine (Urbana-Champaign: University of Illinois Press, 2004), 96.

16. Thompson, *Essays and Reviews*, 585 and 573.

17. "Depend upon it, after all, Thomas, Literature is the most noble of professions. In fact, it is about the only one fit for a man. For my own part, there is no seducing me from the path. I shall be a *littérateur*, at least, all my life; nor would I abandon the hopes which still lead me on for all the gold in California." *The Collected Letters of Edgar Allan Poe*, ed. John Ward Ostrom, rev. Burton R. Pollin and Jeffrey A. Savoye (New York: Gordian Press, 2008), 2;770.

18. The full title is "Closing Statements: Linguistics and Poetics." It was published as a chapter in *Style in Language*, ed. Thomas A. Sebeok (Cambridge, MA: MIT Press, 1960), 350–77.

19. Ferdinand de Saussure's teaching was published posthumously in 1916 as *Cours de Linguistique générale* (Paris: Payot, 1973). The Swiss linguist distinguishes, in his own words, "le rapport syntagmatique (in praesentia)" from "le rapport associatif (in absentia)" (ibid., 170–71).

20. Sebeok, *Style in Language*, 367.

21. "The Rationale of Verse," Thompson, *Essays and Reviews*, 26–70. Poe's ruling principle is "equality" (of rhythmic units) and, as second best, "equivalence" (*passim*).

22. Thompson, *Essays and Reviews*, 244, in Poe's review of *Barnaby Rudge* quoted more fully above.

23. For the following word count, I have used the electronic text available on the Edgar Allan Poe Society of Baltimore website, http://www.eapoe.org.

24. Legrand uses the word "bug" twice in his own name (808), and the narrator, twice too (810, 844). The two white friends resort to "*scarabaeus*" when they discuss genus, and occasionally, to "insect."

25. There are eight occurrences of "goole (-) bug" (with or without the hyphen).

26. See Dwight Thomas and David K. Jackson, *The Poe Log: A Documentary Life of Edgar Allan Poe (1809–1849)* (Boston: G. K. Hall, 1987), 414–16 and 417–29. Also, out of six reprints in other papers during Poe's lifetime, of the two that omit the hyphen, one is a pirated reprint in pamphlet form (London 1846–1847) and the other is titled "The Gold Bug; or, the

Treasures of Kidd," showing little concern for authenticity (*Salem Gazette*, November 1849). See http://www.eapoe.org, "The Gold-Bug," "Reprints."

27. Ostrom et al., *The Collected Letters*, 1:441, 450, 451, and 505. The same tendency to omit the hyphen when attention relaxes might explain why, in the tale, "goole-bug" appears without a hyphen in two instances out of eight.

28. Ibid., 641.

29. I have seen fine specimens at Deyrolle's, Paris, and at "Paradisea," Bligny-sur-Ouche, France. They are of a uniform, metallic, golden color. The black spots suggestive of a human skull belong only, as one would expect, to the specimen found by Legrand.

30. Poe explains, in "The Philosophy of Composition," how he took care to "graduate the stanzas" of "The Raven," adding: "Had I been able, in the subsequent composition, to construct more vigorous stanzas [than the one bringing the repeated 'nevermore' to a climax], I should, without scruple, have purposely enfeebled them, so as not to interfere with the climacteric effect." Thompson, *Essays and Reviews*, 20.

Chapter Ten

"Trust to the shrewdness and common sense of the public"

The Narrative of Arthur Gordon Pym *as a Hoaxical Satire of Racist Epistemologies*

John C. Havard

Since Toni Morrison and others drew attention to the issue in the 1990s,[1] Edgar Allan Poe's representation of race in *The Narrative of Arthur Gordon Pym* has attracted much scholarly attention. This trend challenged the tendency to dehistoricize Poe's work, and while Poe's symbolic ambiguity and structural complexity may lend themselves to New Critical and deconstructionist readings, the turn to race has much to recommend it.[2] Poe published *Pym* in 1838 as the battles between abolitionists and reactionary Southern proslavery ideologues heated up; he had previously published part of the narrative in the proslavery *Southern Literary Messenger*; and the novel trades in constructions of blackness that readers of the time would have recognized as pertinent to the slavery question.

Scholarship on race in *Pym* has been contentious. Initially, many interpreted *Pym* as expressing the racist and/or proslavery attitudes of the antebellum United States and, especially, Poe's South.[3] Many critics, however, have increasingly taken issue with this approach, arguing that roundly condemning Poe's novel as a simple reflection of racist, proslavery thought tells, at best, only part of the story. For these readers, *Pym* reveals a multifaceted, oftentimes conscious engagement on Poe's part with the racial attitudes of his time.[4]

My paper follows the latter view. Poe undoubtedly believed in the inferiority of those of African descent and encoded *Pym* with racist tropes. However, as Terence Whalen compellingly contends, Poe's work should not be read in terms of his personal beliefs, as we know few conclusive specifics about Poe's racial and political stances.[5] Moreover, Whalen claims that labeling Poe as racist is tautological, considering that Poe lived in a time when the vast majority of white Americans, from the most virulent proponent of slavery to the most radical abolitionist, held racist views of some sort. With these points in mind, Whalen argues that we should understand Poe's engagement with issues of race in terms of his relationship to the antebellum literary marketplace. Whalen here claims that Poe's writing exhibits an "average racism [that] was . . . a strategic construction designed to overcome political dissension in the emerging mass audience."[6] In other words, whatever his personal beliefs may have been, we can know with certainty that Poe, as a writer notorious for coveting profit and cultural prestige, strategically filled his work with racialist language that he hoped would appeal to the general assumptions of the time's audience. This audience, importantly, was not solely proslavery and Southern. Thomas White, editor of the *Southern Literary Messenger*, which published the first parts of the work, envisioned a national readership for his magazine. Harper and Brothers, moreover, published the full version of *Pym* for national consumption, keeping in mind their strong readership in the North. As such, Whalen concludes that Poe's work exhibits mild racist tendencies that accorded with those of the range of national readers. These tendencies avoid explicitly engaging divisive issues that might alienate particular portions of that readership, particularly hedging along the lines of the contentious slavery debate.

Whalen's argument renders untenable claims that *Pym* simply reflects antebellum racism by demonstrating that Poe strategically capitulated to audience expectations. We must remember, though, that Poe's relationship with his readers was equivocal, wavering between his desire to win their esteem and his disgust at what he perceived as their less admirable qualities. In this light, we should attend not only to how *Pym* defers to its readers' beliefs but also to how it challenges them. We should not reject Whalen's claims—after all, Poe's writing was multilayered and could ostensibly aim to please his readers all the while subversively attacking them. However, Whalen's claims warrant complication, and this chapter thus explores how *Pym* interrogates racist thinking. To this end, Poe penned the novel as a hoax that satirizes a readership whose intelligence Poe scorned due to what he saw as its tendency to misread and its concomitant inability to comprehend or appreciate his work. In representing Arthur Gordon Pym as a terrible reader, Poe constructed his protagonist as a surrogate who embodies his audience's lack of interpretative competence. Many of Pym's most egregious misreadings stem from his racist assumptions, and through mocking these misreadings, Poe satirizes his readers' tendency to misunderstand race due to their reliance on similarly racist epistemological apparatuses. This readership, as Whalen has shown, was both Southern and Northern and ran the gamut of possible racist positions. Poe not only equally capitulates to, as Whalen contends, but equally savages the different portions of the national readership. In other words, while certain aspects of his satire may speak to particular racisms on the Northern, Southern, antislavery, and proslavery spectrum, Poe unifies these moves to attack a more general racism—something indeed like Whalen's "average racism"—deployed in service of racial hierarchy as it manifested itself in the beliefs of the different constituencies of his national audience. In my reading, Poe's genius in *Pym* finally resides in how Poe shows how blackness and whiteness as construed by racism are constructs and proceeds to subject them and the readership that assumes them to biting hoaxical satire.

A brief discussion of Poe's reasons for and general methods of hoaxing *Pym*'s readers is necessary here. While elements of this background discussion go beyond the racial issues that are my concern, all speak to the generally tense character of Poe's relationship to the publishing industry and his audience. Poe may have chosen to hoax his readership after learning that Harper and Brothers had elected not to publish a collection of his short fiction. In response to the proposal, James Kirke Paulding, Poe's intermediary with Harper's, informed Poe that the publisher had rejected the collection. Paulding suggested that Poe should instead apply his skills "to more familiar subjects of satire; to the faults and foibles of our own people and above all to the ridiculous affectations and extravagancies of the fashionable English Literature of the day."[7] Harper's later returned the manuscript with a letter that advised Poe to leave behind his "learned and mystical" short stories and instead write "a single and connected" work that would please "the multitude."[8] As J. Gerald Kennedy writes, "We can assume that Poe received such counsel with indignation, if not bitterness, for he scorned the American reading public, with its fondness for 'stupid' books, and he objected to the novel on aesthetic grounds."[9] In retaliation, Poe took Paulding's advice that he compose satire—doing so, though, by writing *Pym* as a hoax to avenge himself upon a readership he loathed, a move more subversive than the criticism of literary Anglophilia Paulding had in mind.

To mock his readers, Poe played upon his audience's credulity by presenting his novel under the guise of a true relation of his main character, Pym. While "Mr. Poe" appears in the novel's prefatory and concluding segments as the editor of Pym's writing, Poe's name did not appear on the book's title page or front matter. In the novel's preface, Poe has Pym explain away Poe's acknowledged authorship of the portion of the tale that had appeared in the *Southern Literary Messenger*. While contemporaneous readers saw through the hoax and correctly read *Pym* as fiction, the manner in which Poe mocks his readers warrants notice for what it says about how Poe viewed his audience.[10] Poe begins his covert assault on his readers in the irony-tinged preface. He has Pym relate that "Poe," in his fictional role as editor, had "strongly advised me . . . to prepare at once a full account of what I had seen and undergone, and trust to the shrewdness and common sense of the public—insisting, with great plausibility, that however roughly, as regards mere authorship, my book should be got up, its very uncouthness . . . would give it all the better chance at being received as truth."[11] Pym's words reflect Harper's insistence that unadorned, easily understandable writing appeals to the public. However, the passage inverts Poe's true feelings about his readers, who, Poe believed, possessed little "shrewdness" or "common sense." Similarly, Pym's assertion that Poe as editor has told him that the public will find his relation believable in proportion to its roughness serves as a dig at a readership that Poe felt found literature attractive in proportion to its lack of refinement.[12]

Poe furthers his joke by suggesting an affinity between the reader and Pym. As the tale's protagonist and narrator, Pym is the text's perceptual center; the reader is asked to see the world through and thus to identify with his perspective. The kinship Poe courts, though, between his protagonist and audience is of a devious sort: Poe portrays Pym with the precise characteristic Poe lamented in his readers. Pym's inability to interpret effectively— whether the objects of his attempts are texts or otherwise—is heavily emphasized by Poe.[13] All perceptive readers quickly notice the weight of the appearance-versus-reality theme in *Pym*, which repeatedly comes to light when Pym finds his senses deceived. Critics have traditionally emphasized this theme's resonance with skepticism.[14] While abstract, philosophical considerations are certainly at play, we can also understand Pym's misreadings in terms of the tale's satire of racist epistemology, as doing so recognizes how Poe's representation of Pym as a poor reader works along with Poe's sense of his audience as unperceptive.

Pym's misinterpretations are numerous. His failure to realize Augustus's intoxication before letting his friend man the *Ariel* and his misidentification of the death ship as it approaches the *Grampus* are among the most memorable.[15] These instances both attest to Pym's failures in discerning the difference between perception and reality. What concern me here, though, are his many miscues regarding race. For instance, late in the novel after Pym and Dirk Peters have survived the Tsalalians' attack on the crew of the *Jane Guy*, Pym refers to himself and Peters as "the only living white men upon the island"(1156). However, until this point in the narrative, Pym had identified Peters as a "half-breed Indian" (1007). Upon their meeting, Pym describes Peters by emphasizing what he perceives as Peters's monstrous physical characteristics: "Peters himself was one of the most purely ferocious-looking men I ever beheld" (1043). He describes Peters in racialist terms, among other things noting that Peters's "head was . . . deformed, being of immense size, with an indentation on the crown (like that on the head of most negroes), and entirely bald" (1043). This description reflects how racial science categorized physical difference according to racial type, thus signaling Pym's assumption of such an outlook. Furthermore, while appealing to his audience to believe his story in the preface, Pym equates Peters's racial status with an inability to attest to the narrative's veracity:

> the incidents to be narrated were of a nature so positively marvelous, that, unsupported as my assertions must necessarily be (except by the evidence of a single individual, and he a half-breed Indian), I could only hope for belief among my family, and those of my friends who have had reason, through life, to put faith in my veracity—the probability being that the public at large would regard what I should put forth as merely an impudent and ingenious fiction. (1007)

This passage suggests Pym's sense that his audience might not trust Peters's authority, a notion reflecting how antebellum Southern society did not grant disenfranchised racial groups the right, for instance, to bear witness in court. These passages reveal Pym's understanding of Peters as racially distinct from Pym himself, making his later reference to Peters as white curious.

J. V. Ridgely and Iola S. Haverstick argue that Peters's changing racial status owes to an error on Poe's part.[16] However, ascribing Pym's mistake to Poe's design more satisfactorily addresses the issue. As Evelyn J. Hinz and Dana D. Nelson both point out, Pym refers to Peters as white at the precise moment that the Tsalalians most endanger him. We can, therefore, conclude that Pym does so not because of a mistake by Poe but, rather, because Pym needs an ally who is less racially threatening than the Tsalalians.[17] Poe, here, destabilizes the essentialist racist interpretative framework Pym exercises throughout the novel by revealing how Pym and, by extension, Poe's audience base their readings of race not, as they purport, on essential biological categories but rather on contingencies. Consider the similarities between Pym's move to do so to that of one constituency in Poe's audience: just as Pym understands Peters as a savage "half-breed Indian" while on the *Grampus* but as his fellow white man when the Tsalalians endanger the safety of the two sailors, so too did proslavery thinkers move from arguing that environmental factors led to the inferiority of the African race to a belief in racial essentialism when confronted with the pressures of abolitionism. Poe thus points up the inconsistencies evident in the supposedly stable racist epistemological foundations of his readers.

Poe further emphasizes Pym's assumption of a racist interpretative framework through the novel's generic characteristics, particularly the exploration narrative of the second half.[18] It is common knowledge that Poe excerpted portions of the novel from South Seas exploration narratives. He perhaps, in part, sought to cash in on a popular genre. However, we may just as well here see Poe as using the exploration genre to elaborate further on the epistemological apparatus assumed by Pym. Exploration narratives purported to relate the discovery of the uncharted, but they tended to make sense of that material through classification. When it came to describing formerly unknown peoples, they resorted to a proto-anthropological discourse reliant on the language of hierarchical difference essential to white supremacy. The scientific, classificatory nature of Pym's narration during this portion of the novel demonstrates his investment in the exploration narrative's categorizing impulse. Poe thus develops Pym's assumption of an epistemological outlook that conceives of difference as natural and scientifically grounded by suggesting that Pym sees the world through the lens of the exploration narrative. What is more, that this genre was so widely popular at the time should alert us not only to Poe's attempt to cash in, but rather to his subversive association of Pym with the readerships Poe wished to satirize, as the exploration narrative's popularity suggests its readers' attachment to its manner of understanding difference. Poe here takes a jab at readers who looked to exploration narratives for models for understanding race, perhaps particularly Northern readers whose understanding of difference owed more to such texts than to personal experience interacting with people of color.

As in his inconsistent identifications of Peters, Pym's assumption of a racist interpretative framework does not guide him well in his interactions with the black Tsalalians. Upon meeting them, Pym and the *Jane Guy*'s crewmen immediately understand these natives as radically different. What Pym perceives as their singular and foolish behavior first arrests his attention. First of all, he denies that these people possess linguistic capacity, claiming after initial attempts at conversation that "it was clear they intended their jabbering for" language (1136). Moreover, he perplexedly notes that they appear, for no apparent reason, to fear a number of random objects (1137). Finally, by their actions around the ship's guns, Pym judges: "I do not believe that they had the least suspicion of their actual use, but rather took them for idols, seeing the care we had of them, and the attention with which we watched their movements while handling them. At the great gun their wonder was redoubled" (1138). Pym takes these indications of ignorance to signify the natives' racial inferiority.

Pym's sense of the incomprehensibility of the natives' actions, however, rests on another misunderstanding: Pym believes that "it was quite evident that they had never before seen any of the white race" (1137). This assumption, in fact, may be mistaken, as the behavior patterns Pym notes make more sense if we accept that the Tsalalians had, in fact, previously come into contact with whites before the *Jane Guy*'s arrival.[19] The objects that the natives recoil from, which include sails, eggs, a pan of flour, and the sailors themselves, "from whose complexion, indeed, they appeared to recoil" (1137), are all white, which suggests that the natives have an aversion to whiteness. Nelson claims that this aversion stems from prior experience with whites, that "Pym's account suggests that the Tsalalians were never duped by the crew, but rather acted on their knowledge of the use of firearms *and* the crewmen's sense of security with them in order to trick them into their deaths."[20] This view proves attractive on multiple levels. First of all, Nelson's reading compellingly explains the natives' motive for destroying the crew: they have experienced white colonial perfidy and know how to deal with it. The natives' revulsion at the sight of whiteness, in other words, stems from conscious, provoked hatred. Their interest in the ship's weaponry, which Pym interprets as dumb wonder, especially indicates the natives' feelings of antagonism toward the crew, as this interest suggests prior experience of warfare with gun-wielding whites. What is more, Nelson's claim that Pym misjudges the Tsalalians' actions coheres with the general pattern of misunderstanding that I have been identifying in Pym's behavior. As Pym misinterprets his experiences many times throughout the novel, it makes sense that he does so here as well, especially considering the other evidence present that indicates the natives have seen whites before.

In these passages, Pym assumes an essentialist apparatus much like that of racial science on which to base his understanding of others, much as did Poe's readers. Although racial science purported to explain behavior and capacities by racial classification, Pym's possession of this interpretative framework fails him as he tries to predict the behavior of the Tsalalians, just as it had failed him in his understanding of Peters. The supposedly solid epistemological foundation upon which Pym purports to understand his experience of race does not protect him from inconsistently identifying Peters as a "half-breed Indian" or from misunderstanding the Tsalalians and not foreseeing their attack. If Pym is in fact a stand-in for Poe's readership—and the facts that Poe despised his readers for their lack of interpretative and judgmental skills, that Pym displays the same characteristics, and that both share similar understandings of race strongly argue that he is—then Poe's representation of the Tsalalian episodes suggests that the assumptions governing his readers' understanding of race are dangerously mistaken. Through its hoaxical characteristics, therefore, *Pym* here indicts the folly of a society seeing as natural and essential that which is actually contingent and discursively conditioned.

To further emphasize the faulty nature of the interpretative frameworks that lead to Pym's misreadings, Poe shows how anyone can take on "savage" traits given the circumstances. The novel represents several instances of whites reverting to the savagery they attribute to people of color. The most memorable such instance is probably Pym's, Augustus's, Peters's, and Parker's resort to cannibalism while stranded upon the hulk of the *Grampus*. In this passage, cannibalism—an archetypal form of savagery viewed as taboo by Western civilization—becomes something one assumes when the circumstances require it and not, as racial science would have it, a predilection naturally inhering in people of color. Another significant instance of whites resorting to savagery occurs during the Tsalal episode, when Pym revels in the mass destruction of the Tsalalians when the *Ariel* explodes. The pleasure Pym indulges in during this passage, in which the "full and perfect fruits" suffered by the Tsalalians exceed his "utmost expectations" (1161), does not exhibit the equanimity supposedly natural for a white man but rather the love of revenge Poe's culture often attributed to people of color.[21] Moreover, unlike in the cannibalism passage, Pym here significantly does not indulge in vengeance to survive. The feeling does not occur in response to an extraordinary necessity but rather comes naturally to him; Poe thus suggests that not only is it possible for whites to resort to savagery when circumstances demand it, but that they may also do so when it is not necessary. Through these passages, Poe further shows the faultiness of the interpretative framework of Pym and Poe's audience by demonstrating that their cherished typologies are not essential but rather contingent, that, so to speak, white does not necessarily signify white and black is not always black.

Further playing on the faultiness of racist interpretative frameworks, Poe finally condemns Pym and, by extension, the public Pym represents by revealing the dire consequences of Pym's misreadings of race. *Pym* features two such disasters. These conclude the novel's two major structural divisions—Pym's and Augustus's voyage on the *Grampus* and Pym and Peters's voyage on the *Jane Guy*—and should thus be seen as significant. In the former, Pym and Peters find themselves lost at sea and close to death upon the remains of the *Grampus* after having survived a battle with a gang of mutineers. Kennedy argues that this mutiny alludes to white fears of revolt against society's capitalist and slave-holding bedrock; for Kennedy, the ship's proprietors represent capitalists and slaveholders, while the mutineers, one of whom is significantly black, represent the subversive element.[22] Kennedy proceeds to claim that Pym's, Augustus's, and Peters's countermutiny represents the restoration of the capitalist and slaveholding order. However, their victory is not complete: "By killing the black cook and the rest of the rebellious crew to protect an implicit theory of capital and property, if not maritime slavery, Peters and his confederates (a word I use deliberately, if anachronistically) achieve a hollow victory, for the *Grampus* has become a worthless wreck."[23] For Kennedy, while Pym and other characters in the novel propound a capitalist, instrumentalist attitude toward people of color, Poe represents their enterprise as a failure and thus questions the efficacy of their ideologies. As Pym serves as a surrogate reader, we can conclude that Poe also questions his readers' faith in such ideologies. The countermutiny and the white-supremacist enterprise it represents, Poe claims here, may grant Pym and by extension the society he represents temporary power over blacks, but such victories will prove Pyrrhic in the wake of the social crises embodied in Pym's, Peters's, and Augustus's trials. Racist ideology is here lost at sea and thus an ineffective guide for an unstable society.

The second disaster occurs when most of the *Jane Guy*'s crew dies at the Tsalalians' hands following the misunderstanding between the two groups. If, as Nelson claims, Pym errs in believing the Tsalalians have never seen colonialist whites before, then the slaughter of the sailors results from their inability to recognize the Tsalalians' hatred for the whites and consequent scheme to destroy them. In other words, if Pym and the crewmen had correctly read the signs, they would have managed to predict the Tsalalians' actions and perhaps would have saved themselves. Nelson argues that her reading attests to the blindness of white colonialist knowledge, that the crew's assurance in the stability of its racial codes and hierarchies was misplaced. This erroneous self-understanding, for Nelson, leads to a breakdown in white-black colonial relations on Tsalal. I add that in positing Pym as a stand-in for his readers, Poe suggests that the U.S. society that trusts in the stability of racist organizing principles places its belief in dangerously shaky systems that are close to collapse, built as they are upon an understanding of race that does not lead to predictable results. In this sense, traditional readings that see this part of the novel as projecting fears of black rebellion[24] are partly correct in that *Pym* does express anxiety over societal upheaval in a slave-holding region. However, such readings only get it partly right, as this anxiety about slave revolt results as much from the text's sense of racist ideology's uncertain efficacy as it does from a racist belief in the treacherous nature of blacks.

We can read the narrative proper's final image, that of a shrouded white figure awaiting Pym, Peters, and their recently deceased captive Tsalalian Nu-Nu, in terms of Poe's satirical mockery of racist thinking. The apparent symbolism of this memorable, cryptic image has long puzzled readers and has provoked countless responses from critics.[25] The attention is well warranted, as Poe's aesthetics appreciated images' symbolistically evocative character and capacity to unify effect.[26] We should thus attend to how this image works in terms of *Pym*'s satire. We can read the image as Poe's rendering of Pym's assumption of whiteness as an epistemological organizing principle, a fantasy Poe wishes to mock in the readers Pym represents. As we have seen, Pym's adherence to this principle leads him into trouble many times throughout the novel. Here, Poe shows how this mode of action leads to confusion and uncertainty, the very things whiteness is meant to contain. The image quite literally terminates the narrative proper, leaving the reader with an obscure editorial note from "Mr. Poe." If we read the narrative as Pym's attempt to make sense of his experience and recognize, as we have seen in other instances, that whiteness and the racist epistemological apparatus it organizes are central to how Pym makes sense of the world, then we strikingly find that when Pym confronts an image of monolithic whiteness, he finds himself unable to continue constructing narrative and thus to make any further sense of his experience. His confrontation with the white figure, quite literally, leaves him incapable of rendering experience meaningful, a paradoxical turn of events in that the figure is, as it were, a rendering of that which he had relied upon to structure experience.[27] Here again, Poe shows how his audience's racist epistemology leads to breakdown rather than the certainty it purports to provide. Indeed, whiteness here leads to the utter absence of meaning.

Poe develops this idea in the novel's concluding note, in which the editor reports on Pym's recent death and the confusion the end of the narrative has surely produced in the reader and then attempts to decipher the hieroglyphics Pym and Peters had observed in a cavern on Tsalal. As Paul John Eakin observes, the general purport of this note is to tie up all the loose threads produced by the bizarre, abrupt end of the narrative proper.[28] In this sense, the editor's philological explanation of the hieroglyphics as signifying "to be shady," "to be white," and "the region of the south" (1181)—all significations suggesting the concept of racial difference in that they point to the South and its pro-slavery concerns—serve to do more than simply explain the hieroglyphics. They also point to how we should interpret the narrative's cryptic final image. As that image signifies a breakdown in Pym's assumption of whiteness as an organizing principle, the philological explanations tie up the confusion created by that breakdown by confirming that difference was indeed what was at stake in the strange moment. In this sense, they make sure the reader knows what she or he should have already realized, that Pym's understanding of the relationship between whiteness and blackness and his association with racist thinking are among his most salient characteristics and are at the heart of what Poe's text is satirizing.

I have argued that *The Narrative of Arthur Gordon Pym* satirizes racist beliefs by representing Arthur Gordon Pym as a misreader of race. As Pym serves as a surrogate reader, Poe's mockery of Pym constitutes mockery of the readership Pym represents. Therefore, while in many ways *Pym* exhibits the average racism that Whalen identifies as typical of antebellum literary production, it at the same time questions racism. Should we read Poe's satire on racist epistemologies as a prototype of the extreme deconstruction of identity practiced by cultural critics in recent years? Consider, for example, the words of Paul Gilroy:

> The "postracial" stance I have been trying to develop does not admit the integrity of any avowedly natural perceptual schemes. It does not concede the possibility that "race" could be seen spontaneously, unmediated by technical and social processes. There will be individual variation, but that is not "race." There is no raw, untrained perception dwelling in the body. The human sensorium has had to be educated to the appreciation of racial differences. When it comes to the visualization of discrete racial groups, a great deal of fine-tuning has been required.[29]

Considering Poe's concessions to racism, it would be impossible to confuse Poe with Gilroy. That said, there are significant resonances between the two authors' awareness of the contingent character of racial identification. The issue is an intriguing one that requires further investigation into the precise qualities of Poe's position on race as it relates to his thought and historical context. This chapter, for now, shows that Poe scholars must recognize the complexity of the stance Poe expresses on these issues in *Pym*. Far from simply being a racist statement or an ahistorical text in its concern either for the metaphysical or for placating an audience that might be alienated by historically specific polemics, *Pym* exhibits a multifaceted response to the time's issues that includes a critique of racism that could be said to be, like its author, visionary.

NOTES

I would like to thank Jeffrey Allen Tucker, the audience at my panel at the Poe Bicentennial Conference, and the anonymous reviewers for this volume for their invaluable suggestions on earlier versions of this chapter. I would also like to thank the University of Rochester's Frederick Douglass Institute and Susan Jaffe Tane for funding my trip to the conference.

1. See Toni Morrison, *Playing in the Dark: Whiteness and the Literary Imagination* (New York: Vintage, 1993).

2. For critiques of ahistoricist approaches, see John Carlos Rowe, "Poe, Antebellum Slavery, and Modern Criticism," *Poe's " Pym": Critical Explorations*, ed. Richard Kopley (Durham, NC: Duke University Press, 1992), 117–38; Dana D. Nelson, *The Word in Black and White: Reading "Race" in American Literature, 1638–1867* (New York: Oxford University Press, 1992), esp. 108.

3. Such critics note similarities between Poe's representation of blackness and proslavery tropes. Identifying one such trope, George M. Frederickson (*The Black Image in the White Mind: The Debate on Afro-American Character and Destiny*, 1817–1914 [1971; Middletown, CT: Wesleyan University Press, 1987], 54–55) writes that proslavery ideologues posited that Africans were at heart savages who needed to be tamed by white masters. In this context, Sam Worley ("*The Narrative of Arthur Gordon Pym* and the Ideology of Slavery," *Emerson Society Quarterly* 40, no. 3 [1994]: 230) sees Poe's representation of the Tsalalians as ostensibly faithful servants who in fact have devious intentions as Poe's tacit approval of the views described by Frederickson; the Tsalalians, in effect, have not been fully tamed. For analysis of additional such convergences, see, for example, Sidney Kaplan, introduction to Edgar Allan Poe's *The Narrative of Arthur Gordon Pym* (New York: Hill & Wang, 1960), xxv; A. Robert Lee, *Gothic to Multicultural: Idioms of Imagining in American Literary Fiction* (New York: Rodopi, 2009), 77; Eric Mottram, "Poe's *Pym* and the American Social Imagination," in *Artful Thunder: Versions of the American Romantic Tradition; in Honor of Howard P. Vincent*, ed. Robert J. DeMott and Sanford E. Marovitz (Kent, OH: Kent State University Press, 1975), 48; and J. V. Ridgely, "Tragical-Mythical-Satirical-Hoaxical: Problems of Genre in *Pym*," *American Transcendental Quarterly* 24, no. 1 (1974): 5.

4. For instance, although he points out the novel's debt to proslavery discourse, Worley ("*The Narrative of Arthur Gordon Pym* and the Ideology of Slavery," 242) cautions that "the most plausible interpretation of the relationship between *Pym* and the pro-slavery argument would situate Poe within the discourse of pro-slavery without seeing *Pym* as in any simple sense determined by it." Worley and others have noted intricacies in *Pym* revealing that the novel is not easily complicit with racist or proslavery ideas. For instance, Nelson (*The Word in Black and White*, 90–108) claims that Pym's inability to recognize the Tsalalian's revulsion to

whiteness reveals a critique (not necessarily intentional) of the fallibility of colonialist knowledge. Shaindy Rudoff ("Written in Stone: Slavery and Authority in *The Narrative of Arthur Gordon Pym*," *American Transcendental Quarterly*, n.s., 14, no. 1 [2000]: 77) argues that in *Pym* Poe questions the notion that slavery is divinely ordained. In such analyses, *Pym* exhibits racism's reliance on deceptive, simplistic categories of difference and hierarchy.

5. In addition to being scanty, the material attesting to Poe's views on slavery points to somewhat complex conclusions. It is true that much evidence indicates that Poe held characteristically Southern, proslavery views. These indications have lent credence to the idea that Poe encoded his literary works with proslavery arguments. The most powerful such indication has been the oft-held belief that Poe anonymously authored a favorable 1836 review of two proslavery works (*Slavery in the United States*, by James Kirke Paulding, and *The South Vindicated from the Treason and Fanaticism of the Northern Abolitionists*, by William Drayton; *Southern Literary Messenger* [April 1836]: 336–39). However, recently Terence Whalen (*Edgar Allan Poe and the Masses: The Political Economy of Literature in Antebellum America* [Princeton, NJ: Princeton University Press, 1999]) has compellingly attributed authorship to William and Mary professor and Southern apologist Beverly Tucker. Opinion has long been divided on this question. William Doyle Hull II ("A Canon of the Critical Works of Edgar Allan Poe with a Study of Poe as Editor and Reviewer" [PhD diss., University of Virginia, 1941], Proquest [AAT DP15043]) attributes the review to Tucker on evidence of a letter from Poe to Tucker. Bernard Rosenthal ("Poe, Slavery, and the *Southern Literary Messenger*: A Reexamination," *Poe Studies* 7, no. 2 (1974): 29–38), however, speculated against this position. Many recent scholars, among them Nelson (*The Word in Black and White*, 90–92) and Joan Dayan ("Romance and Race," in *The Columbia History of the American Novel*, ed. Emory Elliott [New York: Columbia University Press, 1991], 96) find Rosenthal's claims convincing, while others, such as J. V. Ridgely ("The Authorship of the 'Paulding-Drayton Review,'" *Poe Studies Association Newsletter* 20, no. 2 [1992]: 1–3) and J. Gerald Kennedy ("'Trust No Man': Poe, Douglass, and the Culture of Slavery," in *Romancing the Shadow: Poe and Race*, ed. J. Gerald Kennedy and Liliane Weissberg [Oxford: Oxford University Press, 2004], 225–58), have, like Whalen, questioned Rosenthal. Other such evidence includes Poe's 19 March 1827 estrangement letter to John Allan, in which an indignant Poe complains, "You suffer me to be subjected to the whims & caprice, not only of your white family, but the complete authority of the blacks—these grievances I could not submit to; and I am gone" (*The Letters of Edgar Allan Poe*, ed. John Ostrom [Cambridge, MA: Harvard University Press, 1948], 1:8). Many have taken Poe's suggestion here that disrespect from blacks is the ultimate insult to indicate Poe's racism. On the other hand, some evidence suggests that Poe's views on race and slavery were more complex than meets the eye. In his review of *The South-West. By a Yankee*, by Joseph Holt Ingraham (*Southern Literary Messenger*, January 1836), Poe laments that many Northerners (Ingraham excluded) "pervert [the South's] misfortunes into crimes—or distort its necessities into sins of volition" (122). Although this review documents Poe's appeals to racist, proslavery views, Poe at the same time expresses ambivalence here, characterizing slavery as a necessary evil rather than as the positive good more virulent apologists would have it be.

6. Whalen, *Edgar Allan Poe and the Masses*, 111–12.

7. Cited in Arthur Hobson Quinn, *Edgar Allan Poe: A Critical Biography* (New York: D. Appleton-Century, 1941), 250.

8. Letter reproduced in Quinn, *Edgar Allan Poe*, 250–51.

9. J. Gerald Kennedy, "The Invisible Message: The Problem of Truth in *Pym*," in *The Naiad Voice: Essays on Poe's Satiric Hoaxing*, ed. Dennis W. Eddings (Port Washington, NY: Associated Faculty Press, 1983), 126. On *Pym*'s publication history, see further Kenneth Silverman, *Edgar A. Poe: Mournful and Never-Ending Remembrance* (New York: HarperCollins, 1991), 132. On Poe's distaste for his readers, see further Lee, *Gothic to Multicultural*, 61–81; Terence Martin, "The Imagination at Play: Edgar Allan Poe," *Kenyon Review* 28 (1966): 195. On Poe's objection to the novel form, see the "The Philosophy of Composition," 1846, in *Poe: Poetry, Tales, and Selected Essays* (New York: Library of America, 1984), 1373–1385.

10. On responses to *Pym*, see Burton R. Pollin, "Poe's *Narrative of Arthur Gordon Pym* and the Contemporary Reviewers," *Studies in American Fiction* 2 (1974): 37–56, and Pollin, "Poe

Viewed and Reviewed: An Annotated Checklist of Contemporary Notices," *Poe Studies* 11 (1980): 17–28.

11. Poe, *The Narrative of Arthur Gordon Pym of Nantucket*, 1838, in *Poe: Poetry, Tales, and Selected Essays* (New York: Library of America, 1984), 1007–1008. Further references to *Pym* are from this edition and are noted parenthetically in the text.

12. See Kennedy, "Invisible Message," 127, on the irony in this passage.

13. See Kennedy, "Invisible Message," 132, on Pym's kinship to Poe's readers.

14. For instance, Edward H. Davidson (*Poe: A Critical Study* [Cambridge, MA: Belknap, 1957], 169) reads the theme as suggesting Poe's interest in philosophical skepticism. On deception in *Pym*, see further J. Gerald Kennedy, "*Pym* Pourri: Decomposing the Textual Body," in *Poe's "Pym": Critical Explorations*, ed. Richard Kopley (Durham, NC: Duke University Press, 1992), esp. 172–73; David Ketterer, "Devious Voyage: The Singular *Narrative of Arthur Gordon Pym*," *American Transcendental Quarterly* 37 (1978): 21–33; and Ketterer, *The Rationale of Deception in Poe* (Baton Rouge: Louisiana State University Press, 1979), esp. 134.

15. In the *Ariel* passage, Pym fails to recognize Augustus's inebriation until the two are upon the seas and it is too late, even though his friend's behavior evidences every stereotypical mark of drunkenness. Predictably, the voyage is nearly fatal. In the *Grampus* passages, Pym and his companions eye an approaching ship with a man on it who ostensibly smiles and waves at them. Thinking that this ship can provide them succor, the men aboard the *Grampus* frantically call out to the vessel. However, as it comes near it assaults them with a horrid smell. The men soon discover that the ship's passengers are dead and decaying; the smiling, waving man only appeared to smile because a gull had eaten the flesh around his mouth and to wave because his body was bobbing with the waves. Thus, instead of helping the *Grampus*, the ship becomes a horrific harbinger of its own possible fate. Pym's words in this passage reveal the depths of his misreading: "I relate these things and circumstances minutely, and I relate them, it must be understood, precisely as they *appeared* to us" (*Pym*, 1085). For the misperceiving Pym, here, perception is an illusion that drastically and tragically diverges from reality.

16. J. V. Ridgely and Iola S. Haverstick ("Chartless Voyage: The Many Narratives of A. Gordon Pym," *Texas Studies in Language and Literature* 7 [1966]: 73) view this inconsistency as one of several that owe to the work being written in separate stages.

17. Evelyn J. Hinz, "'Tekeli-li': *The Narrative of Arthur Gordon Pym* as Satire," *Genre* 3 (1970): 397; Nelson, *The Word in Black and White*, 100–101.

18. For a useful overview of genre and *Pym*, see Ridgely, "Tragical-Mythical-Satirical-Hoaxical."

19. See Nelson, *The Word in Black and White*, 98.

20. *The Word in Black and White*, 100. As opposed to prior experience with whites, Kennedy suggests that the natives' reaction to whiteness owes to a taboo or experience of the uncanny upon viewing the sailors ("'Trust No Man,'" 251). For reasons I discuss momentarily, I find his view less attractive than Nelson's, but it is telling on the significance of race to the novel.

21. Consider that James Fenimore Cooper's Hawk-eye describes revenge as "an Indian feeling" (*The Last of the Mohicans: A Narrative of 1757*, ed. James A. Sappenfield and E. N. Feltskog [1826; Albany: State University of New York Press, 1983], 183) and that the anonymously authored "About Niggers"—although perhaps with some irony—claimed that blacks have "terrible capacities for revenge and hatred" (*Putnam's Monthly Magazine of American Literature, Science, and Art* 6, no. 36 [1855]: 612). Such views were not unusual. In fact, these two texts were relatively sympathetic to minorities. More virulent positions could go farther.

22. "Trust No Man," 246.

23. Ibid.

24. See, for example, Leslie Fiedler, *Love and Death in the American Novel* (1960; Normal, IL: Dalkey Archive Press, 1997), for whom "*Pym* projects on its Negroes the fear of black rebellion" (397).

25. See, for example, Paul John Eakin, "Poe's Sense of an Ending," *American Literature* 45, no. 1 (1973): 1–22; Stephen Mainville, "Language and the Void: Gothic Landscapes in the Frontiers of Edgar Allan Poe," *Genre* 14, no. 3 (1981): 347–62; and Joseph J. Moldenhauer,

"Imagination and Perversity in *The Narrative of Arthur Gordon Pym*," *Texas Studies in Language and Literature* 13, no. 2 (1971): 267–80.

26. See here Eakin, "Poe's Sense of an Ending": as Poe describes the process of capturing consciousness, "a basic plot for the pursuit of such knowledge begins to emerge: a movement of approach and entry, in his claim that he can make this special state of consciousness supervene; and a moment of withdrawal and return, in his claim that he can startle himself from this 'condition' into wakefulness in order to effect its transfer into conscious memory. . . . The moment of revelation itself, that is, the climax of the plot, can be but 'an appreciable *point* of time,' and hence it is rather in terms of an image than as some paraphrase or other exposition that its content can be rendered" (2–3). Note the importance of the image, the "appreciable *point* of time," for narrative function here.

27. In this sense, readings such as that of Moldenhauer ("Imagination and Perversity in *The Narrative of Arthur Gordon Pym*," 278), who views Pym's confrontation with the white figure as the final step in Pym's perverse desire for oblivion, intuit the import of the image. However, they fail to note its imbrications in the novel's interrogation of race as an interpretative basis.

28. Eakin, "Poe's Sense of an Ending," 16.

29. Paul Gilroy, *Against Race: Imagining Political Culture beyond the Color Line* (Cambridge, MA: Belknap, 2000), 42.

Chapter Eleven

Moving Daguerreotypes and Myths of Reproduction

Poe's Body

Lauren Curtright

In his address to the Edgar Allan Poe Society of Baltimore at the society's meeting to mark the centennial of the death of its eponymous author, Allen Tate reminisced about reading his family's works of Poe. He attributed his favoritism for one of these volumes to its resonance with his own precocious ambitions: "In this volume I am sure, for I read it more than the others, was the well-known, desperate, and asymmetrical photograph, which I gazed at by the hour and which I hoped that I should some day resemble."[1] Given that, according to Tate, this set of Poe's works contained the signature of Tate's great-grandfather, who died in 1870, it was probably Rufus Wilmot Griswold's *The Works of the Late Edgar Allan Poe* (1850–1856). Notwithstanding Tate's confidence in his memory, it must be fictitious, because the publishing industry did not use photogravure until the 1880s.

Tate's memory passes as legitimate because it participates in a longstanding tradition of looking to Poe's photographic record to re-view Poe.[2] Tate's misremembered "photograph" matches the *Ultima Thule*, "one of the most celebrated literary portraits of the nineteenth century."[3] Tate recalls the *Ultima Thule* to introduce his argument that Poe's writings are important, despite their "blemishes," or marks of Poe's "provincialism of judgment and lack of knowledge."[4] Tate thus appeals to photography to redeem Poe from Griswold's scathing verbal portraits of the author, in Griswold's infamous obituary of Poe and preface to the aforementioned edition of Poe's works—portraits that long influenced Poe's reception in the United States. Like the title of his lecture, "Our Cousin, Mr. Poe," Tate's substitution of the *Ultima*

Thule for what was probably John Sartain's mezzotint engraving of Poe based on a circa-1845 oil painting by Samuel Osgood illuminates Tate's investment in Poe's legacy. For Tate, positioning Poe within a lineage of renowned American writers required establishing Poe's cousinship with Tate himself and his audience. As an index, a photograph seems a more reliable indicator of genealogy than a painting.

I link Tate's manipulation of the *Ultima Thule* to a prior modernist instance of remaking Poe through mechanical reproductions of Poe's body. The earlier instance comprises two adaptations of images of Poe, one by the literary scholar George Edward Woodberry and the other by the journalist Thomas Dimmock, both of which appeared in the *Century Magazine* around 1895. Their sources are Poe's last two daguerreotypes, taken just weeks before Poe's death—the *Traylor* and the *Thompson*—and one of the *Thompson*'s progeny, a daguerreotyped copy of the *Thompson* named the *Players Club*. Taken together, Woodberry's and Dimmock's adaptations of Poe offered readers of *Century* a means to both fix and fixate on social categories in the face of epistemological and technological change.

INSTANT POE

The altered "mode of perception" that Walter Benjamin attributes to the invention of photography, coupled with the fact that the *Thompson* and the *Traylor* were taken so close in time to Poe's death, inspired reanimations of these daguerreotypes of Poe in an effort to remake Poe's image at the turn of the twentieth century.[5] Literary critic Thomas Carlson claims that a "counterpoint" to the "Griswoldian" image of Poe had been established in the United States by 1900 and that American silent films of this period extended this counterpoint by producing "a view of Poe as brilliant victim."[6] Thus Poe's remaking, which made it possible for him "to join the first rank of American writers," relied as much on moving images as on their still counterparts.[7] However, when D. W. Griffith committed to Poe's reanimation as "a familiar and recognizably beset citizen of early twentieth-century America" with his short biopic *Edgar Allen* [sic] *Poe* and his feature-length film *The Avenging Conscience; or, 'Thou Shalt Not Kill'* (1914), Poe's credence was already tied to photographic renderings of Poe's body.[8]

Poe's alignment with photography seems logical because, like Poe's oeuvre, indexical media are often associated with the supernatural. The discourse on photography envisions this medium as magical, as well as veracious, and endows it with mystery. If the sordid, fantastic, or—to borrow one of Poe's key words—*outré* qualities of the dramas of daguerreotypes of Poe that I present here complement Poe's writings, then they also characterize photography as a quintessentially gothic medium. However, the gothic fea-

Moving Daguerreotypes and Myths of Reproduction 123

Figure 11.1. William Abbott Pratt produced the Traylor daguerreotype in his studio in Richmond, Virginia in 1849. This image of the damaged *Traylor* is reproduced with permission of the Poe Museum.

Figure 11.2. William Abbott Pratt produced the Thompson daguerreotype in his studio in Richmond, Virginia in 1849. The Thompson belongs to the Edgar Allan Poe Collection, Rare Book and Manuscript Library, Columbia University. This image of the *Thompson* is reproduced with the Rare Book and Manuscript Library's permission.

Figure 11.3. William Abbott Pratt produced the *Players Club* daguerreotype, a copy of the *Thompson* daguerreotype, for Thomas Dimmock in Pratt's studio in Richmond, Virginia circa 1855. The *Players Club* daguerreotype belongs to Susan Jaffe Tane. The image here is reproduced with her permission.

tures of daguerreotypes of Poe are also modernist if we define modernism by the epistemological shift that occurred between the nineteenth and twentieth centuries, evident in such diverse arenas as physiology, philosophy, physics, sociology, linguistics, and modernist painting, in which, as Mary Ann Doane argues, reality came to be explained by laws of probability. Doane claims that, during this period, belief in chance grew with modernity because chance makes newness possible; however, chance requires presence. A move away from referentiality eroded confidence in presence, which led to fascination with the possibility of representing the instant. Especially problematic to turn-of-the-century epistemology was the theory of the afterimage, which came to dominate physiological explanations of how spectators perceive motion in film. According to this theory, the image in one frame appears to run into the next because spectators' retinas retain images, creating the illusion of motion and the sense of a continuum between past and present on screen. While the theory of the afterimage helps explain how cinema achieves its effects, it also heightens anxiety about human access to the real; hence "the desire for instantaneity emerges as a guarantee of a grounded referentiality."[9] In response to this anxiety, "photography and the cinema produce the sense of a present moment laden with historicity at the same time that they encourage a belief in our access to pure presence, instantaneity."[10] In their resolute insistence on the power of chance, narratives about the creation, reproduction, and circulation of the last daguerreotypes of Poe assert that these images capture their referent, Poe, in one of his last instants.

While set in the antebellum United States, the story of the final reproductions of the living Poe has its origins in the modernist period: it first appeared in print in Dimmock's 1895 letter to *Century*—a letter titled "Notes on Poe." Despite the actual capacities of the earliest photographic technology, in the same year as film debuts, Dimmock reanimates Poe as an important figure of American letters by presenting a cinematic view of his daguerreotype of Poe. The length of exposure that a daguerreotype requires depends on a number of factors, including devices (e.g., lenses and reflectors) used to produce the (reversed) image inside the *camera obscura*, atmospheric conditions, available light, and chemicals applied to the plate to fix the image. Consequently, the sitting time for a daguerreotype varies according to the times of day and year and the distance from the equator at which the image is made. Still, we know that Poe would have had to sit for many instants while having his "likeness" made in William Abbott Pratt's studio in Richmond, Virginia, in 1849—a sitting that produced two daguerreotypes, which were later named the *Thompson* and the *Traylor*. Regardless, "Notes on Poe" imbues one of these last daguerreotypes of Poe with instantaneity by suggesting that Pratt captured Poe candidly and in motion with his camera. Dimmock, thereby, constructs what Doane calls "a present moment laden with historicity" by giving the impression that the original (the *Thompson*) of Dimmock's daguerreotyped copy of Poe (the *Players Club*) and, indeed, Poe himself are accessible through their reproductions.[11] At a moment when referentiality is in crisis, Dimmock presents his daguerreotype of Poe as an index of its subject—as facilitating the invasion of the present by the past—to reassure his readers that it reproduces the "real" Poe and to validate his own perceptions of Poe crystallized during investigations in Richmond and Baltimore decades before writing his letter to *Century*.

THE FACTS IN THE CASE

Recognizing that a story of origins is antithetical to theorizing reproductions, I am nonetheless compelled to locate another beginning in my analysis of adaptations of Poe: Poe's ending. Although the mystery of Poe's death has long been a favorite topic of Poe aficionados and detractors alike, the equally intriguing stories of the image-objects closely associated with his death have escaped a full investigation. Less than one month before Poe died in Baltimore, Pratt—a daguerreotypist, engineer, and Gothic Revivalist architect—encountered Poe on the street outside Pratt's studio in Richmond, which Pratt soon thereafter named the Virginia Sky Light Daguerrean Gallery at the Sign of the Gothic Window. Against Poe's mild protest that he was not properly dressed to be daguerreotyped, Pratt convinced Poe to come upstairs and sit for what became Poe's final mark on what Poe describes as "the beautiful art of photogeny."[12] Or so Dimmock's story goes in "Notes on Poe."

Exhibited in Pratt's street-level display case until he sold his studio in 1856; presented to John Reuben Thompson, editor of the *Southern Literary Messenger*, who loaned his daguerreotype of Poe to "a number of artists and photographers" for reproduction; and subsequently passed through the hands of a series of inheritors, the *Thompson* is now securely contained in Columbia University's Rare Book and Manuscript Library.[13] Its variant, however, met a dramatic end. Deas speculates that, to the devastation of its namesake and owner at the time (Robert Lee Traylor), the *Traylor* was completely destroyed after it "was damaged beyond repair" when Chicago publishers Stone & Kimball attempted to clean the plate in preparing to reproduce the image as the frontispiece to Woodberry and Edmund Clarence Stedman's *The Works of Edgar Allan Poe* in 1894.[14]

As for the indeterminate number of copies of the *Thompson*, one not only survived the nineteenth century but also made news recently in print, on television, and on the Internet. On October 17, 2006, the *Players Club* was auctioned at Sotheby's in New York for $150,000. Occurring less than a year after its recovery by the FBI, the *Players Club*'s sale benefited its late owner, the Hampden Booth Theatre Library. Sometime after 1981, the *Players Club* went missing from Hampden Booth. It resurfaced in 2004, when one Sally Guest, unaware of the object's provenance, purchased it for $96 from an "antique/junk shop" in Walnut, Iowa.[15] Guest appeared with the *Players Club* on an episode of PBS's *Antiques Roadshow* in early 2005. After displaying it on her mantle for over a year, Guest decided to sell it and contacted the Poe Society to authenticate it. By its signature scratch across the image of Poe's face, Deas, whom the Society consulted, recognized the daguerreotype as belonging to Hampden Booth. The FBI then restored the *Players Club* to the theater, who soon thereafter sold it to the highest bidder at Sotheby's.[16]

AUTHENTICATING POE

The perception that photography grants privileged access of a different order than painting, illustration, sculpture, or writing to the subject it represents has captivated the public's imagination since the invention of daguerreotypy in 1839. This belief accounts for the impressive value accrued by Pratt's daguerreotyped copy of a daguerreotype of Poe. It also belies what Benjamin theorizes as the radical potential of technologies of reproducibility. Writing in exile from Nazi Germany in Paris in the winter of 1935–1936, Benjamin famously characterized the impact of technological reproducibility on the superstructure as the loss of the "aura," or "the here and now of the work of art—its unique existence in a particular place"—which "underlies the concept of [the artwork's] authenticity."[17] The belief that an object possesses authenticity supports "the idea of tradition which has passed the object down as the same, identical thing to the present day."[18] To Benjamin, the concept of authenticity works to suppress the masses; thus photography's demise of the aura enabled what Benjamin calls the politicizing of art. It signaled the possibility of "the liquidation of the value of tradition in the cultural heritage" and the "alignment" of "reality with the masses."[19] At the time of Benjamin's writing, traditional concepts were being "used in an uncontrolled way," which "allow[ed] factual material to be manipulated in the interests of fascism."[20] Likewise, reproductions of Poe's body have been directed toward upholding the concept of authenticity in American racial discourse, which posits "pure" whiteness and mandates the conceptual and biological reproduction of whiteness through laws against miscegenation. Woodberry's and Dimmock's adaptations of Poe engage in this racial discourse as they place Poe at the center of turn-of-the-century negotiations of new forms of technological reproducibility.

Capitalizing on the symbiosis of Poe's images, texts, and biography in the imaginations of the American public and literati, Woodberry featured reproductions of daguerreotypes of Poe in his three-part series "Selections from the Correspondence of Edgar Allan Poe," published in *Century* in the fall of 1894. With a circulation of over 200,000 in 1890, *Century* was famous for its woodcut illustrations and writings by premier authors of the period. However, during the 1890s, publications that converted to the half-tone process for printing photographs began to edge out *Century*, and *Century*'s readership declined to 150,000 by the end of the decade. Through a series of articles in the 1880s that created "a sensation in the magazine press," *Century* reinvigorated debate about the Civil War and promoted reconciliation between white Northerners and Southerners largely through absolution of the South for slavery.[21] As historians have discussed, including Rayford W. Logan, who labels this period the "nadir" of African-American history, the turn of the twentieth century witnessed a rise in violence against African Americans and the endorsement of this violence by national policies of racial segregation and disenfranchisement, exemplified, respectively, by *Plessy v. Ferguson* and the overturning of the Civil Rights Act of 1875.[22] Even as it served as a venue for African-American writers, *Century* was a white magazine implicated in "a snowballing of racist ideas and practices, both of which reached unprecedented vehemence in the 1890s."[23] Thus Woodberry's series on Poe and Dimmock's letter in response to it could be interpreted in relation to technological innovation, historicization, and racism at the turn of the twentieth century.

In "Poe in New York," the final installment in his series on Poe, Woodberry heads Poe's correspondence with an image of an engraved portrait of Poe, captioned as "From a Daguerreotype Owned by Mr. Robert Lee Traylor." The caption identifies the source of this image as the *Traylor*, Pratt's second daguerreotype of Poe, taken during the same sitting as the *Thompson*. A footnote to this caption announces that Woodberry and Stedman's ten-volume edition of Poe's works would also include the images featured in *Century*; thus this footnote converts the *Traylor* into a trailer of sorts. It also gives an abbreviated history of a daguerreotype that was "presented by Poe, a short time before his death, to Mrs. Sarah Elmira (Royster) Shelton" (Poe's last fiancée) and that is "believed to be [Poe's] last portrait."[24] As Deas explains, the *Traylor* differs only slightly from its variant, the *Thompson*.[25] Therefore, the individuality of these images is easy to overlook, especially through a printed copy of an engraved reproduction. It is unsurprising, then, that Dimmock mistook the image heading "Poe in New York" as a copy of the *Thompson*—the daguerreotype that Pratt had copied for him in Richmond forty years earlier. It is remarkable, however, that Woodberry's alleged mistake in identifying the source of this image so disturbed Dimmock that he responded to "Poe in New York" with "Notes on Poe."

The image of Poe heading Woodberry's article is similar to a press photograph in that it is accompanied by texts: a title, subtitle, caption, footnote, and an article composed of Woodberry's introduction and a selection of Poe's letters. Roland Barthes argues that, by analyzing "the code of connotation of . . . the press photograph[,] we may hope to find, in their very subtlety, the forms our society uses to ensure its peace of mind."[26] By captioning the reproduced engraving based on the *Traylor* as "From a Daguerreotype . . . ," Woodberry adorns the image with what Barthes calls "the 'objective' mask of denotation."[27] It is to Woodberry's claim of the denotative status of this image that Dimmock responds. Dimmock's letter is yet another appendage to *Century*'s copy of the *Traylor*. Like a caption, Dimmock's letter "appears to duplicate the image, that is, to be included in its denotation," and it "loads the image, burdening it with a culture, a moral, an imagination."[28] In result, a text, formerly "experienced as connoted[,] is now experienced only as the natural resonance of the fundamental denotation constituted by the photographic analogy and we are thus confronted with a typical process of naturalization of the cultural."[29] Dimmock participates in this "naturalization of the cultural" by claiming that an indexical relation exists between "Notes on Poe" and his daguerreotype of Poe. Barthes's theory of the photographic message helps clarify how, as a mode of communication, "Notes on Poe" functions to "reassure" its readers that Poe was an ideal citizen and that, therefore, his writings were a solid foundation for an American literature.[30] Dimmock does this by molding Poe into a model of white, middle-class masculinity. Just as Tate, in his 1949 lecture to the Poe Society, uses a photograph to reassure his audience that Poe is a relatable figure, Dimmock capitalizes on his readers' belief that a photograph represents indisputable truth in order to make his new, more "gentlemanly" image of Poe seem to reflect reality.

BETTER THAN THE ORIGINAL

In Dimmock's first note on Poe, he describes his viewing of Pratt's original daguerreotype of Poe, his subsequent conversation with Pratt, and his purchase of Pratt's daguerreotyped copy in Richmond "during the Christmas holidays of 1854–1855."[31] Contrary to Woodberry's claim that the *Traylor* was an original daguerreotype that Poe gave to Elmira Shelton, Pratt described Shelton's daguerreotype as a copy to Dimmock, which Pratt sold to her soon after Poe's death. By this, Dimmock presumes that Pratt meant that Pratt made for Shelton—as he did for Dimmock—a daguerreotyped copy of the original daguerreotype in his street-level display case. However, in light of Deas's finding that Pratt did, indeed, give the *Traylor* to Shelton and of the fact that the image of Poe that heads "Poe in New York" is not reversed from the *Thompson*, we may conclude that its unidentified artist worked from one of Pratt's "original" daguerreotypes of Poe. Dimmock's narrative implies that Pratt, recognizing that to deny the originality of the *Traylor* would invest his displayed daguerreotype of Poe with uniqueness and, thereby, advance its copy's sale, misled the journalist to believe that he had produced only one daguerreotype of Poe in his daguerrean gallery in 1849. Nevertheless, based on Dimmock's recollection of his transaction with Pratt, which convinced him that Pratt was an honest man, in "Notes on Poe," Dimmock presents the following flawed correction to Woodberry's account of the *Traylor*:

> Being satisfied then—as I am now—that Mr. Pratt told the truth concerning his daguerreotype, I at once offered to buy it; but naturally enough he declined to sell what, even then, was of considerable value. He told me, however, that he had made an excellent copy for the lady to whom Poe was engaged (not mentioning her name), and would make me one if I so desired. He did so, and this copy is now in my possession, in perfect preservation, after forty years. It

is in every respect, so far as I am capable of judging, quite as good as was the original; but it is *not* the original, nor, I am inclined to think, is that of Mr. Traylor. Where the original now is, I do not know; but whoever examines it, or a good copy, closely, will see that the picture is not such a one as Poe would be likely to give to the lady of his love. . . . Doubtless [Pratt] made several—perhaps many—copies after mine; but I am quite certain of the genuineness and fidelity of my own.[32]

Dimmock's haughty defense of his daguerreotype reveals several aspects of the significance of portrait photography to Americans at the fin de siècle. His admissions that "it is *not* the original" and "not such a one as Poe would be likely to give to the lady of his love" and "doubtless [Pratt] made several—perhaps many—copies after [his]" are essential to counter Woodberry's claims about the *Century*'s source daguerreotype and to justify Dimmock's compulsion to write his letter. However, they also depreciate the value of Dimmock's copy of the *Thompson*.

While Benjamin argues that technological reproduction has the radical potential to abolish the concept of authenticity, Dimmock's letter privileges this concept. However, "Notes on Poe" also reveals the extent to which the belief that a photograph represents reality mutates the idea of authenticity. Dimmock relies on a discourse of originality to describe his portrait of Poe, which he claims "is in every respect, so far as [he is] capable of judging, quite as good as was the original," and of which he "is quite certain of the genuineness and fidelity." However, the mood of his letter disavows its rhetoric and suggests that Dimmock and his readers actually appreciate replication. Dimmock is clearly invested in his daguerreotyped copy and regards it as an index of its subject, Poe. Similarly, a century later, whoever stole the *Players Club* from Hampden Booth, the temporary owner of the image (Sally Guest), its appraiser on *Antiques Roadshow* (C. Wesley Cowan), and the participants in its auction at Sotheby's overlooked the derivativeness of this daguerreotype. By recognizing that a photograph is a copy to begin with, they all saw the *Players Club* as "quite as good as was the original" and, therefore, as possessing "considerable value." In contrast to a photograph, a daguerreotype is a positive print. To mechanically reproduce it, one must take a daguerreotype (or a photograph) of it, as Pratt did for Dimmock. Thus, perhaps one cannot say of the daguerreotype—as Benjamin says of the photograph—that, "to ask for the 'authentic' print makes no sense."[33] However, to ask for its original makes very little sense because a daguerreotype, like a photograph, is constitutively reproducible. This technical aspect of daguerreotype sanctions Dimmock to assert authority over Pratt's first image of Poe even while Dimmock lacks—and dismisses the need to have—full knowledge of the *Thompson*'s provenance.

Ironically, in his second note on Poe, Dimmock unwittingly locates the daguerreotype from which Pratt made the *Players Club*. Here, he "condense[s,] into the briefest possible compass," a story of a live encounter with Poe, using John Reuben Thompson's "own words nearly as memory permits."[34] Dimmock claims that Thompson related this "compass" to him in an interview in Richmond in 1860, during which the subject of Pratt's daguerreotype of Poe apparently did not arise (unbeknownst to Dimmock, Thompson owned the *Thompson* at the time). In his letter, Dimmock uses his reconstruction of Thompson's story of Poe to compensate for his lack of knowledge about the *Thompson*. Dimmock moves easily from discussing a copy of Pratt's daguerreotype of Poe to providing secondhand and even thirdhand knowledge of Poe. His recourse to a verbal portrait of Poe as a substitute for a more complete illustration of the *Thompson* reveals Dimmock's perception, as well as that of his readers, of the interchangeability of a photograph and its subject.

Thompson's story of Poe seems to undermine but actually supports Dimmock's interpretation of the *Players Club*. As Thompson related to Dimmock,

> on going home for lunch my mother told me that a stranger had called to see me, and had left a message to the effect that for a week past a man calling himself Poe had been wandering around Rocketts (a rather disreputable suburb of Richmond) in a state of intoxication and apparent destitution, and that his friends, if he had any, ought to look after him. I immediately took a carriage and drove down to Rocketts, and spent the afternoon in a vain search—being more than once on the point of finding him, when he seemed to slip away. Finally, when night came on, I went to the most decent of the drinking-shops and left my card with the barkeeper, with the request that if he saw the alleged Poe again, he would give it to him. Ten days, perhaps, had passed, and in the press of occupation the matter had entirely gone from my mind, when on a certain morning a person whom I had never seen before entered the office, asked if I was Mr. Thompson, and then said, 'My name is Poe,' without further introduction or explanation. As, singularly enough, I had never met my townsman before, I looked at him with something more than curiosity. He was unmistakably a gentleman of education and refinement, with the indescribable marks of genius in his face, which was of almost marble whiteness. He was dressed with perfect neatness; but one could see signs of poverty in the well-worn clothes, though his manner betrayed no consciousness of the fact.[35]

On the one hand, Thompson's observation that Poe was "dressed with perfect neatness" when he appeared at the office of the *Southern Literary Messenger* in 1849 is opposed to Dimmock's reading of the *Players Club*. According to Dimmock, in his daguerreotype of Poe, Poe's "dress is something more than careless," "a white handkerchief is thrust, as if to conceal the crumpled linen," his "coat is thrown back from the shoulders in rather reckless fashion, and the whole costume, as well as the hair and face, indicates that the poor poet was in a mood in which he cared very little how he looked."[36] On the other hand, Pratt's claim that Poe was reluctant to be daguerreotyped due to his unseemly clothing shows that Poe was, in fact, accustomed to minding his look. As Dimmock says, in the winter of 1854–1855, Pratt told him:

> I knew [Poe] well, and he had often promised me to sit for a picture, but had never done so. One morning—in September, I think—I was standing at my street door when [Poe] came along and spoke to me. I reminded him of his unfulfilled promise, for which he made some excuse. I said, "Come upstairs now." He replied, "Why, I am not dressed for it." "Never mind that," I said; "I'll gladly take you just as you are." He came up, and I took that picture. Three weeks later he was dead in Baltimore.[37]

Pratt's anecdote suggests that, had his camera captured Poe in a less disastrous period than the weeks leading up to his death, Poe's appearance would have been impeccable. Likewise, Thompson's story indicates that Poe's unsuitable attire when he encountered Poe was due, not to Poe's inattention to his person, but to his poverty. Indeed, in Dimmock's note, Thompson goes on to say of Poe, "His face was always colorless, his nerves always steady, his dress always neat."[38] Refuting the facts of Woodberry's footnote, Dimmock asserts that, even in his doomed state in September of 1849, Poe had sufficient presence of mind to recognize that his clothing would offend both his "lady-love" and posterity. Recorded in Pratt's studio, Poe's "disheveled" look—as Columbia University Libraries describe Poe's appearance in this image—seems virtuous when coupled with Thompson's claim that Poe's "manner betrayed no consciousness of" the "signs of poverty in [his] well-worn clothes" when he allegedly appeared at Thompson's office nearly coincidently as Pratt created the *Thompson*.[39]

Thompson's statements about Poe in the flesh balance, rather than contradict, Dimmock's claims about Poe's image on a polished, silver-coated, copper plate. Together, they endow Poe with qualities associated with white, middle-class masculinity at the turn of the twentieth century. In "Notes on Poe," Dimmock testifies that Poe was both attentive to his look and above vanity—that, without sacrificing his duty to his personal appearance, Poe was preoccupied by concerns more lofty than his clothing. Dimmock's various depictions of Poe make a case that the author did, in fact, attend to his person but not excessively so—that is, not in such a way as might compromise Poe's status as subject, not object, of the photographic gaze. Although Dimmock's descriptions of Poe are largely about Poe's clothing, they indicate attributes of Poe's self and insinuate that, even more than a decorum for dress, there is a particular identity best suited for the camera. The seeming contradictions between its narratives make Dimmock's letter function ideologically, at the same time as its basis in facsimile (daguerreotypes and reportage) supports the status of "Notes on Poe" as an index of its subject, allowing Dimmock to claim to, as Pratt did, "take [Poe] just as [he was]."

"Notes on Poe" naturalizes a constructed image of Poe by asserting this image to be revelatory of the "real" Poe. Furthermore, by suggesting that daguerreotypes capture objects in motion (a "thrust" handkerchief, "crumpled linen," and "coat . . . thrown back . . . in rather reckless fashion") and abide by laws of probability, which enable a chance encounter on the street, in his descriptions of Poe in the *Players Club* and of the circumstances surrounding the production of the *Thompson*, respectively, Dimmock compares daguerreotypy to film, a medium even more strikingly veracious than photography because cinema represents motion. This retrospective reconfiguration of the capacities of daguerreotypy obscures that, in reviving Poe, Dimmock fashions Poe with a gendered, classed, and racialized identity.

In Thompson's description of Poe, Dimmock invokes physiognomy, which is implicated in racism: Thompson allegedly claimed that Poe "was unmistakably a gentleman of education and refinement, with the indescribable marks of genius in his face, which was of almost marble whiteness."[40] To readers of *Century*, the daguerreotyped image of Poe connotes knowledge of what constitutes an author at the fin de siècle. As an ideal, Poe is figured to have particular qualities at the same time as their particularity is disavowed in order to naturalize them: whiteness, in "Notes on Poe," blurs into colorlessness. Through Thompson's comparison of Poe to a marble statue, Dimmock imbues his image of Poe with a recomposed aura, performing what Miriam Hansen calls "the simulation of auratic effects."[41] As Benjamin observes, sculpture produces works that "are literally all of a piece"; it is the art form most antithetical to technological reproducibility.[42] "Notes on Poe" tries to solidify Poe as the emblem of "traditional concepts—such as creativity and genius, eternal value and mystery."[43] In the 1930s, Benjamin responded to the fascist corruption of the radical potential of technological reproducibility. In the United States at the turn of the twentieth century, a misuse of mechanical reproduction to reinforce an oppressive ideology also occurred, as exemplified by Dimmock's adaptation of his daguerreotype of Poe.

NOT SEEING POE

Constructions of Poe at the turn of the twentieth century participate in a cultural process of replacing the sense of "the here and now" that is the aura with the "here, now" that is the index.[44] By this shift, reproductions become untied from the original artwork and its "unique existence in a particular place"; they move from one situation to the next, making the objects that they capture present to their beholders.[45] Thompson's narrative about Poe embedded in Dimmock's letter suggests that close encounters with originals leave one with a sense of the uncanny, or "the collapse of boundaries separating fantasy and reality, fiction and life."⁴⁶ Poe's supposedly abrupt appearance at the office of the *Southern Literary Messenger* in 1849 jolts Thompson: the famous writer's sudden presence both startles and delights the editor. By the simple declaration "My name is Poe," Thompson via Dimmock (or vice versa) raises Poe to the author function.⁴⁷ When Poe's body is present to Thompson, Poe's identity as an author is simultaneously sutured to and sundered from his person: it is at once made localizable and distributed everywhere. The singularity of this experience intensifies Thompson's observational impulses; he regards Poe "with something more than curiosity." Thompson's resultant representation of Poe as the living dead registers the effect of this encounter with celebrity, the power that attends eye-witnessing an iconic figure and beholding his aura, but it also highlights the temporariness of Thompson's editorship (a position that Poe had occupied twelve years before him) and provides Thompson with a glimpse of his own mortality.

In "Notes on Poe," Dimmock figures originals of Poe as ghostly—as bodies relegated to the past but haunting the present through their copies. He invests these spectral replicas with greater value—both abstract and material—than their sources; each copy is "quite as good as was the original" precisely because the original merely *was*. In the present, originals are imaginatively if not actually lost, so that only their copies remain. However, truthfully, no originals exist in Pratt's story. Despite the Richmond daguerreotypist's fib, or Dimmock's misinterpretation of Pratt's information, the *Thompson* was not unique but, rather, one of a pair of daguerreotypes. The *Thompson* only became unique after 1894, when the *Traylor* was damaged and lost or destroyed. Furthermore, daguerreotypes are only perceived as originals by virtue of being positive prints. The fantastic logic in privileging the *Thompson* over the *Players Club* contends that by the interaction of light and chemicals, Poe's body was literally captured on one of Pratt's daguerrean plates.

In the modernist reconstruction of Poe bookended by Woodberry's and Dimmock's adaptations of Poe and Tate's reminiscence about the *Ultima Thule*, we witness attempts to vindicate Poe by mechanically aligning him with a particular identity. Photography may be "the first truly revolutionary means of reproduction," but it has also served reactionary politics.⁴⁸ The reproductions of Poe that I have discussed were not employed to meet "*revolutionary demands in the politics of art [Kunstpolitik]*."⁴⁹ They salvage "the value of tradition in the cultural heritage" and accommodate that heritage to a filmic "mode of perception."⁵⁰ By implicating the protocinematic qualities of Pratt's daguerreotypes—their representation of motion and chance—in the cultural transformation of Poe into a norm of white, middle-class masculinity, "Notes on Poe" stymies the radical potential of technological reproducibility. Tate continues Dimmock's operation on Poe a half-century later, as he adapts the *Ultima Thule* to bring Poe into the fold.

NOTES

1. Allen Tate, "Our Cousin, Mr. Poe," in *Essays of Four Decades* (Chicago: Swallow Press, 1968), 385.

2. On the use of daguerreotypes of Poe to explicate his character and biography, respectively, see William A. Pannapacker, "A Question of 'Character': Visual Images and the Nineteenth-Century Construction of Edgar Allan Poe," *Harvard Library Bulletin* 7, no. 3 (1996): 9–24, and Kevin J. Hayes, "Poe, the Daguerreotype, and the Autobiographical Act," *Biography* 25, no. 3 (2002): 477–92.

3. During the last decade of Poe's life, which was the first decade of photography in the United States, Poe sat in front of the camera on six occasions , producing eight daguerreotypes. Each was named after the person or entity who purchased it or who received it as a gift or heirloom, except the *Ultima Thule* , which Sarah Helen Whitman named in allusion to Poe's "Dream-Land." Michael J. Deas, *The Portraits and Daguerreotypes of Edgar Allan Poe* (Charlottesville: Univ ersity Press of Virginia, 1988) , 36 –38.

4. Tate, "Our Cousin, Mr. Poe," 399.

5. Walter Benjamin, "The Work of Art in the Age of Its Technological Reproducibility: Second Version," in *Selected Writings*, volume 3, *1935–1938,* ed. Howard Eiland and Michael W. Jennings (Cambridge, MA: Belknap, 2002), 104.

6. Thomas C. Carlson, "Biographical Warfare: Silent Film and the Public Image of Poe," *Mississippi Quarterly: The Journal of Southern Cultures* 52, no. 1 (1998/1999): 8.

7. Ibid., 7.

8. Ibid., 16.

9. Mary Ann Doane, *The Emergence of Cinematic Time: Modernity, Contingency, the Archive* (Cambridge, MA: Harvard University Press, 2002), 81.

10. Ibid., 104.

11. Doane, *Emergence of Cinematic Time*, 104.

12. Edgar Allan Poe, "A Chapter on Science and Art," *Burton's Gentleman's Magazine, and Monthly American Review*, April 1840, 193.

13. Deas, *Portraits and Daguerreotypes*, 57.

14. Ibid., 58–60.

15. Luke Crafton, "The Purloined Portrait," *Follow the Stories: Omaha, Nebraska (2005)*, Antiques Roadshow, PBS.org, last modified March 27, 2006, accessed August 4, 2012, http://www.pbs.org/wgbh/roadshow/fts/omaha_200402A06.html.

16. Susan Jaffe Tane, owner of the largest private Poe collection and generous supporter of scholarship on Poe, bought the *Players Club* at Sotheby's.

17. Benjamin, "Work of Art," 103.

18. Ibid., 103.

19. Ibid., 104, 105, 101.

20. Ibid., 101–2.

21. Frank Luther Mott, *A History of American Magazines, 1741–1930* (Cambridge, MA: Belknap, 1958–1968), 470.

22. Rayford W. Logan, *The Betrayal of the Negro from Rutherford B. Hayes to Woodrow Wilson* (New York: Collier Books, 1965).

23. Dickson D. Bruce Jr., *Black American Writing from the Nadir: The Evolution of a Literary Tradition, 1877–1915* (Baton Rouge: Louisiana State University Press, 1989), 2.

24. George E. Woodberry, "Poe in New York," *Century Magazine* (October 1894): 854.

25. Deas, *Portraits and Daguerreotypes*, 58.

26. Roland Barthes, *Image, Music, Text*, trans. Stephen Heath (New York: Hill & Wang, 1988), 31.

27. Ibid., 21.

28. Ibid., 25, 26.

29. Ibid., 26.

30. Ibid., 31.

31. Thomas Dimmock, "Notes on Poe," *Century Magazine* (June 1895): 315.

32. Ibid.

33. Benjamin, "Work of Art," 106.
34. Dimmock, "Notes on Poe," 316.
35. Ibid.
36. Ibid., 315.
37. Ibid.
38. Ibid., 316.
39. "Literature, #201," *Jewels in Her Crown: Treasures of Columbia University Libraries Special Collections*, 2004, accessed August 4, 2012, http://www.columbia.edu/cu/lweb/eresources/exhibitions/treasures/html/201.html; Dimmock, "Notes on Poe," 316.
40. Dimmock, "Notes on Poe," 316.
41. Miriam Bratu Hansen, "Benjamin's Aura," *Critical Inquiry* 34 (2008): 336.
42. Benjamin, "Work of Art," 109.
43. Ibid., 101–2.
44. Ibid., 103; Doane, *Emergence of Cinematic Time*, 93.
45. Benjamin, "Work of Art," 103.
46. Fred Botting, *Limits of Horror: Technology, Bodies, Gothic* (Manchester, UK: Manchester University Press, 2008), 6.
47. See Michel Foucault, "What Is an Author?" in *The Book History Reader*, ed. David Finkelstein and Alistair McCleery (London: Routledge, 2002).
48. Benjamin, "Work of Art," 105.
49. Ibid., 102.
50. Ibid., 102, 104.

Index

acrostics, 3
action, 56
adaptation, 101
aesthetics: of Burke, 70; of optimism, 78, 83; of Poe, 3, 4, 23, 54, 57, 62, 115, 120n26. *See also* sublime and sublimity; swerve or deviation
afterimage, 122
"Al Aaraaf"(Poe), 5; Boston Lyceum reading of, 42, 43, 44; epic nature of, 44
Allan, John, xiv; biographical allusions to, 14–17; Poe manipulation of, 16–17; Poe treatment by, 14–15, 22, 24n9, 48
antebellum America: Catholicism treatment in, 29, 30, 32, 32–33, 40n36; Mother Goddess or Virgin Mary treatment in, 30, 34, 38; race and racism in, 108, 110, 111, 116, 119n21
appearance, photographic, 132–134. *See also* photography or daguerreotype, Poe
arabesque: for Schlegel, 61; in "Usher", 60, 61
architecture, 54
Aristotle, 70, 73
armchair detective or flâneur: entertainment over information giving rise to, 87; media on crime giving rise to, 88–89, 90; narration, 93; Poe inventing, xvi, 88; roles played by, 93. *See also* "The Mystery of Marie Rogêt"
Arnold, Elizabeth, xiv

art, 128; for Burke and Kant, 70; "Gold-Bug" title as emblem of, 97; in "Usher", 60–61, 62. *See also* aesthetics
artifice and artificial systems: baroque, 1–2, 9, 10n4; from Fauvel-Gouraud, 8; memory schemes involving, 7–9, 11n45
artist, 13
astonishment: in Dupin trilogy, 75, 76; sublimity in, 75
audience: for Poe, 108–110; for "Pym", 108, 108–110, 112; racism of, 108, 110, 111
aura: photography and lost, 128; of Poe, 134
authenticity: of photograph compared to daguerreotype, 131; technological reproduction abolishing, 131
authority, 17. *See also* paternalism and paternal authority

Bacon, Francis: mnemotechnics employed by, 8; secret writing of, 7
Barnaby Rudge (Dickens), 101
baroque artifice, 1–2, 9, 10n4
Barthes, Roland, 129
Baudelaire, 53, 60, 62
Benjamin, Walter, 122, 128
biography and biographical allusions: paternalism relation to, 14–17; poetry evincing, xii, xiii; in "Tamerlane", 14–15, 17–18

139

Bonaparte, Marie, 53
The Book of Gems: From the Poets and Artists of Great Britain (Hall), 2–4
Boston: Poe association with, 41, 41–42, 46–47, 48–49; Poe criticism of, 49
Boston Lyceum appearance: "Al Aaraaf" reading at, 42, 43, 44; building significance in, 46–47, 47, 48, 51n22; critical history of, 41–42; ego in outcome of, 45; family connection to, 46, 51n22; Higginson on, 43, 51n14; importance of, 45, 46; perverse reaction to, 44; Poe's own criticism concerning, 42–43, 45, 49
brief prose tale: equivalence and contiguity in, 102; from Poe, 101, 102
Brooks, Peter, 20, 25n23
Burke, Edmund, 54; aesthetics of, 70; art for, 70; on language, 70, 81; sublime for, xv, 56, 57, 60, 62, 63, 70, 75, 76; terror and horror for, 56

"Catholic Hymn" (Poe), 28, 34, 38
Catholicism: antebellum America treatment of, 29, 30, 32, 32–33, 40n36; femininity elevated and oppressed by, 33; gender issues in, 32–33; Holy Ghost role in, 30; "Morella" treatment of, 32; Mother Goddess resolution from, 29, 30
Century Magazine, 122, 126, 128–129
Christianity, 31, 38
Civil War, racism following, 128
Clio (Ussher): sublime in, 54, 58; "Usher" compared to, 55, 59, 60, 61; "Usher" impact from, 54
Coleridge, Samuel Taylor, 57–58, 62, 65n31
complexity, xi, xvii
compositional technique, 67, 69
confessional narrative: paternalism and, 15, 18, 22–23, 24n8; pathos in, 17; of self-negation, 18–19, 21, 25n26; of "Tamerlane", 13, 14, 18, 21, 22, 23
"The Conqueror Worm" (Poe), 4, 5
consistency, in "Tamerlane", 13
creation: deviation in, 68; textual sublimity in dissolution and, 78, 81–83
crime: in media, 88–89, 90, 91; sex, 89–90; as urban environment element, 93

critical history: of Boston Lyceum appearance, 41–42; of "Tamerlane", 14, 18, 18–19
Critique (Kant), 70
cryptographic imagination, xii
"Culture" (Greenblatt), 29
Cushing, Caleb, 45

Davidson, Edward, 18
death, 126
"A Decided Loss" (Poe), 9, 11n45
deconstruction: romantic irony compared to, 80; romantic sublimity relation to, 81; textual sublimity and, 81
de Man, Paul, 81
demonic possession, 21–22, 25n29
Derrida, Jacques, 78, 80, 85n39. *See also* deconstruction
destruction and renewal, 78
deviation. *See* swerve or deviation
Diana, 30–31
Dickens, Charles, 101
diegetic sublimity. *See* romantic sublimity
Dimmock, Thomas, 122, 125, 126, 129; Players Club daguerreotype for, 131–132; Poe daguerreotype recontextualized by, 129, 135; on Poe's appearance, 132–134; Traylor daguerreotype for, 130–131
disaster, Boston Lyceum, 41–42
dissolution, 78, 81–83
Doane, Mary Ann, 122, 126
Dupin trilogy (Poe): astonishment in, 75, 76; "Gold-Bug" compared to, 99; "Marie Rogêt" juxtaposed with rest of, 87, 91; narrative order and disorder in, 75, 80; narrator as sublimity carrier in, 77; power and subjection in, 76; sublimity shift from romantic to textual in, 77, 81. *See also* "The Mystery of Marie Rogêt"; "The Purloined Letter"

Edgar Allan Poe Society, 9, 121
ego, 45
emblem and emblematical methods: as baroque artifice, 1–2, 9; in "Gold-Bug" title, 97, 102–104, 104n1, 105n25–106n27; nature and definition of, 2, 10n14; Poe affinity for, 6; from

Quarles, 1, 2, 3, 6; "The Raven" evincing, 6; sublimity through vortex, 53, 63
Emblemes, Divine and Moral (Quarles), 2, 3, 6, 10n14, 10n16, 11n31
Enquiry (Burke), 54, 62
entertainment, 87
epic, 44
Epicurus, 68
epistemology: afterimage in, 122; "Pym" as satirical racist, 108, 110, 111–116, 117n4, 119n20
equivalence and contiguity: in brief prose tale, 102; in "The Gold-Bug", 99, 100, 101, 102, 104, 105n6; in poetic function, 101
"Eulalie" (Poe), 27, 28
Eureka (Poe), 69

"The Fall of the House of Usher" (Poe): arabesque in, 60, 61; architecture in, 59; art in, 60–61, 62; *Clio* compared to, 55, 59, 60, 61; femininity represented in, 62; imagination refigured in, 57, 58, 62; negative sublime in, xv, 53–54, 56–57, 58–59, 59, 61–63, 64n21, 65n31; as parody, 63; Ussher's *Clio* impacting, 54
family, 46, 51n22. *See also* Allan, John
fancy, 57–58, 62
Fauvel-Gouraud, Francis, 1, 7, 8; artifice employed by, 8; for Poe, 8
Feast for Wormes (Quarles), 4–5, 5
feminism and femininity: Catholicism elevation and oppression of, 33; in "Eulalie", 27, 28; negative sublime through, 62; Poe's work evincing, xiv; sexuality disassociation from, 27–28, 38. *See also* "Morella"; Mother Goddess or Virgin Mary
film, 134
flâneur. *See* armchair detective or flâneur
Franchot, Jenny, 28, 29, 32, 33, 40n36
Freud, Sigmund, 24n8

gender, 32–33
German idealism, 67
Gilbert, Sandra, 27
Gilroy, Paul, 116

"The Gold-Bug" (Poe): adaptation applied to, 101; bi-part psyche of Legrand in, 98–99; Dupin compared to, 99; emblem in title of, 97, 102–104, 104n1, 105n25–106n27; equivalence and contiguity in, 99, 100, 101, 102, 104, 105n6; interpretive authority in, 97, 100; Jupiter's nature in, 100, 105n8; narrative role of beetle in, 97, 99–100, 104, 104n3, 105n24, 106n29; secrecy and ciphers in, xvi
Greenblatt, Stephen, 29
Griswold, Rufus Wilmot, 121
grotesque and grotesqueness. *See* quaintness and grotesqueness
Gubar, Susan, 27

Hall, Samuel Carter, 2–4, 6
Halliburton, David, 18–19, 20
Hegel, G. W. F.: identity defined by, 69; sublation from, 69
Higginson, Thomas Wentworth, 43, 51n14
hoax, 108–110
Holy Ghost, 30
horror, 55–56, 57
Hull, Richard, 100

identity: Hegel defining, 69; Poe on, 69, 70; swerve of individual, 69, 70, 71, 73
idol, 31–32, 36
images and pictures, 7. *See also* photography or daguerreotype, Poe
imagination: cryptographic, xii; fancy compared to, 57–58, 62; Poe's reconfiguration of, 57–58, 62; sensuous world less powerful than, 4; "Tamerlane" and Poe's thinking regarding poetic, 14
"The Imp of the Perverse" (Poe): language of, 71; swerve in, 68, 71–73
individual, 76
information, 87
Inquiry (Burke), 70
instantaneity, 126
interpretive authority, 97, 100
intimacy, language for, 23

Jacobs, Robert D., 19
Jakobson, Roman, 101

Jewett, Helen, 89

Kant, Immanuel, 54, 57; art for, 70; on sublimity, 58, 60, 61, 62, 76, 81

language: Burke on, 70, 81; intimacy through, 23; perversity on level of, xv, 72–73; swerve through, 69, 71–73; of textual sublimity, 77
"Linguistics and Poetics" (Jakobson), 101
literature: clinamen in, 70; Poe conception of, 68, 105n17; race and racism in relation to marketplace of, 108, 109; swerve achieved in, 70
Longfellow, Henry Wadsworth, 50, 65n30
Longinus, 58, 61, 76, 77
loss and sorrow, 5
Lucretius, 67, 68–69

madness, 59
The Madwoman in the Attic (Gilbert and Gubar), 27
Maio, Samuel, 17
"The Man of the Crowd" (Poe), 88, 93
maternal longing and identification: of Poe, 47–48; in "Tamerlane", 19, 23
media: account inconsistency, 89, 90, 91; armchair detective and crime in, 88–89, 90; crime in, 88–89, 90, 91; print, rise of, 88; sensationalism, 89, 90, 91
memory, 1; artificial systems for, 7–9, 11n45; images for stimulating, 7
misinterpretation: of race and racism, 113–115, 116; reader, 110, 113, 113–115, 116, 119n15
misrecognition, xii, xviiin6
mnemotechny and mnemotechnics: Bacon employing, 8; nature of, 8; phreno-, 1, 7–8, 8
modernist, photography, 122, 126
"Morella" (Poe): Catholicism treatment in, 32; Mother Goddess demonized in, 34–37, 37; Mother Goddess essence transference in, 31, 34, 36, 37; Mother Goddess in, 28, 30, 33–38; Virgin Mary resemblance to, 30
Morrison, Toni, 107
Morse, Samuel F. B., 28
mortality, 6

Mother Goddess or Virgin Mary, 39n7, 40n35; antebellum America treatment of, 30, 34, 38; in "Catholic Hymn", 28, 34, 38; Catholicism resolution regarding, 29, 30; Christianity treatment of, 31, 38; Diana and other goddess links to, 30–31, 34; as idol, 31–32, 36; in "Morella", 28, 30, 33–38; "Morella" and essence transference of, 31, 34, 36, 37; Morella resemblance to, 30; patriarchal authority demonizing and marginalizing, 31, 34–37, 37–38; Poe experience and treatment of, 29, 31–32, 34–37, 38; worship sites for, 32, 40n28
"The Mystery of Marie Rogêt" (Poe): armchair detective in, 87, 91, 92, 93; crime in urban environment as part of, 93; media inconsistency and sensationalism in, 91; other Dupin tales juxtaposed with, 87, 91; reenactment used in, 92; voyeurism predicted by, 94

narrative: Dupin trilogy order and disorder in, 75, 80; "Gold-Bug" and role of beetle in, 97, 99–100, 104, 104n3, 105n24, 106n29. *See also* confessional narrative
"The Narrative of Arthur Gordon Pym" (Poe): audience and satirical hoax in, 108, 108–110, 112; Pym as author of, 109; Pym as surrogate reader and misinterpretation in, 108, 110–111, 112, 113, 113–115, 116, 119n15; race and literary marketplace in, 108, 109; as satirical racist epistemology, 108, 110, 111–116, 117n4, 119n20; savagery in, 113; scholarship on race in, 107–108, 111, 112, 114–115, 120n27
narrator or narration: armchair detective, 93; overconfidence displayed in, 79; romantic irony of, 79–80; sublimity carried by, 77, 79
"Notes on Poe" (Dimmock), 126, 129, 130–131, 133, 135. *See also* photography or daguerreotype, Poe

object: subject interaction with, 80; sublime and role of, 54, 60, 78

Of the Proficience and Advancement of Learning (Bacon), 7
On the Nature of the Universe (Lucretius), 68
optimism, aesthetics of, 78, 83

parody, 63
paternalism and paternal authority: authority response shaped by, 17; biographical allusions and, 14–17; confessional narrative and, 15, 18, 22–23, 24n8; scapegoat for rejecting, 13, 19; "Tamerlane" rejecting, 13, 14, 17–18, 21, 22–23. *See also* patriarchal authority
pathos, 17
patriarchal authority: female sexuality subverted by, 27–28; Mother Goddess demonized and marginalized under, 31, 34–37, 37–38
penny press. *See* media
perception, altered, 122
Peri Hypsous (Longinus), 76, 77
perversity: Boston Lyceum appearance and reaction of, 44; language and, xv, 72–73; principle of, 72; of sentiment, 25n26; swerve of, 67–68, 72–73
"The Philosophy of Composition" (Poe), 6, 8, 69, 106n30
"The Philosophy of Furniture" (Poe), 88, 93, 94n2
photography or daguerreotype, Poe: appearance in, 132–134; aura lost through, 128; authenticity of, 131; as "brilliant victim", 122; comparison of, 131; death and final, 126–127; denotative status of, 129; film compared to, 134; instantaneity sought in, 126; involvement in, xvii, 136n3; as modernist, 122, 126; nature and time involved in, 126; perception mode altered through, 122; Players Club, 125, 127, 131–132; portrait, significance of, 131; present moment and historicity in, 126; race, racism, technological reproduction, and, 128, 130, 132, 133–134; reanimated and recontextualized through, 121, 122, 126, 129, 133–134, 134–135;

supernatural nature of, 122; Thompson, 124, 126, 127, 129, 131, 131–132, 135; Traylor, 123, 126, 127, 129, 130–131, 135; *Ultima Thule*, 121–122, 135
Phreno-Mnemotechny; or The Art of Memory (Fauvel-Gouraud), 1, 7–8, 8
plagiarism, 62, 65n30
Players Club daguerreotype, 125, 127, 131–132
plot, adaptation in, 101
Poe, David, 46–47
Poe, Edgar Allan: aesthetics of, 3, 4, 23, 54, 57, 62, 115, 120n26; Allan manipulated by, 16–17; Allan treatment of, 14–15, 22, 24n9, 48; armchair detective invented by, xvi, 88; audience for, 108–110; aura of, 134; baroque artifice employed by, 1–2, 9; Baudelaire on sublimity of, 53, 60, 62; Boston association for, 41, 41–42, 46–47, 48–49; Boston criticism from, 49; brief prose tale from, 101, 102; complexity involving, xi, xvii; cryptographic imagination of, xii; death and final image of, 126–127; Fauvel-Gouraud for, 8; feminist undercurrents for, xiv; German idealism evinced by, 67; identity for, 69, 70; imagination reconfigured by, 57–58, 62; literature for, 68, 105n17; Longfellow criticism from, 50, 65n30; maternal identification of, 47–48; misrecognition of, xii, xviiin6; Mother Goddess experience and treatment by, 29, 31–32, 34–37, 38; paternal authority struggle for, 14–17; on plagiarism, 62, 65n30; poetic sentiment treatment by, 6, 62; Quarles affinity from, xiii, 1, 2–3, 4, 5–6, 9; Quarles name appropriated by, 2; race and racism treatment by, xii, xvii, 98, 104n4, 107, 117, 117n3, 118n5; religion treatment by, xiv, 13, 18, 21–22, 32; secret writing resonance for, 7; sublime as interest for, 64n5; subversive in work of, xi, xii, xvii; vortex in fiction of, 53, 63n4; Williams on American literary originality of, 50; Woodberry series on, 128–129, 130. *See also* Boston Lyceum appearance;

Dupin trilogy; photography or daguerreotype, Poe; sublime and sublimity; *specific works*
Poe, Eliza, 46–47
Poe: A Phenomenological View (Halliburton), 18
"Poe in New York" (Woodberry), 129, 130. *See also* photography or daguerreotype, Poe
poetic function, 101
"The Poetic Principle" (Poe), 70
poetic sentiment, 6, 62
poetry, biographical allusions in, xii, xiii
power and subjection: in "The Purloined Letter", 78, 79; as sublimity dynamics, 76, 77
Pratt, William Abbott, 128; background of, 127; Players Club daguerreotype by, 125, 127, 131–132; on Poe's appearance, 132–133; Thompson daguerreotype by, 124, 126, 127, 131, 131–132, 135; Traylor daguerreotype by, 123, 126, 127, 129, 130–131, 135
print media, 88
Protestants. *See* antebellum America
pseudonym, 1, 2
"The Purloined Letter" (Poe), 85n44; armchair detective invented in, xvi; narrator overconfidence in, 79; object in, 78; power and subjection in, 78, 79; romantic sublimity and irony in, 78, 79–80, 81; subject interaction with object in, 80; sublimity in, xv–xvi, 75, 76. *See also* textual sublimity

quaintness and grotesqueness, 4, 6, 9
Quarles, Francis: *Emblemes* from, 2, 3, 6, 10n14, 10n16, 11n31; emblems from, 1, 2, 3, 6; *Feast for Wormes* of, 4–5, 5; Hall on, 6; on mortality, 6; Poe affinity for, xiii, 1, 2–3, 4, 5–6, 9; Poe appropriating name of, 2; quaintness and grotesqueness for, 4, 6, 9; religious reference in work of, 3, 5; Thoreau indebtedness to, 10n8

race and racism: in antebellum America, 108, 110, 111, 116, 119n21; audience, 108, 110, 111; average, 109, 116; contingency-based, 111; literary marketplace in relation to, 108, 109; misinterpretation of, 113–115, 116; photography of Poe and, 130, 132, 133–134; Poe treatment of, xii, xvii, 98, 104n4, 107, 117, 117n3, 118n5; post Civil War, 128; "Pym" as satirical epistemology of, 108, 110, 111–116, 117n4, 119n20; "Pym" scholarship on, 107–108, 111, 112, 114–115, 120n27; subversive for attacking, xvii; technological reproduction and, 128, 135. *See also* "The Narrative of Arthur Gordon Pym"
Radcliffe, Anne, 55–56, 57
"The Raven" (Poe): emblematic construal in, 6; loss unabated in, 5; pseudonym used in, 1, 2
reader: misinterpretation, 110, 113, 113–115, 116, 119n15; "Pym" title character as surrogate, 108, 110–111, 112, 114–115, 116, 119n15
reanimate and recontextualize, through photography, 121, 122, 126, 129, 133–134, 134–135
religion: Christian, 31, 38; Poe's treatment of, xiv, 13, 18, 21–22, 32; Quarles' work referencing, 3, 5; scapegoat in, 22. *See also* Catholicism; Mother Goddess or Virgin Mary
renewal. *See* destruction and renewal
Roads to Rome (Franchot), 28
Rogers, Mary, 87, 89–91, 91–92. *See also* "The Mystery of Marie Rogêt"
roles. *See specific topics*
romantic irony: deconstruction compared to, 80; in "The Purloined Letter", 79–80, 81; romantic and textual sublimity interaction with, 81; of Schlegel, 78–79, 80, 84n26
romantic sublimity: deconstruction relation to, 81; defined, 84n21; in "The Purloined Letter", 78, 81; romantic irony interplay with textual and, 81; textual sublimity replacing, 77, 78, 81–82
Rosenheim, Shawn, xii

savagery, 113

scapegoat: artist as, 13; paternalism rejected through, 13, 19; in religion, 22; in "Tamerlane", 22
Schlegel, Friedrich: arabesque for, 61; romantic irony from, 78–79, 80, 84n26
scholarship, on race and racism, 107–108, 111, 112, 114–115, 120n27
secret writing, ciphers, and cryptology, xii, xviiin2, xviiin4; artificial memory schemes in, 7; of Bacon, 7; in "The Gold Bug", xvi; Poe resonance with, 7
"The Self and the World: Poe's Early Poems" (Jacobs), 19
self-negation, 18–19, 21, 25n26
sensationalism: "Marie Rogêt" commentary on media, 91; media, 89, 90, 91
sensuous world, 4
sentiment, perversity of, 25n26
sex and sexuality: crime involving, 89–90; in "Eulalie", 27, 28; femininity and disassociation from, 27–28, 38; Victorian era and reconfiguring, 27–28, 38
Southern Literary Messenger, 107, 109, 127, 132, 134
subject, 80
sublation, 69
sublime and sublimity: action inspired by, 56; architecture and negative, 59; in astonishment, 75; Baudelaire on Poe's, 53, 60, 62; Burke on, xv, 56, 57, 60, 62, 63, 70, 75, 76; in *Clio*, 54, 58; destruction and renewal of, 78; engagement with, xv–xvi; femininity for negative, 62; individual seeking thrill of, 76; for Kant, 58, 60, 61, 62, 76, 81; language of textual, 77; madness relation to, 59; narrator and narration carrying, 77, 79; negation and reconfiguration of theories of, xv, 53–54, 56–57, 58–59, 59, 61–63, 64n21, 65n31; object role in, 54, 60, 78; power and subjection as dynamics of, 76, 77; romantic to textual shift in, 77, 78, 81–82; terror role in, 54, 55; Ussher on, 54, 56, 58, 59, 60, 61, 63; vortex as emblem of, 53, 63. *See also* "The Fall of the House of Usher"; "The Purloined Letter"; romantic sublimity; textual sublimity
subversive: Poe's work evincing, xi, xii, xvii; racism attacked through, xvii
supernatural, in photography, 122
swerve or deviation: in compositional technique, 67; in creation, 68; in "The Imp", 68, 71–73; of individual identity, 69, 70, 71, 73; through language, 69, 71–73; in literature, 70; perverse, 67–68, 72–73

"Tamerlane" (Poe), 25n24; biographical allusions in, 14–15, 17–18; confessional narrative of, 13, 14, 18, 21, 22, 23; consistency of writing with, 13; critical history of, 14, 18, 18–19; demonic possession in, 21–22, 25n29; maternal longing and identification in, 19, 23; paternalism rejected in, 13, 14, 17–18, 21, 22–23; poetic imagination in, 14; scapegoat in, 22
Tamerlane and Other Poems (Poe), 14
Tate, Allen, 121–122, 130, 135
technological reproduction: authenticity abolished by, 131; race, racism, and, 128, 135
terror: horror juxtaposed with, 55–56, 57; sublime and role of, 54, 55
text. *See* language
textual sublimity: creation and dissolution in, 78, 81–83; deconstruction and, 81; defined, 85n39; language of, 77; romantic sublimity replaced by, 77, 78, 81–82
"The Third International Edgar Allan Poe Conference", xviiin1
Thompson daguerreotype, 124, 126, 127, 129, 131–132, 135
Thompson, John Reuben, 131–132, 134
Thoms, Peter, 75, 77, 79–80, 85n31
Thoreau, Henry David, 10n8
Transcendentalism, 51n10
Traylor daguerreotype, 123, 126, 127, 129, 130–131, 135

Ultima Thule, 121–122, 135
urban environment, crime in, 93

Ussher, James, 54; on sublimity, 54, 56, 58, 59, 60, 61, 63; terror role in sublime from, 55. *See also* Clio

Victorian era, sexuality in, 27–28, 38. *See also* antebellum America
Virgin Mary. *See* Mother Goddess or Virgin Mary
Voller, Jack G., 53, 54, 56–57, 62, 64n21, 84n21
vortex: in Poe's fiction, 53, 63n4; sublimity in emblem of, 53, 63
voyeurism, 94

Weiskel, Thomas, 81
Whalen, Terrence, 107–108
will, overborne, 20, 25n23
Williams, William Carlos, 50
women, xiv. *See also* feminism and femininity
Woodberry, George E., 122, 127, 128; Poe series by, 128–129, 130; on Traylor daguerreotype, 129, 130
The Works of the Late Edgar Allan Poe (Griswold), 121
worship, Mother Goddess, 32, 40n28
writing. *See* secret writing, ciphers, and cryptology

About the Editor and Contributors

Amy C. Branam is an associate professor of English at Frostburg State University. She has published on transatlantic romanticism in the *Edgar Allan Poe Review*, *ANQ*, and various edited collections, including *Edgar Allan Poe: Beyond Gothicism* (2011) and *Edgar Allan Poe in Context* (2012).

Lauren Curtright is an assistant professor of English at Georgia Perimeter College. After earning her doctorate from the University of Minnesota, she was a Marion L. Brittain Fellow at the Georgia Institute of Technology. Her research on Poe explores the ways in which images of Poe and his writings have been adapted to various media, from architecture to photography to cinema, in various cultural contexts, from the antebellum United States to modern Japan.

William E. Engel is a professor of English at Sewanee (The University of the South) and the author of five books on literary and intellectual history, most recently *Early Modern Poetics in Melville and Poe: Memory, Melancholy, and the Emblematic Tradition* (2012). He contributed the entry on "Emblem Books" for Blackwell's *Encyclopedia of Renaissance English Literature* (2012) and currently is coediting a handbook provisionally titled *The Memory Arts in Early Modern England: An Anthology of Images and Texts*.

Daniel D. Fineman is a professor in the Department of English and Comparative Literary Studies at Occidental College in Los Angeles. His primary areas of research are American Literature and Literary Theory. His most recent article on Hegel, Schlegel, and Dickinson is forthcoming in a collection published by Cambridge University Press. He is currently completing a book titled *Becoming Verse: Dickinson and Deleuze*.

Henri Justin lives in Paris, France. He is a "professeur honoraire des universités" and has devoted two books and numerous articles to the study of Poe's work. *Avec Poe jusqu'au bout de la prose* (2009) is an all-round exploration of Poe's exceptional achievement. Having shown the limitations of Baudelaire's *Histoires*, Justin is currently working at a new translation of a selection of Poe's tales into French.

John C. Havard is an assistant professor of English at Auburn University at Montgomery. He specializes in eighteenth- and nineteenth-century U.S. literature, with particular emphases on hemispheric approaches and critical race studies. His book project, tentatively titled *Hispanicism: Spain, Spanish America, and the Emergence of National Identity in U.S. Literature, 1787–1861*, argues that representations of Spain and Spanish America in early U.S. literature inform the emergence of a national literary self-image. In doing so, such representations served as a site of dialogue regarding intersections of national identity, race, and political theory. His essays have appeared in *Intertexts, Hipertexto, Literature in the Early American Republic, American Literary Realism*, and *Studies in the Novel*.

John Edward Martin is an independent scholar and writer from Houston, Texas. He earned his doctorate in English from Northwestern University and has held teaching positions at Northwestern, Wake Forest University, and Louisiana Tech University. He is an editorial board member of *The Edgar Allan Poe Review*, and he has presented scholarly work on Poe at the International Poe Conference, the American Literature Association Conference, and the International Narrative Conference. He has published articles on Poe, H. P. Lovecraft, and nineteenth-century women's writing—most recently an article on teaching horror that will appear in the collection *Fear and Learning: Essays on the Pedagogy of Horror*, edited by Aalya Ahmad and Sean Moreland (2013).

Sean Moreland earned his PhD in English and American literature at the University of Ottawa, where he currently teaches. His research and teaching interests include modern and contemporary American fiction, Gothic and horror fiction and film, gender and psychological theory, and (post)modern poetics. He is coeditor of *Fear and Learning: Essays on the Pedagogy of Horror*, and guest coeditor of the Fall 2012 issue of *The Edgar Allan Poe Review*. He also writes short fiction and poetry, and he coedits and publishes an anthology of weird fiction, *Postscripts to Darkness*.

Philip Edward Phillips (PhD, Vanderbilt University, 1996) is a professor of English and interim associate dean of the University Honors College at Middle Tennessee State University, where he teaches American, British, and early European literature. He received a Mary Catherine Mooney Fellowship from the Boston Athenaeum in 2008–2009 to support his research on Poe and Boston, and he received a W. T. Bandy Fellowship from the W. T. Bandy Center for Baudelaire and Modern French Studies in 2010–2012 to support his research on Baudelaire's translations of Poe. His work on Poe has appeared in *Poe Studies*, *The Edgar Allan Poe Review*, and the MLA *Approaches to Teaching Poe's Prose and Poetry*. He has served on the editorial advisory committee of *The Edgar Allan Poe Review*, and he is currently a member of the Board of Directors of the Edgar Allan Poe Foundation of Boston and a member-at-large of the Executive Committee of the Poe Studies Association.

Stephanie Sommerfeld is a member of the American Studies Program at the University of Göttingen (Germany). She completed her studies at the University of Göttingen and the University of California–Santa Barbara, with a degree in German, French, and American Studies and is currently working on her PhD project, which investigates transfigurations of the sublime in Poe and contemporary literature. She has published articles on Poe, on remediation in digital film, and on teaching drama.

Tim Towslee teaches AP English at Glen Allen High School just outside of Richmond, Virginia. He holds masters' degrees in English literature and teaching secondary English from Virginia Commonwealth University. When his growing family gives him time to do so, he studies nineteenth- and early twentieth-century literature, comics, and popular culture.

Alexandra Urakova works as a senior researcher at the Gorky Institute of World Literature of the Russian Academy of Sciences, and she is an associate professor at the Russian State University for the Humanities in Moscow. She is the author of *The Poetics of the Body in the Short Fiction of Edgar Allan Poe* (2009, in Russian). She published on Poe in *Nineteenth-Century Literature* and in collections including *Poe's Pervasive Influence*, edited by Barbara Cantalupo (2012). She is a member of the editorial boards of *Poe Studies* and *The Edgar Allan Poe Review* and is a member of the *Poe Studies Association Awards Committee*.